Human Strengths and Resilience

Human Strengths and Resilience

Developmental, Cross-Cultural, and International Perspectives

Edited by
Grant J. Rich and
Skultip (Jill) Sirikantraporn

Foreword by
Chris E. Stout

LEXINGTON BOOKS
Lanham • Boulder • New York • London

Published by Lexington Books
An imprint of The Rowman & Littlefield Publishing Group, Inc.
4501 Forbes Boulevard, Suite 200, Lanham, Maryland 20706
www.rowman.com

Unit A, Whitacre Mews, 26-34 Stannary Street, London SE11 4AB

British Library Cataloguing in Publication Information Available

Library of Congress Cataloging-in-Publication Data

ISBN: 978-1-4985-5483-1 (cloth : alk. paper)
ISBN: 978-1-4985-5484-8 (electronic)

∞™ The paper used in this publication meets the minimum requirements of American National Standard for Information Sciences—Permanence of Paper for Printed Library Materials, ANSI/NISO Z39.48-1992.

Printed in the United States of America

Contents

List of Figures vii

List of Tables ix

Acknowledgments xi

Foreword xiii
Chris E. Stout

Introduction: Human Strengths and Resilience: Developmental, Cross-Cultural, and International Perspectives xvii
Grant J. Rich and Skultip (Jill) Sirikantraporn

1 The Concept of Posttraumatic Growth in a Sample of Undergraduates from India: A Mixed-Methods Study 1
Skultip (Jill) Sirikantraporn, Grant J. Rich, and Julie C. Badaracco

2 The Concept of Posttraumatic Growth in an Adult Sample from Port-au-Prince, Haiti: A Mixed-Methods Study 21
Grant J. Rich, Skultip (Jill) Sirikantraporn, and Wismick Jean-Charles

3 The Concept of Posttraumatic Growth in a Cambodian Sample: A Grounded Theory Study 39
Skultip (Jill) Sirikantraporn, Grant J. Rich, and Nashaw Jafari

4 Resilience in Guatemala: Contextual Overview with Future Perspectives 59
Tannia de Castañeda and María del Pilar Grazioso

5 Resilience in Taiwan: The Shaping Forces of its Diverse Cultural Context and Beliefs about Adversity 75
Ching-Yu Huang

6 Contextual Risks and Resilience Enablers in South Africa: The Case of Precious 87
Sadiyya Haffejee and Linda Theron

7 Trauma, Coping, and Resiliency among Syrian Refugees in Lebanon and Beyond: A Profile of the Syrian Nation at War 105
Naji Abi-Hashem

8 Meaningfulworld Trauma Outreach and Prevention across Cultures: Utilizing the 7-Step Integrative Healing Model for Resilience and Meaning-Making 131
Ani Kalayjian and Daria Diakonova-Curtis

9 Resilience and Recovery in Natural Disasters and Epidemics: Comparisons, Challenges, and Lessons Learned from Train-the-Trainer Projects 151
Judy Kuriansky, Alexandra Margevich, Wismick Jean-Charles, and Russell Daisey

Index 193

About the Editors and Contributors 203

List of Figures

Figure 1.1	Grounded Theory for Posttraumatic Growth Model in the Indian Sample (N=9)	11
Figure 2.1	Grounded Theory for Posttraumatic Growth Model in the Haitian Sample (N=11).	31
Figure 3.1	Construction of PTG in the present Cambodian sample	44
Figure 6.1	Image of sangoma produced by Precious	95

List of Tables

Table 1.1	Descriptive Analyses of the Study of Main Variables (N=58)	9
Table 1.2	Reliability Analyses Results	10
Table 2.1	Descriptive Characteristics of the Sample (N=113)	24
Table 2.2	Reliability Analyses Results	27
Table 2.3	Intercorrelation Matrix of PTGI, MLQ, ARM, and SWLS (N=113)	29

Acknowledgments

A book is a major project indeed, and the editors are grateful to the many persons who have helped us along the way. We would like to thank Kasey Beduhn at Lexington Books for ably assisting us through the process. Also essential to mention are the faculty, staff, and students in Cambodia, Haiti, and India who contributed to the research described in several chapters in this book. Grant J. Rich expresses his appreciation for their help, hospitality, and guidance during his time in each of these nations. Not only was their assistance invaluable during the research process for the chapters on these nations in this book, but these international experiences also deepened our own understanding of resilience and posttraumatic growth. We'd also like to emphasize our gratitude to mentors, teachers, and colleagues who have encouraged us throughout the process. In particular, Grant Rich notes that Uwe P. Gielen, Harold Takooshian and Danny Wedding must be acknowledged for their exemplar work as international psychologists, and for help along the way above and beyond the ordinary. Jill Sirikantraporn acknowledges Debra Kawahara and Neil Ribner for their ongoing support and mentorship since she started embarking on her academic journey as a junior professor with a specialization in international psychology, Michael Ungar for inspiration in high-quality international resilience work, and her coeditor, Grant Rich, for a truly exceptional collaboration and for being her role model as a dedicated international psychologist. We'd also like to thank loved ones who offered moral support both during the process of producing this book and during the sojourns abroad to conduct the research, often far away from family. Grant Rich singles out his parents, models of resilience in the face of challenge. Jill Sirikantraporn would like to thank her parents in Thailand, Kasem and Wandee Sirikantraporn, and her husband, Kevin Hart, for their unwavering support and belief in her work. Finally, to everyone who believed in this project and its value, a huge thank you!

Foreword

Innovation, Inspiration, and Hope

Chris E. Stout

In other writings, I have often quoted from an excerpt from The Reverend Dr. Martin Luther King's Nobel acceptance speech "*Of all the forms of inequality, injustice in health care is the most shocking and inhumane.*" It is sad that a person of King's stature had to make this point; sadder still is that it was said some 50-odd years ago, and not much has changed. But, from reading the work of the authors in this book, I am now experiencing equal parts of hope and inspiration that we may be upon a change . . .

I am not an economist nor a policy wonk or even a political scientist. I am trained as a clinical psychologist, experienced as a health system administrator, learned as a medical school professor, matured as a result of numerous start-ups, and passionate about the work of my not-for-profit Center that focuses on global health inequity projects. All this led me to look positively at the impact of the efforts of the projects described herein and to see what this group of talented professionals will be up to next.

Drs. Rich and Sirikantraporn have created a unique book that crosses borders as well as paradigms in the analyses and synthesis of resilience across the spectrum of human experience and trauma presented. One of the founding directors of my Center, the late Edith Grotberg, PhD, spent five years in Sudan, teaching at the Ahfad University for Women in Omdurman, where she began her work on resilience. This work culminated in an international study of the promotion of resilience with data gathered from 22 countries. Her books on resilience include *A Guide to Promoting Resilience in Children: Strengthening the Human Spirit* (1995), *Tapping Your Inner Strength: How to Find the Resilience to Deal with Anything* (1999), and *Resilience for Today: Gaining Strength from Adversity* (2003), during the production of which we first met. She always coached me to look at the resilience aspects of any project we may undertake at our Center, and those projects were always the better for it. I feel her aspirations live on in this book and in the efforts of the authors.

I am also reminded of one of my favorite books, William Easterly's *The White Man's Burden* (2006), wherein he examines the power of the small project, and *Human Strengths and Resilience: Developmental, Cross-Cultural, and International Perspectives* further demonstrates this power acted out in a global way. The contributing authors, as well as the coeditors, are a who's who of experts in the field today, consolidated in this impressive work. This book provides a wonderful opportunity to take a look into both their world and their work at a fine-grain level.

While written by psychologists, social workers and other behavioral health care professionals, the readership audience is not limited to such. I think policy experts, political scientists, economists, humanitarian organizations' leadership, along with global health practitioners/thought leaders, and undergraduate and graduate students in various programs will gain much from learning about their work. This book represents a *tour de force* of various voices and perspectives bound together by the uniting thread of human strengths and resilience. In some instances, we learn how such are organic or indigenous to some individuals surviving in extraordinary situations and circumstances. In others, it is a hopeful indication that trauma can alternatively produce growth via the informed aid and in collaboration with a psychologist or other behavioral health care specialist.

This also reminds me of what a dear friend, Jonathan Granoff, president of the Global Security Institute, said to me while I was working on my three-volume book set, *The New Humanitarians* (2009, p. 8), "(this work) is a counter to the pervasive 'pornography of the trivial' that infects much of what is in print these days." I feel this is also the case for *Human Strengths and Resilience: Developmental, Cross-Cultural, and International Perspectives*, but even more so from an academic publishing context.

Speaking as a psychologist, and as I have said before, I feel that many of us too often sit on the global health sidelines, feeling like we're in the wrong arena. There has historically been a great divide between behavioral health and its potential in dealing with the health aspects of the overall human sequelae of disasters—both natural and human caused. The late Norine Johnson, PhD, changed that during her tenure as president of the American Psychological Association (APA), when she had its council of representatives add the word "health" to the APA's mission statement (Garcia-Shelton, 2006). Similarly, another APA past president, and dear, dear friend and mentor, Patrick DeLeon (2003), rightfully chided us psychologists, noting that, as a science and a profession, psychology has not yet developed a highly visible and proactive international agenda. Shame on us, as I believe that psychologists are better prepared by our training than those in most other disciplines to provide culturally competent services along with a myriad of psychological tools necessary to effect change in individuals, families, systems of care, and policy. This book is yet another piece of evidence.

I think that reading the words and the works of those in this book will help expand our vision and, hopefully, our participation. Those who know me will attest that I am a bit of a broad thinker and integrator of often diverse disciplines and perspectives; thus, readers of this important work will understand why I was so impressed with not only the authors' scholarship and their fundamental work that their writing is predicated upon, but perhaps even more so their humanity.

REFERENCES

DeLeon, P. (2003, July). A time for psychology's proactive involvement. *International Psychology Bulletin, 7*(3), 10, 18, 20.

Easterly, W. (2006). *The White man's burden: Why the West's efforts to aid the rest have done so much ill and so little good.* New York: Penguin Press.

Garcia-Shelton, L. (2006). Meeting US health care needs: A challenge to psychology. *Professional Psychology: Research and Practice, 37*(6), 676.

Grotberg, E. H. (1995). *A guide to promoting resilience in children: Strengthening the human spirit.* The Hague, The Netherlands: Bernard van leer foundation.

Grotberg, E. H. (1999). *Tapping your inner strength: How to find the resilience to deal with anything.* Oakland, CA: New Harbinger.

Grotberg, E. H. (Ed.). (2003). *Resilience for today: Gaining strength from adversity.* Westport, CT: Greenwood Publishing Group.

Stout, C. E. (2009). *The new humanitarians: Inspiration, innovations, and blueprints for visionaries, Volume 1, Changing global health inequities.* Santa Barbara, CA: ABC-CLIO.

Introduction

Human Strengths and Resilience: Developmental, Cross-Cultural, and International Perspectives

Grant J. Rich and Skultip (Jill) Sirikantraporn

HUMAN RESILIENCE AND POSTTRAUMATIC GROWTH: INTERNATIONAL AND CROSS-CULTURAL PERSPECTIVES

Over the past several generations, psychology is emerging from a discipline dominated by the United States to a much more international discipline. In fact, Zoma and Gielen (2015) estimate that approximately 76 percent–78 percent of the world's approximately one million psychologists now reside outside the United States. However, most textbooks in the field continue to rely almost exclusively on research conducted in North America and Europe (Takooshian, Gielen, Plous, Rich, & Velayo, 2016) despite recent trends and efforts to internationalize the teaching of psychology (e.g., Leong, Pickren, Leach, & Marsella, 2012; Rich, Gielen, & Takooshian, 2017).

In addition to the internationalization of psychology, another trend over the past fifteen years or so has been the development of positive psychology, led by Martin E.P. Seligman, Mihaly Csikszentmihalyi, and other leaders. Since its formal launch in the late 1990s, positive psychology has resulted in a number of advancements in psychology. In particular, by emphasizing human strengths and virtues it has offered a welcome corrective to what has been termed as the "business as usual" or "doom and gloom psychology" that has been the principle focus of most of the discipline since its nineteenth-century origins (e.g., Peterson, 2006; Seligman, 2011). Positive psychologists state that they aim for an evidence-based, rigorous methodological approach and work to avoid a naïve Pollyanna-like view of human nature (Rich, 2016, 2017; Seligman, 2002; Seligman & Csikszentmihalyi, 2000). Among the topics considered by positive psychologists are positive emotions, positive traits, and positive institutions, including such foci as happiness, life satisfaction, subjective well-being, positive coping, and resilience. It should be noted that work in strength-based social work (e.g., Saleeby, 2008) also relates to the positive psychology discipline, as does the recently emerging fields of positive anthropology and anthropology of well-being (e.g., Mathews & Izquierdo, 2009).

Our book is intended to serve as a bridge between these two rapidly expanding disciplines by focusing on the critical issue of human strengths and resilience in cross-cultural and international perspective. Additionally, many of the chapters in this book adopt a developmental, lifespan perspective, and many of the chapters utilize child or youth samples, and/or emphasize growth over time during the lifespan.

Later in this chapter we describe some other books which address similar themes, but we succinctly note here now that our book is special, unique, and timely in that it specifically focuses on a strengths-based positive psychology approach to posttraumatic growth (PTG) and resilience, rather than merely on PTSD or trauma. In addition, we find only two other books that focus on resilience and PTG in international context, though the present volume focuses on different, understudied, yet worthy of attention nations and groups, such as post-earthquake Haiti, post-genocide Cambodia, contemporary political, caste, and gender violence in India, Syrian refugees, PTG in Armenian disaster survivors, PTG for aid workers in the African Ebola crisis, sexual trauma in South African adolescent girls, resilience in post-conflict Guatemala, and cultural and historical factors impacting resilience in Taiwan. This research, from many international regions, is special, and much needed for positive social change around the globe, and to inform researchers, clinicians, and policymakers about conditions in these regions and the implications they have both internationally and for research and practice in the United States. Among the questions examined include how human strengths, resilience, and PTG manifest themselves in diverse regions of the world, and how and why these qualities are similar and different from such strengths as evident in North American, Western European, and other wealthy, industrialized nations. Furthermore, the book explores how existing theories and research on resilience and PTG apply or do not apply to the international contexts examined in our book, thus sharpening thinking and understanding of these processes.

To achieve these ambitious goals, the editors have assembled an international group of leading contributors who, taken together, have taught, counseled, consulted, and conducted research in all regions of the world, including North America, Europe, Asia, Africa, the Pacific Region, Latin America, the Caribbean Region, and the Middle East. Among the contributors are numerous Fellows of the American Psychological Association, editors of several books on trauma/resilience (e.g., Kalayjian's *Mass Trauma and Emotional Healing Around the World* and *Forgiveness and Reconciliation* and Theron's

Youth Resilience and Culture) and international psychology (e.g., Kuriansky's *The Psychosocial Aspects of a Mass Epidemic: Ebola, Beyond Bullets and Bombs: Grassroots Peacebuilding Between Israelis and Palestinians* and *Living in an Environmentally Traumatized World*), award winners (e.g., Kalayjian's 2016 APA's Trauma Division D56 "Outstanding Contributions to the Practice of Trauma Psychology" award and Theron's 2013 Education Association of South African award for contributions to understanding and promoting resilience processes), and advocates (e.g., Kalayjian's and Kuriansky's work for the UN, Abi-Hashem's consultations to many institutions and groups on trauma and issues in the Middle East). In brief, the book represents a dynamic collaboration of leading scholars on issues of significance and value to the psychology of today and the future.

The editors are experienced academics and psychologists, and together form an effective collaboration that bridges applied practice and academic research. Grant Rich has an abiding interest in international psychology and positive psychology. He has published two recent edited books in international psychology, *Pathfinders in International Psychology* (Rich & Gielen, 2015) and *Internationalizing the Teaching of Psychology* (Rich, Gielen, & Takooshian, 2017), and also has served as editor for various special issues of journals, and for publications including APA's *International Psychology Bulletin*. Dr. Rich has taught in Cambodia and India as well as the United States, publishing on topics in cross-cultural and strengths-based psychology. Dr. Sirikantraporn, originally from Southeast Asia, is a licensed psychologist with extensive experience teaching and counseling in trauma, resilience, and PTG in the context of international psychology, also publishing and conducting research on resilience and PTG. Together, Drs. Rich and Sirikantraporn have extensive clinical and research experience, informing both their ongoing research projects in Cambodia, India, and Haiti, among other nations, and their editing of the present volume.

It is helpful to mention several books that are relevant to the present volume, and which likely will interest its readers. Though there are many books that examine PTSD, resilience, or posttraumatic growth, as noted earlier, the present book is specially positioned to fill an important gap in the literature by explicitly focusing on international work concerning (1) positive psychology, strengths-based approaches to PTG, and resilience, in (2) understudied nations (e.g., Haiti, Cambodia, India, Syria) that clearly face significant challenges.

Youth Resilience and Culture: Commonalities and Complexities (Cross-cultural advancements in positive psychology) (2015), edited by Linda Theron, Linda Liebenberg, and Michael Ungar targets some similar issues as this book and is international in nature. In general, Theron, Liebenberg, and Ungar examine such nations as Canada, Zimbabwe, New Zealand, China, and

Colombia, and have a narrower focus on youth only, compared to samples in this book that range from youth through adulthood and, indeed, old age. Importantly, the present volume focuses largely on different nations/groups (e.g., Haiti, Cambodia, India, Guatemala, Syrian refugees, and Armenia—ones that indeed have large numbers of traumatized persons, and which are underrepresented in the resilience literature).

In *Posttraumatic Growth and Culturally Competent Practice: Lessons Learned from Around the Globe*, Weiss and Berger (2010), two social work faculty members also examine a topic similar to ours, but they focus on very different nations than those in the present book. For instance, their book explores Spain, the Netherlands, Israel, Japan, Germany, and Australia. Additionally, they write from a social work rather than a psychology perspective. Finally, though ten years old, Rhoades and Sar's *Trauma and Dissociation in a Cross-Cultural Perspective* (2005) does focus on some related content on trauma, though, unlike our book, it focuses on dissociation, and their book largely predates the current work on positive psychology and strengths-based work on PTG and resilience. Additionally, it focuses on very different nations than our book (e.g., Argentina, China, Ireland, Australia, France, and Japan).

Several other valuable books do examine PTG but do not have an international orientation. Among these books are Calhoun and Tedeschi's *Handbook of Posttraumatic Growth: Research and Practice* (2006), which has no international focus, and Calhoun and Tedeschi's more recent *Posttraumatic Growth in Clinical Practice* (2013), which has one chapter on "multicultural" issues. Joseph and Linley's *Trauma, Recovery, and Growth: Positive Psychological Perspectives on Posttraumatic Stress* (2008) does take a strengths-based approach, but it only has one chapter that can be considered somewhat international (one on immigrants). Paton, Violanti, and Smith edited *Promoting Capabilities to Manage Posttraumatic Stress: Perspectives on Resilience* (2002), though this older book does not have an international focus, except one chapter on South Africa, nor an explicitly positive psychology approach. Harvard's Bessel van der Kolk wrote an important and best-selling book with *The Body Keeps Score: Brain, Mind, and Body in the Healing of Trauma* (2015), but his book is largely a literature review reporting on his significant, influential work; he mostly focuses on the United States and does not explicitly take a strengths-based positive psychology approach. Paul Wong's edited book, *The Human Quest for Meaning* (2012), has an important focus on life meaning that relates in some ways to resilience and positive coping, but the focus in his book is more on existential psychology, and only one chapter focuses (as indicated by its title) on resilience; in addition, it is not internationally focused in its samples, though one of its chapters does utilize Chinese adolescents from Hong Kong.

Several other books focus on trauma in individual nations, but are not focused internationally around the globe in multiple nations such as the present book. Nor do these otherwise helpful books take a positive psychology strengths-based approach focused on PTG and resilience; rather they focus mostly on posttraumatic stress disorder (PTSD) and related anxiety and depression issues. For instance, Van Schaack, Reicherter, and Chhang (2011) take a mostly psychiatric approach to Cambodia in their book *Cambodia's Hidden Scars: Trauma Psychology in the Wake of the Khmer Rouge*. Likewise, well-known Harvard physician and anthropologist Paul Farmer writes a book-length view of the situation in Haiti post-2010 earthquake (*Haiti: After the Earthquake* (2010)), but it focuses on many medical, social, and health issues beyond resilience and posttraumatic stress, and focuses only on Haiti.

In sum, the present book fills an important gap by bridging the rapidly expanding disciplines of positive psychology and strengths-based work with a focus on PTG and resilience, with a much-needed international and often developmental focus, in nations that clearly have underserved, understudied populations with a significant prevalence of trauma.

The target audience for this book includes scholars and researchers in the discipline of trauma and PTG and resilience, as well as those in related fields, such as positive psychology, strengths-based social work, and cross-cultural and international psychology. We also anticipate our book finding an audience with advanced undergraduates and graduate students, in addition to some therapists, practitioners, and clinicians. The present book may be utilized in a broad range of courses; it is especially timely, given the increased need and desire to internationalize courses (Takooshian, Gielen, Plous, Rich, & Velayo, 2016). The following is a nonexhaustive list of courses for which the proposed book may be used: stress and coping, disaster and mental health, diversity and trauma, cross-cultural psychology, cultural psychology, international psychology, counseling psychology, clinical psychology, positive psychology, developmental psychology, trauma and resilience across cultures, and courses in related nonpsychology disciplines, such as allied health professions, including transcultural psychiatry, transcultural nursing, medical anthropology, and public health.

In the following section, the plan and chapter contents of the book are briefly summarized.

BRIEF REVIEW OF CHAPTERS

The book is loosely organized with more empirical research chapters near the start of the book, review chapters of research around the middle of the book, and chapters based on clinical, consulting, and humanitarian aid experience toward the end of the book. That said, the boundaries are fuzzy indeed, and many chapters, or parts of chapters, could be categorized in multiple categories, as research informs practice, and practice informs research.

The first three chapters in the book are coauthored by the book editors Jill Sirikantraporn and Grant Rich and their colleagues, based on their work in India, Haiti, and Cambodia. Each of these three studies utilizes a mixed-methods design, and each study includes both qualitative interviews and quantitative data. Among the quantitative measure utilized in these three studies are: a demographic form, the life events checklist (LEC), the posttraumatic growth inventory scale (PTGI), and the Adult Resilience Measure (ARM). The India study also used the General Health Questionnaire-28 (GHQ-28), and the Haiti study also utilized the Meaning in Life Questionnaire (MLQ) and the Satisfaction with Life Scale (SWLS). While some quantitative data are reported in the chapter on Cambodia, here we focus more on the qualitative interview data. Each of these three chapters begins with a review and analysis of trauma in the respective nation, and these chapters also note recent events that may have impacted results and conclusions. For instance, in India, the Jat agitation of 2016 involved caste-based violence that closed the university at which data were collected for one week during the term of the study. In Haiti, all participants were impacted by the 2010 earthquake there, but a very deadly 2016 Hurricane that occurred about one month prior to data collection also likely impacted participants. Finally, for Cambodia, while many are aware of the nation's brutal Pol Pot time in the 1970s that resulted in the deaths of one-fourth of Cambodia's population, fewer outside Cambodia are aware of its current challenges with crime, corruption, poverty, and lack of adequate health care. Reading the three chapters together one can begin to find both commonalities and uniqueness in the experiences of each nation's participants, as well as similarities and differences to existing models of PTG mostly developed in Europe, the United States, and other developed nations. Results from these studies have implications for development of culturally appropriate clinical applications in each respective nation, and likely implications for work with refugees or immigrants from these nations to other nations, such as to the United States.

Like Cambodia, Guatemala is surfacing from years of violence and war. Tannia de Castañeda and María del Pilar Grazioso describe the historical background to the situation in that nation, as well as offer some cultural orientation before describing a range of research projects and applications, predominately targeting youth, that aim to build resilience and strengths capacities in this population to the benefit of both the individual participants and the society as a whole. Ching-Yu Huang's chapter examines resilience in Taiwan, focusing in particular about the special culture there, and how it is both similar to and different from the culture and history of mainland China.

Her chapter reviews ample historical, sociological, cultural, and psychological evidence to lead to suggestions for more effective, more nuanced clinical practice with Taiwanese or immigrant Taiwanese families. Next, in their chapter, Sadiyya Haffejee and Linda Theron examine contextual risks and resilience enablers in South Africa with a powerful case study and participatory study. Their work is methodologically rich, with an approach involving participatory diagramming, interviews, and digital stories to explore the life histories of seven sexually abused adolescent girls.

The final three chapters, by Naji Abi-Hashem, Ani Kalayjian and Daria Diakonova-Curtis, and Judy Kuriansky and her colleagues, are more practice based and more consultant oriented. Naji Abi-Hashem focuses on trauma, coping, and resilience among Syrian refugees in Lebanon and environs. His helpful chapter first describes the historical and contextual events from the Middle East that are relevant to the present situation, and he also explains his own point of view in terms of relevant education and experience to the present population. His chapter, based on extensive applied work with the population, offers numerous examples of both the types of challenges faced by the Syrian refugees and the strengths they bring and cultivate to help them meet these challenges with enduring resilience. Ani Kalayjian and Daria Diakonova-Curtis describe Dr. Kalayjian's Seven-Step Integrative Healing Model for Resilience and Meaning-Making and how it has been applied extensively in several regions around the globe, including work by her Meaningfulworld group after traumatic events in Armenia, a Hurricane in Florida, the 9/11 attacks in New York, and the tsunami in Sri Lanka, and following Palestinian-Israeli tensions. Finally, Judy Kuriansky and her colleagues examine how the prevalence of natural disasters as well as epidemics impacting nations around globe emphasize the need for quality psychological supports in both the short and the long term. The authors describe a stepped pyramid model used to train community members that they implemented over several years in post-earthquake Haiti and in Sierra Leone after the Ebola epidemic. The authors review existing research and their own studies and applications in these nations, and make evidence-based recommendations for research and policy for disaster recovery, especially that aimed at reducing treatment disparities in developing nations and underserved communities.

REFERENCES

Calhoun, L. G., & Tedeschi, R. G. (Eds.). (2006). *Handbook of posttraumatic growth: Research and practice*. New York: Psychology Press.

Calhoun, L. G., & Tedeschi, R. G. (2013). *Posttraumtic growth in clinical practice*. New York: Routledge.

Farmer, P. (2011). *Haiti after the earthquake*. New York: Public Affairs.
Joseph, S., & Linley, P. A. (Eds.). (2008). *Trauma, recovery, and growth: Positive psychological perspectives on posttraumatic stress*. Hoboken, NJ: John Wiley.
Kalayjian, A., & Eugene, D. (Eds.). (2010). *Mass trauma and emotional healing around the world*. Santa Barbara, CA: ABC-CLIO.
Kalayjian, A., & Paloutzian, R. F. (Eds.). (2010). *Forgiveness and reconciliation*. New York: Springer.
Kuriansky, J. (Ed.). (2007). *Beyond bullets and bombs: Grassroots peacebuilding between Israelis and Palestinians*. Westport, CT: Praeger.
Kuriansky, J. (Ed.). (2016). *The psychosocial aspects of a mass epidemic*. Santa Barbara, CA: ABC-CLIO.
Leong, F. T. L., Pickren, W. E., Leach, M. M., & Marsella, A. J. (Eds.). (2012). *Internationalizing the psychology curriculum in the United States*. New York: Springer.
Mathews, G., & Izquierdo, C. (Eds.). (2009). *Pursuits of happiness: Well-being in anthropological perspective*. New York: Berghahn Books.
Nemeth, D., Hamilton, R. B., & Kuriansky, J. (Eds.). (2012). *Living in an environmentally traumatized world*. Santa Barbara, CA: ABC-CLIO.
Paton, D., Violanti, J. M., & Smith, L. M. (Eds.). (2002). *Promoting capabilities to manage posttraumatic stress: Perspectives on resilience*. Springfield, IL: Charles C. Thomas.
Peterson, C. (2006). *A primer in positive psychology*. New York: Oxford University Press.
Rhoades, G. F., & Sar, V. (Eds.). (2005). *Trauma and dissociation in a cross-cultural perspective*. New York: Routledge.
Rich, G. (2016). The promise of qualitative inquiry for positive psychology: Diversifying methods. *Journal of Positive Psychology, 12*(3), 220–231. doi: 10.1080/17439760.2016.1225119.
Rich, G. (2017). Positive psychology and humanistic psychology: Evil twins, sibling rivals, distant cousins or something else? *Journal of Humanistic Psychology*. doi: 10.1177/0022167817698820.
Rich, G., & Gielen, U. (Eds.). (2015). *Pathfinders in international psychology*. Charlotte, NC: IAP- Information Age Publishing.
Rich, G., Gielen, U., & Takooshian, H. (Eds.). (2017). *Internationalizing the teaching of psychology*. Charlotte, NC: IAP- Information Age Publishing.
Saleeby, D. (Ed.). (2008). *The strengths perspective in social work practice* (5th ed.). Boston: Allyn & Bacon.
Seligman, M. E. P. (2002). *Authentic happiness*. New York: Free Press.
Seligman, M. (2011). *Flourish*. New York: Free Press.
Seligman, M. E. P., & Csikszentmihalyi, M. (2000). Positive psychology: An introduction. *American Psychologist, 55*, 5–14.
Takooshian, H., Gielen, U., Plous, S., Rich, G., & Velayo, R. (2016). Internationalizing undergraduate psychology education: Trends, techniques, and technologies. *American Psychologist, 71* (2), 136–147.
Tedeschi, R. G., & Calhoun, L. G. (1996). The posttraumatic growth inventory: Measuring the positive legacy of trauma. *Journal of Traumatic Stress, 9* (3), 455–471.

Theron, L., Liebenberg, L., & Ungar, M. (Eds.). (2015). *Youth resilience and culture: Commonalities and complexities (Cross-cultural advancements in positive psychology).* New York: Springer.

Van Schaack, B., Reicherter, D., & Chhang, Y. (Eds.). (2011). *Cambodia's hidden scars: Trauma psychology in the wake of the Khmer Rouge.* Phnom Penh, Cambodia: Documentation Center of Cambodia.

Van der Kolk, B. (2015). *The body keeps the score: Brain, mind, and body in the healing of trauma.* New York: Viking.

Weiss, T., & Berger, R. (Eds.). (2010). *Posttraumatic growth and culturally competent practice: Lessons learned from around the globe.* Hoboken, NJ: John Wiley and Sons.

Wong, P. (Ed.). (2012). *The human quest for meaning* (2nd ed.). New York: Taylor and Francis.

Zoma, M., & Gielen, U. P. (2015). How many psychologists are there in the world? *International Psychology Bulletin, 19*(1), 47–50.

Chapter 1

The Concept of Posttraumatic Growth in a Sample of Undergraduates from India

A Mixed-Methods Study

Skultip (Jill) Sirikantraporn, Grant J. Rich, and Julie C. Badaracco

Resilience is increasingly studied cross-culturally to better capture the nuances of the recovery/thriving process after trauma in different cultures/nations. This chapter focuses upon posttraumatic growth (PTG) in a sample of undergraduate students at an academically rigorous university in northern India, in Haryana state. As India is an exceptionally diverse nation, generalizing results from this present study to other regions or populations in India should be viewed with caution.

Located in South Asia, India shares borders with Pakistan, China, Nepal, Bhutan, Myanmar (Burma) and Bangladesh. India is presently the second most populous nation in the world, with 1.2 billion people, and is expected to become the world's most populous nation by 2028 (Sirikantraporn, Rich, Badaracco, Valsaint, & Krukeja, 2017). India consists of 29 states and 7 union territories, with New Delhi being its capital. Official languages are Hindi and English. Hindi and English are the main languages in the Haryana region, where the data collection site for the present study is located, and Punjabi is an additional official language there. The language of instruction at the research site was English.

Census figures (2011) indicate great religious diversity in India: Hinduism (79.8 percent), Islam (14.23 percent), Christianity (2.3 percent), Sikhism (1.72 percent), Buddhism (0.70 percent), Jainism (0.36 percent) and others such as Zoroastrianism and Baha'i. In Haryana, the research site, the 2011 Census finds that Hindus were 87.46 percent, Sikhs 4.91 percent and Muslims 7.03 percent of the state population. Also notable is that the 2011 Census finds that the sex ratio nationally was 940 females per 1,000 males. Haryana state has perhaps the greatest disparity (903 to 1,000, in 2015) (Sirikantraporn, Rich, Badaracco, Valsaint, & Krukeja, 2017).

India is considered the world's fourth-largest economy. While India has steadily enjoyed fast economic gross domestic product (GDP) growth rate (about 9 percent), the World Bank's current estimation of the number of people below the poverty line in India is above 20 percent (the World Bank, 2017). Poverty in India is largely pervasive in rural areas, where 70 percent of India's population lives. Poverty rates in India's poorest states are three to four times higher than those in the more advanced states. India experiences one of the worst social and economic inequity situations in the world. Inequity in all dimensions, including religion, health, caste and gender, is virtually omnipresent in India.

Poverty-stricken areas often face many infrastructural and public health problems, including road safety, inadequate quality health care services and ongoing threats of land acquisition by the government state in farming areas (Parwez & Sen, 2016). The issue of gender inequality and gender-based violence in India has been raised very fervently in international media in recent years. These social, economic and cultural stressors affecting numerous lives in India bring attention to the impact of extreme life stress or trauma in Indians.

TRAUMA IN INDIA

While there is no one single definition of trauma, it has been broadly and universally defined as life events that bring about extreme distress in individuals, including threats to physical and/or emotional integrity. Trauma can be experienced directly, or indirectly, by witnessing it happening to loved ones. Trauma involves experiencing, witnessing, anticipating or being confronted with an event or events that involve actual or threatened death or serious injury, or threat to the physical integrity of one's self or others (APA, 2013).

Political Trauma

Historically and politically, India has experienced political conflicts for decades (and indeed centuries), both prior and after its independence in 1947. For instance, much has been written on abuses under the British Colonial Empire, and their psychological impact on the present generations of Indians (e.g., Kakar & Kakar, 2011; Linstrum, 2016; Sen, 2005).

In terms of violence, some argue that India has been a success story overall, in that, post-Independence, it has avoided involvement in wars of the magnitude of World Wars I and II. In addition, it must be mentioned that India has nuclear weapons, currently has the world's third largest standing army and is rated sixth in military expenditure internationally. That said, one must remember on the other hand the many violent conflicts/events that have transpired over the past nearly seventy years. For example, estimates of those killed around the 1947 partition with Pakistan range from 200,000 to 2,000,000 with 14 million displaced persons. Furthermore, India has continued strained relations with Pakistan, with wars/conflicts in 1947, 1965, 1971 and 1999, particularly involving Kashmir and Bangladesh. Interactions with Pakistan remain tense, as is even witnessed by public reactions surrounding sporting matches between the two nations. The 1962 Sino-Indian War should also be noted, as well as the continued strong military presence along borders with both Pakistan and China. Finally, it should be noted in addition to its violent engagements with other nations, there is notable violence and political instability within India itself. For instance, one should mention the issues and events involving the Maoist-influenced Naxalite insurgents, Jammu/Kashmir separatists, and continued religious and caste-related violence (India, 2017).

Natural Disasters

It has been reported that in India, there have been a total of 431 natural disasters from 1980 to 2010 (Chadha, Malhotra, & Srivastava, 2013). The most recent devastating one was the Indian Ocean tsunami in December 2004, which resulted in the most devastating earthquake in recent history, caused massive destruction in eight Asian countries and had over 250,000 casualties (John, Russell, & Russell, 2007).

Traffic- and Infrastructure-Related Traumas

India has the largest amount of fatal road traffic accidents in the world (Rastogi et al., 2014). Indian studies have estimated that road traffic accidents are increasing at the annual rate of 3 percent; a vehicular accident is reported every two minutes and a death every eight minutes on Indian roads. A trauma-related death occurs in India every 1.9 minutes. The majority of fatal road traffic accident victims are pedestrians, two-wheeler riders and bicyclists. India loses approximately 2–2.5 percent of its GDP to road traffic injuries alone (PreventionWeb, 2014).

Gender-Based Violence against Women

Gender-based violence against women and girls has been a public health issue in India that has received wider international attention in recent years (Ganapathy-Coleman, 2017). For instance, a 2012 gang rape and murder of a 23-year-old physiotherapy student who had boarded a bus after seeing a movie with a male friend led to riots and ample discussion in India about the rape issue and about gender violence more generally. A film based on the event was scheduled to be released on International Women's Day in India, but a court order by the Indian police prevented that broadcast, though the film aired widely outside India and was uploaded to YouTube, though the Indian government ordered YouTube to block access to it in India (Udwin, 2015).

It has been reported that overall, about 50 percent of women reported experiencing at least one abusive behavior at least once in their married life; 43.5 percent reported at least one psychologically abusive behavior, and 40.3 percent reported experiencing at least one form of violent physical behavior (Ahuja et al., 2000). Two million women in India are HIV positive, and often they are infected by husbands who visit brothels or who have multiple partners (Ganapathy-Coleman, 2017).

TRAUMA RESPONSES

High-impact trauma disrupts known ways of living for trauma victims. Trauma can have adverse and chronic effects on its victims. Culture plays a major role in how trauma manifests in its members. Like many other Asian cultures, India has exhibited collectivistic, fatalistic and interdependent preferences (Sinha & Verma, 1994). This has been demonstrated in a study of victims of the Asian Tsunami, and results reflect the importance of community support, collectivistically constructed meaning after the trauma and public mourning (Rajkumar, Premkumar, & Tharyan, 2008).

RECENT TRAUMATIC EVENTS: THE JAT AGITATION OF 2016 AND STUDENT SUICIDES

In February 2016, India faced riots due to the Jat agitation in Haryana, India. The riots were a result of caste-based violence in which the Jat caste made demands for reservations in jobs/education (an issue somewhat reminiscent of US affirmative action debates). Jats are listed as upper caste but desired job quotas similar to those granted to lower castes (Sirikantraporn, Rich, Badaracco, Valsaint, & Krukeja, 2017). The agitation led to 30 deaths, and over 1,000 arrests, with numerous incidences of arson, as well as blockading of the national highway, and allegations of mass rape of ten women by a mob of 30 men. Estimates of damage are in the range of $US5 billion. More than ten million people in the capital, Delhi, had to go without water after the protesters also sabotaged a key canal supplying water to the city. There were thousands of troops in Haryana. The Indian army was called to Rohtak and other towns such as Sonepat, in which the data collection site for the present study is located. In Sonepat, protesters vandalized a hotel and college owned by a member of Parliament (MP). At the university in which data for the present study were collected, some staff members took personal risk to escort vehicles of food supplies to campus. In addition, some alumni/staff were generous in offering accommodation to students stranded in Delhi (Sirikantraporn, Rich, Badaracco, Valsaint, & Krukeja, 2017).

Another event that caused anxiety and stress to many Indians, especially university students, was a highly publicized 2016 suicide of a student, Rohith Vemula, and media coverage of other earlier student suicides as alleged incidences of discrimination against Dalits and backward classes. Though India's stated goals and policies frequently promote religious and class tolerance and equality, these realities and events show that in practice, laws, policies and publicly stated beliefs may not always align with actual behaviors and with statistics that show enduring inequalities and disparities (Sirikantraporn, Rich, Badaracco, Valsaint, & Krukeja, 2017).

Notably, the Jat agitation occurred in February 2016, in the midst of the academic term at the data collection site in Haryana, India. The university (along with other such institutions) closed for one week during the peak of the violence. Quantitative data for the present study were collected about one month later, in March 2016, and qualitative interviews were conducted several months later in May 2016.

METHODS

Participants

For the quantitative portion of this study, there were 58 participants. The sample comprised undergraduate students at an academically rigorous university in northern India, in Haryana state. The demographic questionnaire revealed that participants were relatively young, with a mean age of 18.71 (SD= 1.02, range=18–24). The majority of the sample were females (74.1 percent). All were identified as single and were currently college students. About 45.5 percent reported moderate income, and 45.5 percent reported high to very high income. Slightly over 50 percent self-identified as Hindu (54.4 percent), 5.3 percent as Buddhist, 3.5 percent as Muslim and 3.5 percent as Sikh. One hundred percent of the sample reported having experienced at least 3 types (out of 17) of traumatic events, with 51 percent reporting at least 11 traumatic events. When compared to a previous trauma study of undergraduates at a Midwestern university in the United States (Osei-Bonsu, Weaver, Eisen, & Vander Wal, 2011), which reported 44.6 percent (*n*=166) recounting one lifetime traumatic incident and 55.4 percent recounting two or more traumatic events, the rates are much higher in the present study.

9 participants, five female and four male, out of 58 total participants participated in part 2 of the study, the in-depth interview.

Measures

Fifty-eight participants were administered a survey consisting of five questionnaires: a demographic form, the life events checklist (LEC), the PTG inventory (PTGI) scale, the Adult Resilience Measure (ARM) and the General Health Questionnaire-28 (GHQ-28).

Life Events Checklist

The LEC scale (Gray, Litz, Sue, & Lombardo, 2004) is a self-report measure of participants' lifelong exposure to traumatic events according to the posttraumatic stress disorder (PTSD) criterion A diagnosis in the *Diagnostic and Statistical Manual of Mental Disorders* (DSM)-5. Subjects are given a list of 17 traumatic stressors to choose as to whether the trauma happened to them, they witnessed it, they learned about it, and it was part of their job, or else they indicate they are not sure, or that the question doesn't apply (Gray, Litz, Sue, & Lombardo, 2004). Psychometric properties were reported to have good reliability (Kappa coefficients above .50 ($p< .001$); Gray, Litz, Sue, & Lombardo, 2004).

Posttraumatic Growth Inventory Scale

The PTGI scale (Taku, Cann, Calhoun, & Tedeschi, 2008) is a 21-item Likert scale measuring participants' degree of PTG according to Tedeschi and Calhoun (1996) in the following five subscales: relating to others, new possibilities, personal strength, spiritual change and appreciation of life. Each subscale consisted of possible responses from a Likert scale of 1–6 (1= I did not experience this change as a result of my crisis, and 6= I experienced this change to a very great degree as a result of my crisis).

The PTGI scale has been shown to have satisfactory internal consistency among the total and subscales scores and test-retest reliability with Cronbach's alpha ranging from .67 to .85 (Tedeschi & Calhoun, 1996). Studies have examined the cross-cultural validity of the PTGI scale and whether the items are more influenced by personality or culture. A study by Taku and Oshio (2015) assessed whether the items in the subscale truly measured PTG variables, using a Japanese sample. The results showed that PTG measured by the scale is more likely to occur when core beliefs are challenged, and few occur without cognitive effort. Thus, the significant personality factor in PTG measured by the PTGI scale shows that it is a largely universal phenomenon. Additional cross-cultural studies have suggested that differences in the degree of PTG dimensions are culturally influenced (Cormio, Romitto, Giotta, & Mattioli, 2015; Ho, Law, Wang, Shih, Hsu, & Hou, 2013).

Adult Resilience Measure-28

The ARM (Ungar & Liebenberg, 2011) is a 28-item Likert scale that was adapted from the Child and Youth Resilience Measure-28 (CYRM-28), one of the most culturally sensitive resilience measures (Windle, Bennett, & Noyes, 2011). The measure was derived from data collected in 12 different countries over three different continents. The ARM-28 has three subscales (individual, relational and contextual resilience). Reliability analyses were conducted, and they demonstrate that the CYRM-28 and its subscales are internally consistent with Cronbach's alpha ranging from .80 to .84 (Leibenberg, Ungar, & Van de Vijver, 2012).

General Health Questionnaire-28

Developed by Goldberg in 1978 (Goldberg, 1978), the GHQ-28 aims to detect those with high psychological distress and likely to develop psychiatric disorders. The GHQ-28 has four subscales (somatic symptoms, anxiety/insomnia, social dysfunction and severe depression). Numerous studies have shown high reliability and validity of the GHQ-28 with test-retest reliability being reported between .78 and .9 (Robinson & Price, 1982) and interrater reliability known to be excellent (Cronbach's .9–.95; Falide, Ramos, & Fermandex-Palacin, 2000).

Semi-structured Interview Guide

An interview guide included 20 open-ended questions and aimed to explore in-depth experiences and understanding of the concept of PTG. The questions were based on recent research and clinical literature on PTG and on cultural literature on the Indian culture and society (e.g., Kakar & Kakar, 2011; Misra, Matthijs Cornelissen, & Verma, 2010). To help better ensure confidentiality and data quality and integrity, the qualitative interviews were conducted in May 2016 by an Indian MSW social worker who is a faculty member at a different university in India from the institution at which the sample was selected.

DATA ANALYSES

Quantitative Data

Descriptive statistics were used for frequency findings on the demographic variables, PTGI, ARM, GHQ-28 and LEC. Reliability analyses were utilized to test each measure's internal reliability (Cronbach alpha's). T-test analyses were used to examine whether there were any mean differences of PTGI, ARM, GHQ-28 and LEC among different demographic groups. Pearson correlation analyses were used to analyze correlations between the study of main variables. All significant results are set at p value < .05.

Qualitative Data

Grounded theory was used to generate an emergent theory through the discovery of themes (Glaser & Strauss, 1967). Theoretical sampling was used to increase the maximum variable sampling (Maykut & Morehouse, 1994) by recruiting from the pool of the quantitative sample participants, which reflected a wide variation of trauma experiences, assessed by LEC. The sample size was determined by the concurrent process of data collection and coding procedures until the saturation point was met, the point at which no new categories were forthcoming (Maykut & Mayhouse, 1994). Constant comparative analysis through three stages of coding (open coding, axial coding and selective coding) was used to discover emerging themes and an overarching theory (see Glaser & Strauss, 1967). There were several strategies utilized to increase trustworthiness of the study findings. First, peer scrutiny of the research project was used where three coders independently coded the data and compared emerging categories and themes until the final version of categories and themes was agreed upon. Second, an audit trail and journaling among researchers was utilized to increase researchers' reflexivity and progressive subjectivity (Lincoln & Guba, 1985) to minimize the intrusive influence of the researchers' own biases on the research procedures and findings.

RESULTS AND DISCUSSION

Quantitative Results

Fifty-eight college students at an academically rigorous university in India participated in the study by completing five measures, including the demographic form. The characteristics of the sample included 74 percent female, mean age of 18.71 years (*SD*=1.02, min-max=18–24), 100 percent single (not married), 45.5 percent reporting moderate income, 45.5 percent reporting high to very high income and 54 percent reporting Hinduism as their religion.

Table1.1 revealed the descriptive results of each main variable of the study. Reliability analyses (see Table1.2) revealed that all subscales of PTGI, except one (PTGI-spiritual change), had satisfactory internal reliability, ranging from .67 to .93. All subscales of GHQ-28 had satisfactory internal

Table 1.1 Descriptive Analyses of the Study of Main Variables (*N*=58)

Variables	*% (n)*	*Mean (SD)*	*Min–Max*
LEC (happened to them and witnessed it combined)			
Natural disaster	89.7 (52)		
Transportation accident	87.9 (51)		
Sudden violent death (e.g., homicide, suicide)	86.2 (50)		
Life-threatening illness or injury	79.3 (46)		
Sudden accidental death	77.8 (45)		
Physical assault	75.9 (44)		
Any other very stressful event/ experience	71.9 (41)		
Fire explosion	65.5 (38)		
Other unwanted or uncomfortable sexual experience	62.1 (36)		
Severe human suffering	60.3 (35)		
Assault with weapon	47.4 (27)		
Sexual assault	44.8 (26)		
Serious accident at work or home	43.1 (25)		
Exposure to toxic substance	43.1 (25)		
Combat or exposure to war zone	36.2 (21)		
Captivity	24.1 (14)		
Serious injury, harm, death you cause to someone else	17.2 (10)		
PTGI			
New possibilities		16.71 (5.89)	5–28
Personal strength		13.91 (4.79)	4–22
Relating to others		20.52 (8.08)	6–37
Appreciation of life		10.01 (4.09)	3–17
Spiritual change		2 (1.53)	1–6
PTGI-Total		174.62 (29.24)	102–242
ARM			
Individual		36.61 (4.30)	26–40
Relational		33 (4.34)	23–40
Contextual		29.64 (6.14)	18–44
ARM-Total		107.40 (13.23)	79–137
GHQ			
Somatic symptoms		15.32 (3.31)	8–23
Severe depression		11.42 (5.44)	7–28
Anxiety		15.60 (5.13)	7–28
Social dysfunction		16.32 (3.31)	10–27

Table 1.2 Reliability Analyses Results

Variables	*Number of Items*	*Cronbach's Alpha*	*Response scale*
PTGI			
New possibilities	5	.75*	1–6
Personal strength	4	.67*	1–6
Relating to others	7	.83*	1–6
Spiritual change	2	.26	1–6
Appreciation of life	3	.77*	1–6
PTGI-Total	21	.93*	1–6
GHQ-28			
Somatic symptoms	7	.67*	1–5
Severe depression	7	.61*	1–5
Anxiety	7	.69*	1–5
Social dysfunction	7	.80*	1–5
GHQ-Total	28	.85*	1–5
ARM-28			
Individual	11	.73*	1–4
Relational	7	.76*	1–4
Contextual	10	.79*	1–4
ARM-Total	28	.88*	1–4

* $p<.05$.

reliability, ranging from .61 to .85. All subscales of ARM-28 had satisfactory reliability, ranging from .73 to .88.

Bivariate Correlation Analyses

PTG and Resilience. Pearson correlations revealed that PTGI-total is significantly correlated to ARM-individual, r=.36, ARM-relational, r=.56, ARM-contextual, r=.44 and ARM-total, r=60. PTGI-new possibilities is significantly correlated to ARM-individual, r=.44, ARM-relational, r=.43, ARM-contextual, r=.32 and ARM-total, r=.37. PTGI-personal strength is significantly correlated to ARM-individual, r=.32. PTGI-relating to others is significantly correlated to ARM-individual, r=.39, ARM-relational, r=.42 and ARM-total, r=.37.

PTG, Resilience and Health Outcomes. Pearson correlations revealed that several subscales of PTGI and GHQ are significantly correlated in the negative direction. These include PTGI-total and GHQ-severe depression, r=–.51, PTGI-new possibilities and GHQ-social dysfunction, r=–.31, PTGI-relating to others and GHQ-social dysfunction, r=–.30.

Results also reveal that several subscales of ARM and GHQ are significantly correlated in the negative direction. These include ARM-total and GHQ-social dysfunction, r=–.29, ARM-total and GHQ-severe depression, r=–.32, ARM-individual and GHQ-severe depression, r=–.34, ARM-individual and

GHQ-social dysfunction, *r*=–.30, ARM-relational and GHQ-total, *r*=–.36, and ARM-relational and GHQ-severe depression, *r*=–.39.

Qualitative Results

Nine (five female and four male) participants who completed the quantitative part volunteered to participate in the in-depth interview for the qualitative analysis. Overall, three of the four categories (gratitude for life, personal growth and interpersonal growth) in the original PTG model proposed by Tedeschi and Calhoun (1996) were supported in this Indian qualitative sample; two categories (spiritual change and new possibilities) were not supported, and one new category for this particular sample (healing as a process) emerged.

This section presents exemplary quotations (F means the quotation was from a female participant and M means the quotation was from a male participant) that capture the major categories, together with the major themes associated with each category; discusses the themes of PTG that emerged from the data by the Grounded Theory method; and compares these themes with previous literature on Tedeschi and Calhoun's model of PTG. Four categories and ten themes emerged from the data (see Figure 1.1)

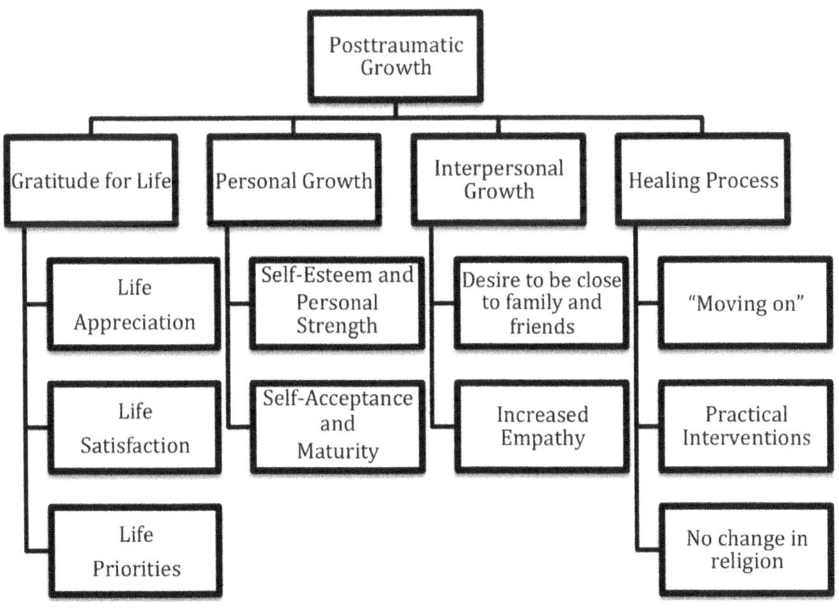

Figure 1.1 Grounded Theory for Posttraumatic Growth Model in the Indian Sample (*N*=9).

Category 1: Gratitude for Life

Gratitude is defined as the feeling of thankfulness and appreciation for kindness and life opportunity. This category has two themes (increased sense of appreciation of life and life satisfaction and contentment leading to happiness).

Theme 1: Increased Sense of Appreciation of Life

It was reported by 100 percent of the sample (nine out of nine) that feeling grateful stemmed from an appreciation of life as a result of the experience of surviving the trauma. Increased appreciation of life was also reported by Calhoun and Tedeschi (2006) as one of the major components of PTG. This is consistent with trauma and recovery literature that suggests that recovery involves recognizing that trauma does not define one's entire identity; rather it is just part of what happened in one's life that needs to be integrated (Herman, 1992).

Quotes from participants to illustrate this theme include:

> Death is part of life. I just want to live my life the best I can. I appreciate life more when I accept this fact. (P#7, M)

> So the fragility of your health and what you can do in life and so that sort of helped me understand. (P#4, M)

Theme 2: Increased Contentment and Life Satisfaction

It was reported by 100 percent of the sample (nine out of nine) that after experiencing the traumatic event, their contentment and satisfaction in things they had in life had increased.

Quotes from participants to illustrate this theme include:

> For me to be happy is to achieve satisfaction with where you are in your life becoming happy means making sure I work hard enough so that wherever I am in terms of my job, in terms of my relationships. (P#2, M)

> My definition of happiness…is feeling good about something you achieved or you know, just small things which make you, give you joy. (P#6, F)

Theme 3: Shifting in Life Priorities

Eighty-eight percent (eight out of nine) reported that components of their life priorities have shifted and/or are more focused after the trauma. According to Lindstrom, Cann, Calhoun and Tedeschi (2011), PTG involves the reconstruction of cognition, which often results in the individual changing their life priorities. This may be related to the appreciation of small things in life, refocusing on what is truly meaningful in life and learning new things (Taylor, Lichtman, & Wood, 1984).

Quotes from participants to illustrate this theme include:

> Life is fragile and finite: the finiteness of life. Like at some point everybody is going to die…I want to focus on what and who is important to me. (P#4, M)

> Shifting priorities and commitment from myself and merely family to building career for future. (P#1, F)

Category 2: Personal Growth

Personal growth refers to responses that pertain to the participants' personal aspects of growth as a result of coping with trauma. This category consists of two themes (increased self-esteem and personal strength and increased self-acceptance and maturity)

Theme 1: Increased Self-esteem and Personal Strength

Hundred percent of the participants (nine out of nine) reported elements of increased personal strength after trauma. Self-esteem is defined as confidence in one's own worth and ability. Self-esteem is associated with psychological well-being and positive mental health (Paradise & Kernis, 2002). As a result of PTG, it also has been shown to increase self-esteem and positive affect in one meta-analysis by Helgeson, Reynolds and Tomich (2006).

Quotes from participants to illustrate this theme include:

> I've gone through something so hard and that means that in the future this happens I will be able to cope with that too. (P#1, F)

> I would call it…empowerment, stronger, I can deal with any problems now. (P#9, F)

> I realized I'm stronger than I ever thought I am. (P#8, F)

Theme 2: Increased Self-acceptance and Maturity

Acceptance emerges throughout the nine transcripts (100 percent) in the context of increase in the ability to accept self and accept past experiences and move on after trauma. Acceptance has been shown to also be an important PTG theme in an Australian sample (Shakespeare-Finch & Copping, 2010). In addition, this theme is consistent with the concept of acceptance in Hinduism and Buddhism, two of the most influential religions in India. Both religions view acceptance as a logical attitude toward one's life, including pain and suffering (Whitman, 2007).

Quotes from participants to illustrate this theme include:

> Because I feel like I'm in control and I feel like I'm acting in a much more mature manner. (P#2, M)

> That there was no like precursor or anything or something like that. It was just random and suddenly he had to be rushed to the hospital. So the fragility of your health and what you can do in life and so that sort of helped me understand. I gained maturity on that. (P#4, M)

Category 3: Interpersonal Growth

This category refers to themes that contain growth element in the relationships with others domain. Relating to Others is one of the five domains in the PTG model (Calhoun & Tedeschi, 2006; Tedeschi & Calhoun, 1996); it emphasizes significant changes in relationships, which may include increased compassion and closeness. This category consists of two themes: seeking to be closer to family and friends and increased empathy for people with similar life struggles.

Theme 1: Desire to be Closer to Family and Friends

Eight out of nine participants (88 percent) reported that after experiencing the traumatic event, they have appreciated the support from family and friends more and have attempted spending more time with them.

Quotes from participants to illustrate this theme include:

> We have limited time here together…we should cherish it. (P#7, F)

> I started making more friends. I want to be a good friend to my friends. I have become a better daughter. It sorta hit me that my family loves me. (P#8, F)

> You know previously I would be so busy with my own work I wouldn't talk with them [his family] for weeks and uh things like that. But uh I know that's a very uh—because you're they sent me away and they know probably about me a lot so it's yeah, it's sort of like a mutually, I think we've grown close to each other. So yeah. (P#4, M)

Theme 2: Increased Empathy for People with Similar Life Struggles

Seventy-seven percent (seven out of nine) endorsed that they have had increased empathy and desire to help people with similar struggles. Empathy is defined as an understanding of another's emotional state, and it often co-occurs with mirroring emotional responses that are similar to another person's emotional responses (Lawrence, Shaw, Baker, Baron-Cohen, & David, 2004). Empathy has been found to act as a mediating factor for gender and PTG (Swickert, Hittner, & Foster, 2012).

Quotes from participants to illustrate this theme include:

> Want to help others who go through a similar thing that I did. (P#1, M)

> I can relate to a lot of people with medical conditions. (P#3, F)

Category 4: The Process of Healing

This category contains themes that pertain to the concept of healing process. Three themes that emerged are "healing takes time," "healing involves practical interventions," and "religion plays no role in the healing process." While this category is a new domain that is not part of the five-factor PTG model (Tedeschi & Calhoun, 1996), the process of healing and growth after trauma are often used interchangeably in the PTG literature. Healing, recovery and growth after trauma are often addressed together in the PTG literature as a multidimensional process, involving specific and individualized steps of recovering one's sense of safety, self-control/hope and sense of connection (Harvey, 1996; Herman, 1996).

The emerging themes in this category elucidate specific aspects of the process of healing endorsed by the majority of the participants.

Theme 1: Healing from Trauma Involves the Process of "Moving on"

Seventy-seven percent of participants (seven out of nine) endorsed the idea that part of their healing and coping is to determine to move on from the crisis.

Quotes from participants to illustrate this theme include:

> But after that, I think once that happened, um I dealt with it. The way I deal with these things is I don't, so if I don't get in the whole phase of what is happened I move on. (P#1, F)

> You know, if you realize how to deal with the situation and move on and make it, accept it, into part of your life. (P#3, M)

Theme 2: Healing from Trauma Involves Practical Interventions

Seventy-seven percent of participants (seven out of nine) stated that practical help, such as medical treatment and family intervention, gave them hope and strength to heal from trauma.

Quotes from participants to illustrate this theme include:

> medical care. He's in the best hospital in eastern India for neurology and so uh he [his father] yeah, so he's, so I know he's in very good care. So I'm pretty hopeful. (P#4, M)

> Medical treatment and practical treatment for my condition makes me feel more hopeful. (P#3, M)

Theme 3: No Change in One's Religion in the Healing Process

Interestingly, 100 percent of the participants (nine out of nine) responded that there was no change in their religion in the healing process, which is contrary to the Tedeschi and Calhoun's model (Tedeschi & Calhoun, 1996), which suggests spiritual change as one of the main PTG domains. Past research also suggests that people who utilize religious coping (e.g., attending religious gatherings, having intrinsic spiritual beliefs) are more likely to report PTG (Askay & Magyar-Russell, 2015).

Quotes from participants to illustrate this theme include:

> Religion has no role: Um so I'm an atheist, and uh for me I don't think so, I because I don't have any belief, that didn't really play any part in my recovery. (P#2)

> Religion plays no role. (P#5, F)

> I'm not a religious person so I really…my religious beliefs have not changed at all. (P#4, M)

CONCLUSION

PTG studies have increasingly shown promising findings on positive changes as a result of traumatic experience. Cross-cultural studies in this line of research have also continued to expand in order to gain better understanding of the concept of PTG in different cultural contexts. India, while enjoying fast economic growth, has also faced many psychosocial, political and environmental challenges that put its citizens at risk for trauma, such as political violence, gender-based violence, poverty and natural disasters with limited infrastructural support. This mixed-methods study revealed that high PTG subscales were positively related to resilience subscales. In addition, some PTG subscales were negatively related to depression and social dysfunction. Qualitatively, this study showed a four-category model of PTG (gratitude for life, personal growth, interpersonal growth and healing process). These mixed-methods findings may give culturally appropriate insight for mental health professionals in India who work on fostering growth after trauma for people exposed to trauma or life crisis.

REFERENCES

Ahuja, R. C., Bangdiwala, S., Bhambal, S. S., Jain, D., Jeyaseelan, L., Kumar, S., Lakshman, M., Mitra, M. K., Nair, M. K. C., Pillai, R., Pandey, R. M., Peedicayal, A., Sadowski, L., Suresh, S., & Upadhyaya, A. K. (2000). *A summary report of a multi-site household survey*. International Clinical Epidemiologists Network (INCLEN). Washington, DC: International Centre for Research on Women.

American Psychiatric Association (APA). (2013). *Diagnostic and statistical manual of mental disorders: DSM-5*. Washington, DC: American Psychiatric Association.

Askay, S. W., & Magyar-Russell, G. (2015). Posttraumatic growth and spirituality in burn recovery. *International Review of Psychiatry, 21*(6), 570–579.

Calhoun, L. G., & Tedeschi, R. G. (Eds.). (2006). *The handbook of posttraumatic growth: Research and practice*. Mahwah, NJ: Lawrence Erlbaum Associates Publishers.

Chadha, M., Malhotra, S., & Srivastava, P. (2013). Issues in the psychological assessment of trauma victims. *Delhi Psychiatry Journal, 16*(1), 193–203.

Cormio, C., Romitto, F., Giotta, F., & Mattioli, V. (2015). Post-traumatic growth in the Italian experience of long-term disease-free cancer survivors. *Stress & Health, 31*(3), 189–196.

Falide, I., Ramos, I., & Fermandex-Palacin, F. (2000). Comparison between the GHQ-28 and SF-36 (MH 1-5) for the assessment of the mental health in patients with ischaemic heart disease. *European Journal of Epidemiology, 16*(4), 311–316.

Ganapathy-Coleman, H. (2017). About Asian Indian Women. In C. Brown, U. Gielen, J. Gibbons, & J. Kuriansky (Eds.), *Women's evolving lives: Global and psychosocial perspectives* (pp. 39–58). New York: Springer.

Glaser, B. G., & Strauss, A. L. (1967). *The discovery of grounded theory: Strategies for qualitative research*. New Brunswick, NJ: Aldine Transaction.

Goldberg, D. (1978). *Manual of the general health questionnaire*. Windsor: NFER-Nelson.

Gray, M. J., Litz, B. T., Hsu, J. L., & Lombardo, T. W. (2004). Psychometric properties of life events checklist. *Assessment, 11*(4), 330–341. doi: 10.1177/1073191104269954.

Harvey, M. (1996). An ecological view of psychological trauma and recovery. *Journal of Traumatic Stress, 9*, 3–23.

Helgeson, V. S., Reynolds, K. A., & Tomich, P. L. (2006). A meta-analysis review of benefit finding and growth. *Journal of Consulting and Clinical Psychology, 74*(5), 797–816.

Herman, J. L. (1992). *Trauma and recovery*. New York: Basic Books.

Ho, S. M., Law, L. S., Wang, G. L., Shih, S. M., Hsu, S. H., & Hou, Y. C. (2013). Psychometric analysis of the Chinese version of the Posttraumatic Growth Inventory with cancer patients in Hong Kong and Taiwan. *Psychooncology, 22*(3), 715–719.

India. (2017). Retrieved from https://en.wikipedia.org/wiki/India

John, P. B., Russell, S., & Russell, P. S. (2007). The prevalence of posttraumatic stress disorder among children and adolescents affected by tsunami disaster in Tamil Nadu. *Disaster Management Response, 5*(1), 3–7.

Kakar, S., & Kakar, K. (2011). *The Indians.* New York: Penguin.

Lawrence, E. J., Shaw, P., Baker, D., Baron-Cohen, S., & David, A. S. (2004). Measuring empathy: Reliability and validity of the Empathy Quotient. *Psychological Medicine, 34*(5), 911–919.

Leibenberg, L., Ungar, M., & Van de Vijver, F. (2012). Validation of the Child and Youth Resilience Measure-28 (CYRM-28) among Canadian youth. *Research on Social Work Practice, 22*(2), 219–226.

Lincoln, Y. S., & Guba, E. G. (1985). *Naturalistic inquiry.* Newbury Park, CA: Sage Publications.

Lindstrom, C. M., Cann, A., Calhoun, L. G., & Tedeschi, R. G. (2011). The relationship of core belief challenge, rumination, disclosure, and sociocultural elements to posttraumatic growth. *Psychological Trauma: Theory, Research, Practice, and Policy, 4,* 400–410.

Linstrum, E. (2016) *Ruling minds: Psychology in the British Empire.* Cambridge, MA: Harvard University Press.

Maykut, P., & Morehouse, R. (1994). *Beginning qualitative research: A philosophic and practical guide.* London: Falmer Press.

Misra, G., Matthijs Cornelissen, R. M., & Verma, S. (2010). *Foundations of Indian psychology, Volume 1: Theories and concepts.* Delhi, India: Pearson.

Osei-Bonsu, P. E., Weaver, T. L., Eisen, S.V., & Vander Wal, J. S. (2011). Posttraumatic Growth Inventory: Factor structure in the context of DSM-IV traumatic events. *ISRN Psychiatry.* doi: 10.5402/2012/937582.

Paradise, A. W., & Kernis, M. H. (2002). Self-esteem and psychological well-being: Implications of fragile self-esteem. *Journal of Social and Clinical Psychology, 21,* 345–361.

Parwez, S., & Sen, V. (2016). Special economic zone, land acquisition, and impact on rural India. *Emerging Economy Studies, 2*(2), 223–239.

PreventionWeb. (2014). India: *Disaster & risk profile.* Retrieved August 23, 2017 from http://www.preventionweb.net/countries/ind/data/

Rajkumar, A. P., Premkumar, T. S., & Tharyan, P. (2008). Coping with the Asian tsunami: Perspectives from Tamil Nadu, India on the determinants of resilience in the face of adversity. *Social Science Medicine, 67*(5), 844–853.

Rastogi, D., Meena, S., Sharma, V., & Singh, G. K. (2014). Epidemiology of patients admitted to a major trauma center in northern India. *Chinese Journal of Traumatology, 17*(2) 103–107.

Robinson, R. G., & Price, T. R. (1982). Post-stroke depressive disorders: A follow-up study of 103 patients. *Stroke, 13*(5), 635–641.

Sen, A. (2005). *The argumentative Indian.* New York: Farrar, Straus, and Giroux.

Shakespeare-Finch, J., & Copping, A. (2010). A grounded theory approach to understanding cultural differences in posttraumatic growth. *Journal of Loss and Trauma, 11*(5), 355–371.

Sinha, J. B. P., & Verma, J. (1994). Social support as a moderator of the relationship between allocentrism and psychological well-being. In U. Kim, H. C. Triandis, C. Kagitcibasi, S. C. Choi, & G. Yoon (Eds.). *Individualism and collectivism: Theory, method and application* (pp. 267–275). Thousand Oaks, CA: SAGE.

Sirikantraporn, J., Rich, G., Badaracco, J., Valsaint, M., & Krukeja, S. (2017). *Posttraumatic growth in India: Quantitative and qualitative approaches.* Paper presented at the annual meeting of the American Psychological Association. Washington, DC.

Swickert, R. J., Hittner, J. B., & Foster, A. (2012). A proposed mediated path between gender and posttraumatic growth: The roles of empathy and social support in a mixed-age sample. *Psychology, 3*(12A), 1142–1147.

Taku, K., Cann, A., Calhoun, L. G., & Tedeschi, R. G. (2008). The factor structure of the Posttraumatic Growth Inventory: A comparison of five models using confirmatory factor analysis. *Journal of Traumatic Stress, 21*(2), 158–164.

Taku, K., & Oshio, A. (2015). An item-level analysis of the Posttraumatic Growth Inventory: Relationships with an examination of core beliefs and deliberate rumination. *Personality and Individual Differences, 86*, 156–160.

Taylor, S. E., Lichtman, R. R., & Wood, J. V. (1984). Attributions, beliefs about control, and adjustment to breast cancer. *Journal of Personality and Social Psychology, 46*(3), 489–502.

Tedeschi, R. G., & Calhoun, L. G. (1996). The posttraumatic growth inventory: Measuring the positive legacy of trauma. *Journal of Traumatic Stress, 9*(3), 455–471.

The World Bank. (2017). *Poverty & equity*. Retrieved August 23, 2017 from http://povertydata.worldbank.org/poverty/country/IND

Udwin, L. (Dir.). (2015). *India's daughter* [DVD]. United Kingdom: Assassin Films.

Ungar, M., & Liebenberg, L. (2011). Assessing resilience across cultures using mixed methods: Construction of the Child and Youth Resilience Measure. *Journal of Mixed Methods Research, 5*(2), 126–149.

Whitman, S. M. (2007). Pain and suffering as viewed by the Hindu religion. *The Journal of Pain, 8*(8), 607–613.

Windle, G., Bennett, K. M., & Noyes, J. (2011). A methodological review of resilience measurement scales. *Health Quality of Life Outcomes, 9*(8). doi: 10.1186/1477-7525-9-8.

Chapter 2

The Concept of Posttraumatic Growth in an Adult Sample from Port-au-Prince, Haiti

A Mixed-Methods Study

Grant J. Rich, Skultip (Jill) Sirikantraporn, and Wismick Jean-Charles

In recent years, resilience has been examined more frequently in cross-cultural contexts in order to better capture the nuances of the recovery/thriving process after trauma as it varies around the globe. This chapter focuses upon posttraumatic growth (PTG) in a sample of adult Haitians from Port-au-Prince, Haiti's largest city and capital, and the site of its devastating 2010 earthquake.

A BRIEF HISTORY OF TRAUMA IN HAITI

Haiti is a Caribbean nation that is located in the Greater Antilles archipelago, where it occupies the western quarter of the island of Hispaniola (the eastern portion of the island is the Dominican Republic). It population is estimated at between 10 and 11 million, and thus it is the second most populous nation in the Caribbean (Dash, 2010). Today, French is spoken, though Haitian Kreyòl predominates, and the population is 95 percent white and 5 percent white or mixed (Haiti, 2017). Its Gini index indicates extremely high economic inequality between the wealthy and the poor, and it ranks very low on the UN Human Development Index, a composite measure of life expectancy, education, and per capita income, ranking 163rd out of 188 nations in 2016 (list of countries by Human Development Index, 2017).

Haiti has a diverse history. The region was originally inhabited by the indigenous people, the Taínos. Christopher Columbus landed there on his first voyage in 1492, near the present-day cities of Limonade and Cap Haitian.

The Spanish brought infectious diseases, creating small pox epidemics, and maltreatment of the natives included the forced labor *encomienda* system and forced conversions to Catholicism. The native population was decimated over time and piracy flourished. After Spanish rule from 1492 to 1625, French rule dominated, and the western part of the island was renamed Saint Domingue (the 1697 Treat of Ryswick formally ended the French-Spanish hostilities). The French imported and enslaved thousands of Africans, transporting them to Saint Domingue to work in the sugarcane and coffee plantations. The colonial whites became vastly outnumbered by the enslaved Africans, and other additional social groups emerged, such as free blacks and free coloreds (Dubois, 2004; Geggus, 2014; Girard, 2010; James, 1963).

Eventually, free coloreds, as well as enslaved and free blacks, agitated for rights and freedom. In the 1790s, revolts such as that led by Ogé and Chavannes paved the way for the Haitian Revolution, which was led by Toussaint L'Ouverture, a former slave (and notably slave owner himself), and was in part inspired by the 1789 French Revolution. The Haitian Revolution resulted in the end of slavery and the defeat of Napolean Bonaparte's army. Thus, in 1804 Haiti became not solely the only nation in the world that was created as a result of a successful slave revolt (in 1804), it also became the first independent country in Latin America and the Caribbean, and the second republic in the Americas (Dubois, 2004; Geggus, 2014; Girard, 2010; James, 1963).

Unfortunately, the ensuing decades were tumultuous ones politically, socially, and economically for Haiti, with many leadership transitions, including an almost 20-year-long occupation by the United States and its forces from 1915 to 1934. Soon after arrival, the US Marines took control of Port-au-Prince and the banks, declared martial law, and censored journalists (Dash, 2010; Dubois, 2004, 2013; Farmer, 2005; Girard, 2010). During the Duvalier dynasty (1957–1986), severe abuses and corruption continued under both Papa and Baby Doc Duvalier, as evidenced by the rulers' use of the *Tontons Macoutes* group, which kept order by terrorizing the general public, especially political opponents. Political instability continued, with *coups d'etat* in 1991 and 2004 especially notable. The most significant event of the past decade was the magnitude 7.0 earthquake that struck Haiti on January 10, 2010. Estimates of the death toll ranged from 100,000 to over 200,000. Over 1.6 million were left homeless, and infrastructure was decimated, especially in Port-au-Prince, the national capital and largest city. The aftermath of the earthquake included a large cholera outbreak, adding to and prolonging the devastation. Haiti was the poorest nation in the Western hemisphere before the earthquake, and its institutions and recovery were further destroyed by the earthquake. Humanitarian aid from foreign governmental and nongovernmental groups was not always received, was not received in timely fashion, or was distributed in corrupt fashion, causing further problems for Haitians (Dubois, 2013; Farmer, 2011; Katz, 2013). Indeed, Haiti often ranks among the most corrupt countries in the world on the Corruption Perceptions Index, and crime, especially in Port-au-Prince, is a continuing concern, especially in areas such as Cité Soleil (e.g., Schwartz, 2010). Poverty is often associated with social problems, and indeed in Haiti, there is a notable challenge of modern-day slavery (known as *restavec*), in which poor, vulnerable children are sent to live and work with an adult, sometimes a distant relative, in what amounts in many cases to brutal servitude (Cadet, 1998; Haiti, 2017).

In October 2016, Hurricane Matthew struck Haiti as a Category 4 storm. Death toll estimates ranged from the official figure of 546 to over 1,000 and damage estimates approached US$2 billion, with approximately 175,1000 left homeless (Hurricane Matthew, 2017). Much of the worst of the hurricane was in southern Haiti, though gusts of 60 MPH reached Port-au-Prince. Data collection for the present chapter was conducted in Port-au-Prince, Haiti, approximately one month later in November 2016.

METHOD

Participants

For the quantitative portion of this study, there were 113 participants. They were sampled from Port-au-Prince, Haiti's largest city, and the site of the 2010 earthquake. Table 2.1 revealed the descriptive results of the demographic variables. The demographic questionnaire revealed that the mean age of the participants was 26.56 (*SD*= 5.60, min-max= 19–48). The sex ratio of the participants was relatively equal with 46.9 percent female and 52.2 percent male. For marital status, 83.8 percent identified as single and 6.3 percent reported being married. About 55.1 percent reported having a four-year college education and 17.8 percent a master's degree; 40.4 percent reported moderate income and 50.5 percent low to very low income; and 80.9 percent self-identified as Christian. One Hundred percent of the sample reported having experienced at least 3 types (out of 17) of traumatic events with 50.8 percent reporting at least 11 traumatic events.

In part 2 of the study, that is, the in-depth interview, 11 out of 113 total participants participated. All participants were female.

Measures

A total of 113 participants were administered a survey consisting of six questionnaires: a demographic form, the life events checklist (LEC), the PTG

Table 2.1 Descriptive Characteristics of the Sample (*N*=113)

Variables	*Number (%)*	*Mean*	*Range*
Age		26.56	19–48
Gender			
Female	53 (46.9)		
Male	59 (52.2)		
Marital Status			
Single	93 (83.8)		
Married	7 (6.3)		
Divorced	1 (.9)		
Decline to answer	9 (8.1)		
Income			
Very high	2 (1.8)		
High	8 (7.3)		
Moderate	44 (40.4)		
Low	38 (34.9)		
Very low	17 (15.6)		
Education			
High school	3 (2.8)		
Two-year college	21 (18.6)		
Four-year college	59 (55.1)		
Master's	19 (17.8)		
Advanced degree	2 (1.9)		
Decline to answer	3 (2.8)		
Employment			
Employed for wages	14 (12.7)		
Self-employed	2 (1.8)		
Out of work for more than one year	5 (4.5)		
Out of work for less than one year	4 (3.6)		
Student	84 (76.4)		
Religion			
Christianity	89 (80.9)		
Other (but did not specify)	14 (12.7)		
Decline to answer	7 9 (6.40)		
Life Event Total		11	3–17
Frequency			
3–5 events	3 (6.1)		
6–10 events	28 (43.2)		
11–13 events	20 (30.8)		
14–17 events	13 (20)		
Type of event			
Natural Disaster	81 (95.3)		
Fire or Explosion	61 (65.6)		
Transportation Accident	67 (71.3)		
Serious accident at work, home	51 (54.3)		
Exposure to toxic substance	40 (43.5)		
Physical assault	62 (64.6)		
Assault with a weapon	54 (58.8)		
Sexual assault	42 (44.2)		

Other unwanted or uncomfortable sexual experience	42 (43.8)
Combat or exposure to a war zone	35 (36.5)
Captivity	22 (23.7)
Life-threatening illness or injury	64 (67.4)
Sexual human suffering	70 (76.1)
Sudden, violent death	48 (53.9)
Sudden, unexpected death of someone close to you	78 (85.7)
Serious injury, harm, or death you caused to someone else	28 (30.1)
Any other extremely stressful life even t or experience	74 (79.5)

inventory (PTGI) scale, the Adult Resilience Measure (ARM), the Meaning in Life Questionnaire (MLQ), and the Satisfaction with Life Scale (SWLS).

Life Events Checklist

The LEC scale is a self-report measure of participants' lifelong exposure to traumatic events according to the posttraumatic stress disorder (PTSD) criterion A diagnosis in the Diagnostic and Statistical Manual of Mental Disorders (DSM)-5. Subjects are given a list of 17 traumatic stressors to choose whether the trauma happened to them, they witnessed it, they learned about it, or it was part of their job, or else they indicate they are not sure, or that the question doesn't apply (Gray, Litz, Sue, & Lombardo, 2004).

Posttraumatic Growth Inventory Scale

The PTGI scale is a 21-item Likert scale measuring participants' degree of PTG according to Tedeschi and Calhoun (1996) in the following five subscales: relating to others, new possibilities, personal strength, spiritual change, and appreciation of life. Each subscale consists of possible responses from a Likert scale of 1–6 (1= I did not experience this change as a result of my crisis; 6= I experienced this change to a very great degree as a result of my crisis).

The PTGI scale has been shown to have satisfactory internal consistency among the total and subscales scores and test-retest reliability (Taku, Cann, Calhoun, & Tedeschi, 2008). Studies have examined the cross-cultural validity of the PTGI scale and whether the items are more influenced by personality or culture. A study by Taku and Oshio (2015) assessed whether the items in the subscale truly measured PTG variables, using a Japanese sample. The results showed that PTG measured by the scale is more likely to occur when core beliefs are challenged, and few occur without cognitive effort. Thus, the significant personality factor in PTG measured by the PTGI scale shows that it is likely a largely universal phenomenon, or at least one present in multiple cultures. Additional cross-cultural studies have suggested that differences in the degree of PTG dimensions are culturally influenced (Cormio, Romitto, Giotta, & Mattioli, 2015; Ho, Law, Wang, Shih, Hsu, & Hou, 2013).

Adult Resilience Measure-28

The ARM is a 28-item Likert scale that was adapted from the Child and Youth Resilience Measure-28 (CYRM-28; Ungar & Liebenberg, 2011), one of the most culturally sensitive resilience measures (Windle, Bennett, & Noyes, 2011). The measure was derived from data collected in 12 different countries over 3 different continents. The ARM-28 has three subscales (individual, relational, and contextual resilience). Reliability analyses were conducted, which demonstrated that the CYRM-28 and its subscales were internally consistent (Leibenberg, Ungar, & Van de Vijver, 2012).

Meaning in Life Questionnaire

The MLQ is a ten-item scale rated on a seven-point scale from "Absolutely True" to "Absolutely Untrue" on the person's perception of meaning in life. There are two subscales: the presence of meaning subscale, measuring how full individuals feel their lives are of meaning (Steger, Frazier, Oishi, & Kaler, 2006), and the search for meaning subscale, measuring how motivated individuals are in finding meaning in their lives. The MLQ has good reliability (presence: $\alpha = .82$, and search: $\alpha = .87$), test-retest stability, and good fit factor structure (Steger, Frazier, Oishi, & Kaler, 2006).

Satisfaction with Life Scale

The SWLS is a five-item scale measuring cognitive judgments of one's life satisfaction (Diener, Emmons, Larsen, & Griffin, 1985). Respondents answer how much they agree or disagree with each of the five items, using a seven-point scale that ranges from 7 = strongly agree to 1 = strongly disagree. A meta-analysis study found that 62 articles that investigated the reliability of the SWLS in different populations found an average of .76 reliability coefficients (Vassar, 2007).

Semi-structured Interview Guide

An interview guide included 20 open-ended questions in French and aimed to explore in-depth experiences and understanding of the concept of PTG. The questions were based on recent research and clinical literature on PTG and on cultural literature on the Haitian culture and society (Cadet, 1998; Dash,

2010; Dubois, 2013; Girard, 2010). Participants could answer the interview questions in French or in Haitian Kreyòl.

DATA ANALYSES

Quantitative Data

Descriptive statistics were used for frequency findings on the demographic variables, LEC, PTGI, ARM, MLQ, and SWLS. Reliability analyses were utilized to test each measure's internal reliability (Cronbach alpha's; see Table 2.2 for the reliability results). T-test analyses were used to examine whether there were any mean differences of LEC, PTGI, ARM, MLQ, and SWLS among different demographic groups. Pearson correlation analyses were used to analyze correlations between the study main variables. A multiple linear regression model was used to examine the effects of independent variables (demographic variables, PTGI, MLQ, SWLS) on the dependent variable (ARM subscales). All significant results were set at p value < .05.

Qualitative Data

The Grounded Theory was used to generate an emergent theory through the discovery of themes (Glaser & Strauss, 1967) from a purposively recruited

Table 2.2 Reliability Analyses Results

Variables	*Number of Items*	*Cronbach's Alpha*	*Response Scale*
PTGI			
New possibilities	5	.72*	1–6
Personal strength	4	.72*	1–6
Relating to others	7	.81*	1–6
Spiritual change	2	.49	1–6
Appreciation of life	3	.74*	1–6
PTGI-total	21	.93*	1–6
MLQ			
Presence of meaning	5	.70*	1–7
Search for meaning	5	.76*	1–7
ARM-28			
Individual	11	.74*	1–4
Relational	7	.76*	1–4
Contextual	10	.70*	1–4
ARM-total	28	.85*	1–4
SWLS			
Total life satisfaction	5	.77*	1–7

* p<.05.

group of people who have experienced the same phenomenon, which is the 2010 Earthquake. Maximum variable sampling (Maykut & Morehouse, 1994) was attempted by recruiting from all adult age groups and socioeconomic status. The sample size was determined by the concurrent process of data collection and coding procedures until the saturation point was met, the point at which no new themes were forthcoming (Maykyt & Mayhouse, 1994). Constant comparative analysis through three stages of coding (open coding, axial coding, and selective coding) was used to discover emerging themes and an overarching theory (see Glaser & Strauss, 1967). There were several strategies utilized to increase trustworthiness of the study findings. First, peer scrutiny of the research project was used where three coders independently coded the data and compared emerging categories and themes until the final version of categories and themes were agreed upon. Second, an audit trail and journaling among researchers was utilized to increase researchers' reflexivity and progressive subjectivity (Lincoln & Guba, 1985) to minimize the intrusive influence of the researchers' own biases on the research procedures and findings.

RESULTS AND DISCUSSION

Quantitative Results

Reliability Analysis Results

A total of 113 Haitians participated in the study by completing six questionnaires. The reliability analysis (Cronbach's alpha) was utilized to examine internal reliability of PTGI, ARM, MLQ, and SWLS with p value < .05. The results showed acceptable to great reliability for PTGI subscales (except for spiritual change) as follows: relating to others (α = .81), new possibilities (α = .72), appreciation of life (α = .74), personal strength (α = .72), total PTG (α = .93), and spiritual change (α = .49). The results showed good reliability for ARM subscales as follows: individual (α = .74), relational (α = .76), contextual (α = .70), and total resilience (α = .85). The results showed acceptable reliability for MLQ subscales as follows: presence of meaning in life (α = .70) and search for meaning (α = .76). Lastly, the results showed acceptable reliability for SWLS (α = .77).

Table 2.3 revealed the descriptive results of each main variable of the study and correlation matrix of the main variables.

Bivariate Correlation Results

As shown in Table 2.3, Pearson correlation analyses showed the relationship between PTGI and other main variables as follows: (1) PTGI-relating to others was significantly related in the positive direction to all subscales of ARM, the

Table 2.3 Intercorrelation Matrix of PTGI, MLQ, ARM, and SWLS (*N*=113)

Constructs	*M (SD), min-max*	*1*	*2*	*3*	*4*	*5*	*6*	*7*	*8*	*9*	*10*	*11*	*12*	*13*
1. PTGI Relating to others	32.85 (6.22), 8–42	1.00												
2. PTGI New possibilities	23.86 (4.79), 7–30	.85**	1.00											
3. PTGI Personal strength	18.70 (4.10), 5–24	.76**	.85**	1.00										
4. PTGI Spiritual change	4.45 (1.46), 1–6	.61**	.39**	.37*	1.00									
5. PTGI Appreciation of life	15.24 (2.97), 3–18	.79**	.82**	.78**	.52**	1.00								
6. PTGI total	96.58(17.46), 23–120	.84**	.90**	.81**	.57**	.83**	1.00							
7. Presence of meaning	25.02 (4.77), 11–33	**.37****	**.39****	**.35****	.21	.24	**.30****	1.00						
8. Searching for meaning	26.28 (8.06), 5–35	-.01	-.00	.00	.00	.12	.12	.01	1.00					
9. Individual resilience	45.26 (5.27), 31–55	**.58****	**.49****	**.40****	**.19**	**.30****	**.45****	**.30****	-.00	1.00				
10. Relational resilience	25.99 (5.61), 11–35	**.39****	**.26***	.16	.08	.14	.21	.22.	-.19	.69**	1.00			
11. Contextual resilience	37.89 (4.96), 21–45	**.38****	**.31****	.21	**.25***	.17	**.25***	.20	-.06	.49**	.48**	1.00		
12. Total resilience	114.70 (12.97), 81–140	**.51****	**.37****	**.27***	.21	.22	**.30***	.24	-.10	.82**	.87**	.75**	1.00	
13. SWLS	22.71(6.75), 5–35	**.45****	**.46****	**.35****	**.35****	**.25***	**.50****	**.37***	-.18	**.37****	**.48****	.20	**.39****	1.00

*p < .05,
** p < .01,
Bold: significant correlations between posttraumatic growth inventory, Meaning in Life Questionnaire, Adult Resilience Measure (ARM), Satisfaction With Life Scale.

presence of meaning subscale of MLQ, and SWLS; (2) PTGI-new possibilities was significantly related in the positive direction to all subscales of ARM (except for relational resilience), the presence of meaning subscale of MLQ, and SWLS; (3) PTGI-personal strengths was significantly related in the positive direction to individual resilience and contextual resilience, the presence of meaning subscale of MLQ, and SWLS; (4) PTGI-appreciation of life was significantly related in the positive direction to the presence of meaning subscale of MLQ and SWLS; and (5) PTGI-total was significantly related in the positive direction to all subscales of ARM (except for relational resilience), the presence of meaning subscale of MLQ, and SWLS. Lastly, PTGI-spiritual change was found to be significantly related in the positive direction to SWLS only.

Pearson correlation analyses showed the relationship between MLQ and other main variables as follows: (1) the presence of meaning subscale was significantly related in the positive direction to all subscales of ARM, all subscales of PTGI, and SWLS; (2) the search for meaning subscale was found to not be significantly related to any other variables.

Pearson correlation analyses showed the relationship between SWLS and other main variables as follows: (1) total life satisfaction was significantly related in the positive direction to all subscales of ARM; (2) total life satisfaction was significantly related in the positive direction to all subscales of PTGI; (3) total life satisfaction was significantly related in the positive direction to the presence of meaning subscale of MLQ but not the search for meaning subscale of MLQ.

Multiple Linear Regression Results

To clarify the relationship between PTG construct and resilience construct, a multiple linear regression was calculated to predict the effects of PTGI subscales and other main variables (MLQ and SWLS) on resilience (ARM) subscales. A significant regression equation was found for individual resilience ($F(8,56) = 7.226$, $p < .000$), with R^2 of .508. Participants' predicted individual resilience is equal to 28.40 (B) + 1.004 (PTGI-total) + 1.239 (PTGI-relating to others) + 1.811 (PTGI-new possibilities) +1.224 (PTGI-personal strength) + .264 (presence of meaning).

A significant regression equation was found for relational resilience ($F(8,52) = 2.484$, $p < .023$), with R^2 of .276. Participants' predicted relational resilience is equal to 23.304 (B) + 1.194 (PTGI-new possibilities) + 2.75 (presence of meaning).

Qualitative Results

Eleven (all female) participants who completed the quantitative part volunteered to participate in the in-depth interview for qualitative analysis. There are five emergent categories (appreciation of life, personal strength, change in interpersonal relations, the role of religion in trauma recovery, perceived happiness) and eight themes.

This section presents exemplary quotations that capture the major categories found, together with their major themes (at least 60 percent of participant endorsement); discusses the themes of PTG that emerged from the data by the Grounded Theory method; and compares these themes with previous literature on Tedeschi and Calhoun's model of PTG. Five categories and ten themes emerged from the data (see Figure 2.1).

Category 1: Appreciation of Life

This category depicted themes that are related to the participants' endorsement of the sense of appreciation of life. This category is closely aligned with appreciation of life, one of the main domains in the original PTG model by Tedeschi and Calhoun (1996). There are two prominent themes in this category.

Theme 1: "Do not Take Life for Granted"

Ten of 11 participants (90 percent) mentioned statements that they learned to not take life for granted after having experienced life trauma. Quotes from participants to illustrate this theme include:

> What gives you hope: Because I was alive, and there were other people who did not have that chance. (P#3)

> The fact that I'm living and I'm not sick. I wake up everyday, I come here and I can see my friends. (P#6)

> I see that life is short so we have to make our mark during our time here because like fire, it goes by fast. (P#7)

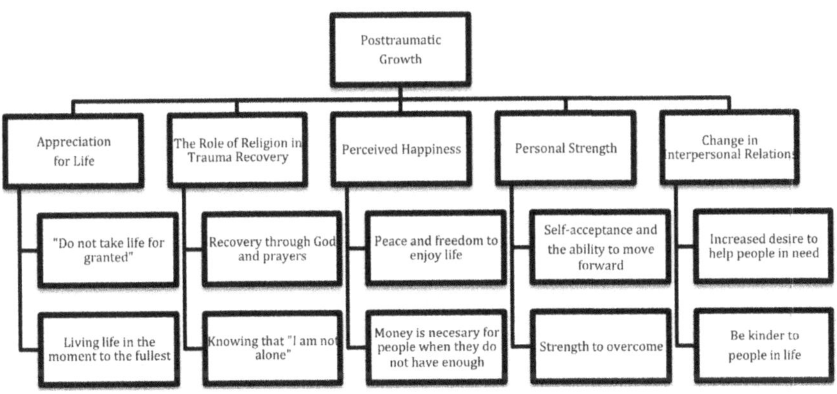

Figure 2.1 Grounded Theory for Posttraumatic Growth Model in the Haitian Sample (*N*=11).

> I always hear other says life is short, and it can be gone in one instant (very quickly). (P#9)

Theme 2: Living Life in the Moment to the Fullest

Nine of 11 participants (81 percent) also stated that they learned to live life in the moment and accept all the good and the bad that it presents. Quotes from participants to illustrate this theme include:

> To take advantage of the present moment because we do not know when we're going to die, or when we will perish somewhere in the world or at least when life will end on earth, we do not know, so we must take advantage of the experience, the present moment to enjoy life fully. (P#1)

> You come to realize that everything is temporary, just live the present moment....It's like enjoying every moment whether it was good or bad because it's all of the little things together which makes life. (P#9)

> We should...as long as we're living, we should live life to the fullest and realize that we're alive and after this trauma that we have experienced. Try to live as much as we can. (P#4)

> It is to celebrate the present moment. (P#10)

Category 2: The Role of Religion in Trauma Recovery

This category is closely related to spiritual change domain in the Tedeschi and Calhoun's model (1996). This category captures themes that participants mentioned how religion has helped them cope with trauma and crisis in life. There are two themes in this category.

Theme 1: Recovery through God and Prayers

Eleven of 11 participants (100 percent) endorsed that they have recovered from life crisis through God, their connection with God, or prayers. Quotes from participants to illustrate this theme include:

> Sometimes I don't even want to live, I even thought of killing myself sometimes, but my God helps me stay hopeful. (P#4)

> Religion...yes, it's true after a traumatic event I lean more toward prayer. (P#5)

> I always referred to the Bible, I'm always...the people who often support me are the priests, so I can say religion influenced [my recovery]. (P#6)

> Spirituality because I truly believe in God. When I know that I am really traumatized and I pray often. (P#7)

Theme 2: Knowing that "I am not alone" with Support from Church

Seven out of 11 participants (63 percent) mentioned that the reason that regularly going to church helped them cope with life problems is because they got to learn about other people's struggles, which helped them know that they were not alone in their struggles and life hardship. Quotes from participants to illustrate this theme include:

> I'm also a choir member. Although there are difficulties in life that does not mean that you are the only one who's going through it. (P#4)

> I pray often, I go to church, I sing and because I sing and pray so I forget what has just happened, and get out of myself. And I see that I'm not the only one who is in this situation and that there are other people who has been through it as well. (P#7)

Category 3: Perceived Happiness

As part of trauma recovery, the concept of happiness was tapped into, and two different themes with regards to perceived happiness were identified.

Theme 1: Peace and Freedom to Enjoy Life

Ten out of 11 participants (90 percent) stated that happiness to them means "being free," "being at peace with oneself," and/or "having the freedom to enjoy life." Quotes from participants to illustrate this theme include:

> I believe that happiness is being free to take life as it is without resigning oneself of the bad thing of life or at least, the traumatic experience, to learn to be guided by the good thing of life without worrying about the problems that happen to us every day. (P#1)

> You're free with your choices, your actions, and to be the person that you want to be, to have good friends and family. (P#3)

> Happiness is when I am at peace with myself. (P#4)

> You are happy when you're feeling good and at peace in your place. (P#11)

Theme 2: Money is Necessary for People when they do not have Enough

While none of the participants endorsed money as their own source of happiness, 10 out 11 participants (90 percent) believed that money is a source of happiness for other Haitians. Quotes from participants to illustrate this theme include:

> ¾ of Haitians would say they want to have money because we do not have enough. (P#3)

> Money is more important for Haitians because we live in a society that is poor I can say that money will always be more important to them. (P#8)

> I will not speak in general; I will speak about my friends who are Haitians. They think that having a lot of money is what can make them happy. (P#10)

Category 4: Personal Strength

This category depicts the themes in relation to the recognition of their personal assets in overcoming trauma in life.

Theme 1: Self-acceptance and the Ability to Move Forward

Eight out of 11 participants (72 percent) endorsed the idea that accepting one's self and one's ability to move forward helped them cope with the tragic incident. Quotes from participants to illustrate this theme include:

> It is to overcome…I mean to surpass what has happened and use it as a lesson, yes that's it. (P11)

> Then you learn to accept yourself for who you are after these things, I think. (P3)

> It's accepting that you have been through what happened. Try to live with it day by day until the pain is completely gone. (P#4)

> Accept that it when something bad happened to you then you learn from the traumatic experience, it helped you to blossom personally. (P#8)

Theme 2: Strength to Overcome

Nine out of 11 participants (81 percent) reported that they saw their own inner strength as a way to get through trauma. Quotes from participants to illustrate this theme include:

I learned that that I was stronger than I thought. (P#3)

I think I was a child also whom could not face a series of traumatic events but after I become stronger when going through traumatic events. (P#5)

I always believe in my strength....I learned that I am someone who is strong of character after I'm traumatized (P#6)

I simply told myself I have been through this already so I can overcome other obstacles and there is no need to be afraid. (P#7)

Category 5: Change in Interpersonal Relations

This category captured the ways in which the participants' relationships with others have changed after trauma. Two themes emerged in this category.

Theme 1: Increased Desire to Help People who are in Need

Eight out of 11 participants (72 percent) stated that they have an increased desire to help people in need. Quotes from participants to illustrate this theme include:

I take time to help others who are weaker than me. (P#7)

I now concentrate more in my studies and said to myself that I will be a future psychologist, I would like to be more present for the people who surround me and need my help. (P#4)

I now dedicate my life to help others. It helps and comforts me. (P#11)

Theme 2: Be Kinder to People in Life

Eight out of 11 participants (72 percent) mentioned the change in their approach when it comes to their existing and new relationships. More specifically, the participants want to be kinder to their family and close friends and "treat them right," but when it comes to new relationships, many of them responded that they are being less open and more discriminative about who they can trust. Quotes from participants to illustrate this theme include:

I have learned to respect people, to love people, and to treat people as they should be treated. One must also learn to honor people, learn how to tell people

> how wonderful they, how important they are in our lives since we do not know exactly when that person may leave the world. (P#1)
>
> I think that this person if I approached him/her, I would speak to him/her more gently, and not rush him because the earthquake really marked the Haitian people. They (my family) did their best to be there for me as much as possible also. (P#4)
>
> It is to spend time with my family and the people I love. They mean a lot to me. (P#11)

CONCLUSION

Haiti has suffered much trauma in its history. In addition to the legacy of colonialism and slavery, occupation by foreign powers, and, in recent decades, frequent political turmoil and corruption, Haiti has suffered tragic natural disasters. Most significantly, the 2010 earthquake led to deaths estimated between 100,000 to over 200,000 persons, leaving 1.6 million homeless and decimating much infrastructure. In 2016, shortly before data collection for the present study, Hurricane Matthew struck Haiti, leading to deaths estimated from over 500 to over 1,000, leaving approximately 175,000 homeless, with damages estimated at nearly US$2 billion.

Studies from several disciplines have shown that the trauma exposure has taken a societal and psychological toll on Haitians (Cadet, 1998; Dubois; 2013; Farmer 2013; Girard, 2010; Katz, 2013; Nicolas, 2013; Schwartz, 2010). Internationally, outside of Haiti, the PTG literature has revealed promising results related to the positive changes that may result from the struggle to cope with trauma, enhancing scholars' and practitioners' understanding of the effects of trauma on individuals (Calhoun & Tedeschi, 2006, 2013; Joseph & Linley, 2008; Theron, Liebenberg, & Ungar, 2015; Weiss & Berger, 2010). This study was one of the first attempts aiming to understand the concept of PTG from local Haitians in Port-au-Prince, all of whom were affected by the 2010 earthquake. Quantitative results indicate correlations between various PTGI subscales and various subscales of the ARM and the MLQ. Additionally, total life satisfaction (SWLS) was significantly correlated with all subscales of both the PTGI and the ARM. The study found that PTGI (except for the spiritual change subscale) may be a culturally appropriate measure to assess PTG. The Grounded Theory analysis of the qualitative data revealed five prominent categories and ten themes that are essential for the experience of PTG in the Haitian sample. Qualitative results suggest growth components including gratitude and appreciation for life, increased role of religion, a changed sense of perceived happiness and role of money, increased personal growth and personal strength, and enriched connections with others. In sum, these results carry significance for clinical application development.

REFERENCES

Cadet, J. R. (1998). *Restavec: From Haitian slave child to middle-class American.* Austin, TX: University of Texas Press.

Calhoun, L. G., & Tedeschi, R. G. (Eds.). (2006). *Handbook of posttraumatic growth: Research and practice.* New York: Psychology Press.

Calhoun, L. G., & Tedeschi, R. G. (2013). *Posttraumtic growth in clinical practice.* New York: Routledge.

Cormio, C., Romitto, F., Giotta, F., & Mattioli, V. (2015). Post-traumatic growth in the Italian experience of long-term disease-free cancer survivors. *Stress & Health, 31*(3), 189–196.

Dash, M. (2010). *Culture and customs of Haiti.* Westport, CT: Greenport Press.

Diener, E., Emmons, R. A., Larsen, R. J., & Griffin, S. (1985). The satisfaction with life scale. *Journal of Personality Assessment, 49*(1), 71–75.

Dubois, L. (2004). *Avengers of the New World: The story of the Haitian Revolution.* Cambridge, MA: Harvard University Press.

Dubois, L. (2013). *Haiti: The aftershocks of history.* New York: Henry Holt and Company.

Farmer, P. (2005). *The uses of Haiti.* Monroe, Maine: Common Courage Press.

Farmer, P. (2011). *Haiti after the earthquake.* New York: Public Affairs.

Geggus, D. (2014). *The Haitian revolution: A documentary history.* Indianapolis, IN: Hackett Publishing Company.

Girard, P. (2010). *Haiti: The tumultuous history: From pearl of the Caribbean to broken nation.* New York: Palgrave MacMillan.

Glaser, B. G., & Strauss, A. L. (1967). *The discovery of grounded theory: Strategies for qualitative research.* New Brunswick, NJ: Aldine Transaction.

Gray, M. J., Litz, B. T., Hsu, J. L., & Lombardo, T. W. (2004). Psychometric properties of life events checklist. *Assessment, 11*(4), 330–341. doi: 10.1177/1073191104269954.

Ho, S. M., Law, L. S., Wang, G. L., Shih, S. M., Hsu, S. H., & Hou, Y. C. (2013). Psychometric analysis of the Chinese version of the Posttraumatic Growth Inventory with cancer patients in Hong Kong and Taiwan. *Psychooncology, 22*(3), 715–719.

James, C. L. R. (1963). *The Black Jacobins: Toussaint L'Ouverture and the San Domingo revolution.* New York: Random House.

Joseph, S., & Linley, P. A. (Eds.). (2008). *Trauma, recovery, and growth: Positive psychological perspectives on posttraumatic stress.* Hoboken, NJ: John Wiley.

Katz, J. M. (2013). *The big truck that went by: How a world came to save Haiti and left behind a disaster.* New York: St. Martin's Press.

Leibenberg, L., Ungar, M., & Van de Vijver, F. (2012). Validation of the Child and Youth Resilience Measure-28 (CYRM-28) among Canadian youth. *Research on Social Work Practice, 22*(2), 219–226.

Lincoln, Y. S., & Guba, E. G. (1985). *Naturalistic inquiry*. Newbury Park, CA: Sage Publications.

Maykut, P., & Morehouse, R. (1994). *Beginning qualitative research: A philosophic and practical guide*. London: Falmer Press.

Nicolas, G. (2013). Haiti's "resilience" and mental health. *Caribbean Journal*. Retrieved from https://www.caribjournal.com/2013/05/10/haitis-resilience-and-mental-health/#

Rich, G. (2013). *Bien-être psychologique et massothérapie: Résultats de recherche pour la pratique professionnelle. Psychological well-being and massage therapy*. La Troisième Conférence Internationale sur la Spiritualité et la Psychothérapie en Haiti.

Schwartz, T. T. (2010). *Travesty in Haiti: A true account of Christian missions, orphanages, food aid and drug trafficking* (2nd ed.). Booksurge Publishing.

Steger, M., Frazier, P., Oishi, S., & Kaler, M. (2006). The meaning in life questionnaire: Assessing the presence of and search for meaning in life. *Journal of Counseling Psychology, 53*(1), 80–93.

Stewart, S. (2017). National Hurricane Center Tropical Cyclone Report: Hurricane Matthew. *National Weather Service*. Retrieved from http://www.nhc.noaa.gov/data/tcr/AL142016_Matthew.pdf

Taku, K., Cann, A., Calhoun, L. G., & Tedeschi, R. G. (2008). The factor structure of the Posttraumatic Growth Inventory: A comparison of five models using confirmatory factor analysis. *Journal of Traumatic Stress, 21*(2), 158–164.

Taku, K., & Oshio, A. (2015). An item-level analysis of the Posttraumatic Growth Inventory: Relationships with an examination of core beliefs and deliberate rumination. *Personality and Individual Differences, 86*, 156–160.

Tedeschi, R. G., & Calhoun, L.G. (1996). The posttraumatic growth inventory: Measuring the positive legacy of trauma. *Journal of Traumatic Stress, 9*(3), 455–471.

Theron, L., Liebenberg, L., & Ungar, M. (Eds.). (2015). *Youth resilience and culture: Commonalities and complexities (Cross-cultural advancements in positive psychology)*. New York, NY: Springer.

Ungar, M., & Liebenberg, L. (2011). Assessing resilience across cultures using mixed methods: Construction of the Child and Youth Resilience Measure. *Journal of Mixed Methods Research, 5*(2), 126–149.

United Nations (UNDP). (2016). *Human Development Report 2016*. Retrieved from http://hdr.undp.org/sites/default/files/2016_human_development_report.pdf

United Nations, Office for the Coordination of Humanitarian Affairs (UNOCHA). (2016, October). *Haiti: Struggling to survive*. Retrieved on August 30, 2017 from http://www.unocha.org/country/top-stories/all-stories/haiti-struggling-survive

Vassar, M. (2007). A note on the score reliability for the Satisfaction with Life Scale: An RG Study. *Social Indicators Research, 86*, 47–57.

Weiss, T., & Berger, R. (Eds.). (2010). *Posttraumatic growth and culturally competent practice: Lessons learned from around the globe*. Hoboken, NJ: John Wiley and Sons.

Windle, G., Bennett, K. M., & Noyes, J. (2011). A methodological review of resilience measurement scales. *Health Quality of Life Outcomes, 9*(8). doi: 10.1186/1477-7525-9-8.

Chapter 3

The Concept of Posttraumatic Growth in a Cambodian Sample

A Grounded Theory Study

Skultip (Jill) Sirikantraporn, Grant J. Rich, and Nashaw Jafari

Studies have documented that people do report growth or positive outcomes as a result of their struggle to cope with trauma or stressful life events (Bonanno, 2005; Calhoun & Tedeschi, 2006; McMillen, 1999). The term "posttraumatic growth" (PTG) was developed to conceptualize the phenomenon. Most Western studies have suggested that the core elements of PTG include improved relating to others, seeing new possibilities in life, spiritual change, and increases in personal strength and appreciation of life (Tedeschi & Calhoun, 1996). More recently, the concept of PTG has begun to be investigated across cultures in both quantitative and qualitative studies. For instance, relevant research includes samples from Australia (Shakespeare-Finch & Copping, 2006), Japan (Taku, Calhoun, Tedeschi, Gil-Rivas, Kilmer, & Cann, 2007), Bosnia (Powell et al., 2003), and China (Ho et al., 2013), and from cancer survivors across cultures (Diaz, Cordova, & Spiegel, 2012). The cross-cultural findings suggest that the five dimensions of PTG (personal strength, appreciation of life, relating to others, spiritual change, and new possibilities; Tedeschi & Calhoun, 1996) may or may not vary across cultures, especially for cultures in which the self is defined as individualistically oriented, compared to collectivistically oriented (Helgeson, Reynolds, & Tomich, 2006; Yang, 2003). This indicates that more in-depth examinations for different cultures are warranted.

Since the end of the horrific and tragic era of the Khmer Rouge, which peaked between 1975 and 1979, and which killed approximately two million people, a quarter of the whole Cambodian population at that time, from execution, disease, starvation, and overwork (Chandler, 2007; Hinton, 2004; Kierman, 2008), Cambodia continues to be plagued by the trauma and cycles of violence and victimization due to ongoing political and social instability, high rates of poverty, and limited access to resources (Jarl, Cantor-Graae,

Chak, Sunbaunat, & Larsson, 2015). A recent survey of nearly 3,000 adults from 9 of the 25 provinces in Cambodia found that an estimated 31 percent of women and 18.4 percent of men suffer from probable anxiety disorders and 19.7 percent of women and 10.2 percent of men suffer from probable depressive disorders. This survey also found that of those who experienced the civil war, 92.3 percent experienced at least one traumatic event, with a mean of seven events, and that among younger participants who did not experience the civil war, 70.2 percent experienced at least one traumatic event (RUPP, 2012).

Living in the posttraumatic era after the experience of the atrocity of the genocide, Cambodians have had to find ways to cope with the psychological impact. Throughout the past decades of research, many cultural studies, including work in medical anthropology, have examined the cultural meanings of trauma and trauma responses among Cambodians as a result of the Khmer Rouge (Becker, Gay, Beyene, & Ken, 2000; Hinton et al., 2009; Hinton, Howes, & Kirmayer, 2008; Ratliff, 1997; Van Schaack, Reicherter, & Chhang, 2011). However, to understand the complete picture of trauma study in cultural context, it is also important to explore cultural meanings of growth and positive changes after trauma. This study, therefore, aimed to investigate the concept of PTG among a Cambodian sample from both etic and emic perspectives of cultural psychology.

Trauma studies in Cambodia have evolved in their attempts to understand the effects of trauma on Cambodians' psychological and cultural health. A trauma-based cultural syndrome was defined as the set of salient culturally specific trauma-related symptoms of survivors of the Khmer Rouge, and include *kyol goeu* (wind overload), which causes one to become unconscious, fall to the ground, turn pale, and sweat (Hauff, 2001), sleep paralysis ("the ghost pushes you down"), nightmares, and panic attacks (Hinton, Pich, Chhean, & Pollack, 2005). Another important Cambodian trauma phenomenon is "broken courage" or "*baksbat*," which overlaps to some degree with posttraumatic stress disorder (PTSD) (Chhim, 2013). *Baksbat* is the idiom of distress experienced by Khmer persons as a lack of trust in others, submissiveness, feeling fearful, and being "mute and deaf" (Chhim, 2013). The interpersonal nature of many of the above symptoms, such as sleep paralysis and *baksbat,* may partially explain why healing practices found to be important for Cambodian trauma survivors are interpersonal by nature. Some of these identified practices among Cambodian trauma survivors are making merits to the deceased, holding a festival for loved ones, and healing the wider community (Agger, 2015).

The struggle of Cambodians over the past few decades has been further complicated by the intergenerational effects of trauma (intergenerational transmission of trauma) to the younger generation Cambodians. Often the adverse effects of intergenerational transmission of trauma are referred to as "unspoken trauma." Although the young Cambodians experienced their own suffering acquired from post-genocide effects, coupled with the direct damage done to the country's current human and socioeconomic development, these effects and impacts on the country's youth have been under-acknowledged (Rich, 2015). One proposed path of transmission is through family interactions. Such a pathway suggests that the enduring effects of violence experienced by the survivors of the genocide have significantly impacted the ability of their children and young adults to form a stable sense of security and attachments. A study of Cambodian mothers, who experienced the Khmer Rouge, and their daughters confirmed and expanded this path by revealing that the mother's PTSD was predictive of her daughter's anxiety (Field, Muong, & Sochanvimean, 2013). In addition, the mother's role-reversing parental style mediated the relationship (Field, Muong, & Sochanvimean, 2013).

Another path of transmission of effects is through lingering effects of socioeconomic issues stemming from the Khmer Rouge, which have kept Cambodia in severe poverty decades after the genocide. Corruption and abuse of power in the government and military present during the Khmer Rouge era have continued to affect the post-genocide country's poor research infrastructure and accessibility as well as have led to mistrust in the government among young-generation Cambodians (Hinton, 2002). These effects of intergenerational trauma have caused many young Cambodians to continue to suffer from trauma stemming from the Khmer Rouge era despite the fact that they were not even there themselves.

The focus of the above studies in Cambodia has been on the negative outcomes of trauma, which is understandable, because it enables researchers and practitioners to establish culturally appropriate diagnosis and treatment. However, a more complete, culturally appropriate understanding of recovery from trauma, and of growth after trauma, is also necessary to cultivate ways of coping and thriving after any type of trauma. The purpose of the present study is to fill a gap in the existing Cambodia trauma studies by exploring the concept of PTG to conceptualize this term from within the culture. Thus, a primary goal of the current study was to identify specific factors associated with PTG in the Cambodian context, examining whether more universalist and Western assumptions in the preexisting PTG literature apply to the present sample.

METHODS

Participants

Twelve participants participated in the in-depth interview. These participants were drawn from a larger mixed-methods study of 70 participants (mean age = 20.86) conducted in Phnom Penh, Cambodia's largest city (Rich, 2015). There were six female and six male participants in the qualitative portion of the study. Most identified as single (83 percent), and as from mid-level socioeconomic status (SES; 75 percent). Most reported they had completed high school (66 percent) and were currently students (75 percent) and self-identified as Buddhist (91 percent). All of them reported having experienced at least one traumatic experience.

Data using the life events checklist (Gray, Litz, Hsu, & Lombardo, 2004) from the larger quantitative sample found that 97 percent endorsed at least *one* type of trauma, and 84 percent endorsed 5+ types of traumas (Sirikantraporn, Rich, Jafari, & Chandhok, 2016). The most frequent number of traumas endorsed by the quantitative sample was 9 (17 percent of the sample). The most frequently endorsed types of traumas were: (1) transportation accident, 90 percent; (2) natural disaster, 86 percent; and (3) severe human suffering, 73 percent. To protect participant confidentiality, researchers are not able to link specific qualitative interviewees to specific quantitative measure responses.

Measures

Semi-structured Interview Guide

An interview guide included 20 open-ended questions in the Khmer language and aimed to explore in-depth experiences and understanding of the concept of PTG. The questions were based on recent research and clinical literature on PTG and on cultural literature on the Khmer culture and society (e.g., Chandler, 2007; Ratliff, 1997).

Data Analysis

Grounded theory was suitable for this study because the study proposed to examine the phenomenon of PTG from the point of view and insight of the local people, a topic and approach which has not yet been explored in-depth within the Cambodian context. Grounded theory was used to generate an emergent theory through the discovery of themes (Glaser & Strauss, 1967). Theoretical sampling was used to increase the maximum variable sampling (Maykut & Morehouse, 1994). The sample size was determined by the concurrent process of data collection and coding procedures until the saturation point was met, the point at which no new categories were forthcoming (Maykyt & Mayhouse, 1994). Constant comparative analysis through three stages of coding (open coding, axial coding, and selective coding) was used to discover emerging themes and an overarching theory (see Glaser &

Strauss, 1967). There were several strategies utilized to increase trustworthiness of the study findings. First, peer scrutiny of the research project was used, where three coders independently coded the data and compared emerging categories and themes until the final version of categories and themes were agreed upon. Second, an audit trail and journaling among researchers was utilized to increase researchers' reflexivity and progressive subjectivity (Lincoln & Guba, 1985) to minimize the intrusive influence of the researchers' own biases on the research procedures and findings.

Procedure

This research was a collaborative project between Alliant International University and the American University of Phnom Penh (AUPP). This chapter focuses on the qualitative portion of a mixed-methods study; the quantitative portion of the study includes data utilizing such measures as the life events checklist (LEC), PTG inventory (PTGI) scale, and the Adult Resiliency Measure (ARM) (Sirikantraporn, Rich, Jafari, & Chandhok, 2016). The Institutional Review Board (IRB) approval was obtained from both institutions. This was the first research project conducted at AUPP, a new university founded in 2014. AUPP created an IRB specifically to facilitate our work, and this IRB included faculty as well as student board members. Thus, the timeframe for approval was somewhat extended and the IRB approval process began in early Autumn 2014, and approval was received in Winter/Spring 2015. The voluntary nature of student participation was emphasized. Planning for data collection was involved, especially as summer student schedules were only finalized around time of the researcher's arrival to Cambodia from the United States. Because student schedules were very full, extra credit for research participation was not permitted, and since several field trips for summer classes conflicted with previously arranged data collection schedules, multiple data collection sessions were conducted. Two bilingual Khmer English student teaching assistants (TAs) arranged and conducted the interviews. At the end of the data collection period, a debriefing session was held by one of the faculty coauthors with the student TAs also present, and all students were invited; the session was well attended and students demonstrated an interest both in social science research methods and in the work's relevance and potential value for Cambodia.

RESULTS AND DISCUSSION

Overall, the model of PTG proposed by Tedeschi and Calhoun was supported in this Cambodian qualitative sample (N = 12. 50 percent female).

This section presents exemplary quotations (F means the quotation was from a female participant and M means the quotation was from a male participant) that capture the major categories found, together with their major themes; discusses the themes of PTG that emerged from the data by the Grounded Theory method; and compares these themes with previous literature on Tedeschi and Calhoun's model of PTG. Four categories and ten themes emerged from the data (see Figure 3.1).

Category 1: Personal Growth

Personal growth is defined as personal strengths and positive personal aspects of growing as a result of one's struggle to cope with trauma. This category was made up of three themes (i.e., self-efficacy, acceptance, and self-actualization).

First Theme: Self-efficacy

Reported by 66 percent of the participants (8 out of 12), self-efficacy, which refers to one's belief in one's ability to successfully execute behaviors necessary to produce specific performance attainments (Bandura, 1986), is reflected in the selective code by the catch phrase, "I now know I can overcome future

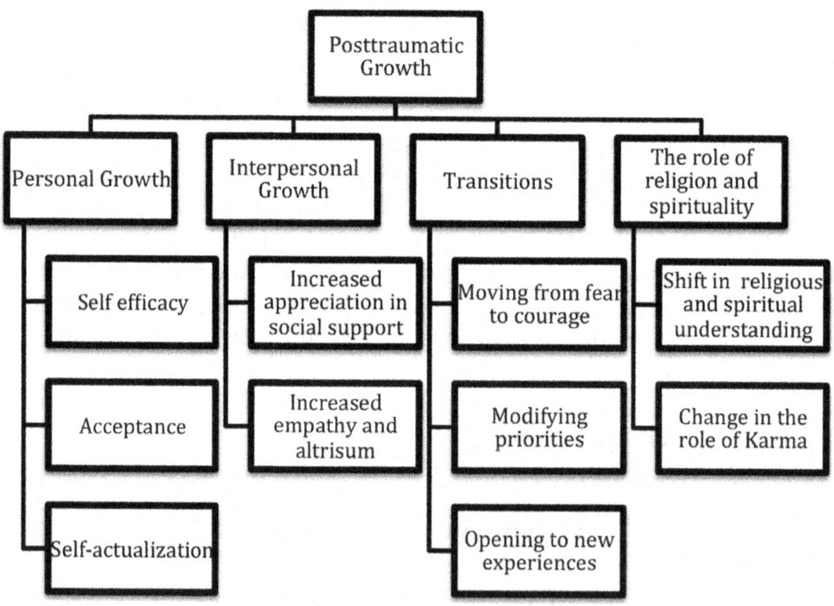

Figure 3.1 Construction of PTG in the Present Cambodian Sample.

stressful events." The experience is seen as a turning point at which the person feels a sense of independence for having been able to cope with and survive the event because they have done so with the last trauma. This theme has also been found in an Australian sample (Shakespeare-Finch & Copping, 2006), and it can be considered in line with the increased personal strength dimension of the five-factor Tedeschi and Calhoun model that found that individuals have a strong belief in one's ability to face life problems after enduring a stressful life event. Some of the responses to illustrate this theme are:

> At the end it makes me stronger, but before it [the trauma] makes me stronger it…it kind of destroys me a little bit until I knew that I shouldn't be there because it's not going too good for me, then I got stronger. But I always got stronger after everything that happened. (F)

> Like I'm the most important person who can makes me a better person and also the one who can keep myself going so… I have a feeling that everything is possible if I want it to happen. (M)

> I am able to pick myself up and start over, like not dwelling on some uh, bad experience in the past that hinders me from achieving other things that I want in life. (M)

Second Theme: Acceptance

The second theme refers to personal growth that stems from the ability to accept the situation and to accept the good and not-so-good qualities of life, of self, and of others, and to recognize that "no one and no family is perfect." This theme was mentioned by 66 percent of the participants (8 out of 12), and is exemplified by the quote, "so it changed about my life—[xxx] no one is perfect and people have their own flaws" (M). More responses to illustrate this theme include:

> Learned to accept that you are not perfect and you still have something to improve. (F)

> For anything or about anything it's just kind of whatever happens, happens, whatever doesn't, doesn't … sometimes things happen for a reason. (F)

> I feel like open to that be more accepting. And I'm more willing to try to accept other peoples' flaws but I also at the same time am more close and accepting about my own feelings. (M)

While this theme was not explored and measured in the original five-factor model of Tedeschi and Calhoun's PTGI (1996), it was viewed later by the authors as a precursor (and not an outcome) of growth (Tedeschi & Calhoun, 2004).

This theme was also found to be a salient PTG theme in the Australian sample (Shakespeare-Finch & Copping, 2006). While Acceptance is viewed as a precursor and not an outcome of growth when Tedeschi and Calhoun explained that valuing the event itself can be a catalyst for growth (Tedeschi & Calhoun, 2004), in this study's sample, acceptance implied not only accepting what happened but also accepting different qualities (positive and negative) in oneself and others, which suggests that acceptance may function as both a precursor and an outcome of PTG. After trauma, a less extreme and more balanced way of viewing the world has also been found in a longitudinal PTG study of tsunami survivors to be serving as a coping resource after the disaster, in which both positive and negative experiences are integrated (Siqveland, Nygaard, Hussain, Tedeschi, & Heir, 2015).

Third Theme: Self-actualization

Self-actualization is defined in this study as increased self-knowledge and self-realization of one's life priorities and one's capabilities (Heylighen, 1992). This theme, found in 75 percent of the participants (9 out of 12), appears to be more related to inner satisfaction of self and self-awareness, rather than outward satisfaction in career or intellectual achievements. The self-actualizing process has been believed to potentially be interrupted and "forfeited" in trauma sufferers (George & Sar, 2006). As the person learns to confront and grow from trauma, this process may resume and become available to survivors again (Dass-Brailsford, 2007). This supports the notion in the PTG literature that self-actualization is an outcome of one's acceptance and confrontations of the trauma (Joseph & Linley, 2005). Exemplary quotes of this theme include:

> I don't think it has affected, like I said earlier, what I wanted in life is still what I want in life, just I improve on that goal, improve on the, on the process of how I want to achieve it. Instead of just wanting it, I know I have a better idea, a clearer idea in order to reach that goal. (M)

> I know that I'm strong and I can focus on what is important to me and my goals. (M)

Self-efficacy, acceptance, and self-actualization emerged as three salient and interconnected themes that appear important for the participants' sense of increased personal strength.

Category 2: Interpersonal Growth

The second category, interpersonal growth, is defined as the growth-promoting factors that are related to one's interpersonal relationships as a result of trauma. Two major themes were identified as supporting interpersonal growth: (1) increased appreciation for social support and (2) increased empathy and altruism.

First Theme: Increased Appreciation for Social Support

Eighty-three percent of the participants (10 out of 12) reported the importance of support from family, friends, and community. This support can be in the form of having at least one person to think of when they experienced high stress. One participant captured this dimension by stating, "without such support, I wouldn't have been where I am today." Social support has been identified as one of the essential dimensions of growth after trauma (Tedeschi & Calhoun, 2004), and further studies suggested that the relationship between social support and growth may be the perceived availability of emotional support (Schroevers, Helgeson, Sanderman, & Ranchor, 2010), which allows successful cognitive coping and recovery after trauma (Tedeschi & McNally, 2011).

In addition, this theme illustrates the closer and warmer interpersonal relationships that often exist post-trauma in comparison to prior to the trauma. These findings strongly support the literature of PTG, which highlights the warmer, more intimate relations with others after a stressful life event. One important quality of closer interpersonal relationship among this sample is good listening, which was reported by 58 percent of the participants, such as is reflected in this quote: "My friends and family help me a lot because they are good listeners" (M). This finding potentially expands the PTG literature by clarifying that good listening from one's social support person(s) is one of the important qualities of a good relationship, and such supportive listening may help one feel better as one struggles to cope with stressful life events. While this dimension of good listening has not be directly explored in relation to PTG, Woodward and Joseph (2003) indicated that having relationships where the traumatic individuals can feel nurtured and validated and experience genuine acceptance from others through "active, attentive, and compassionate listening" may not only help them recover, but also foster PTG. As the finding from this study suggested, this person may be anyone, including a close friend, family member, spiritual leader, and/or mentor. Some of the exemplary quotes for this theme are:

> I, first of all, I didn't realize that he was that sick. I just don't know what, and then, after his recovery, I realized *how much he meant to me and I really appreciate it*. Every single day I tell him I love him and take care of him more and we've become much closer. (F)

> Friends and family help me a lot. They keep encouraging me to go on and live happily. (M)

> I learned, like, people in the fear factor, people are like, frightened. So, we all know that most, mostly when we are frightened, we are frightened and feeling down. So, I learned that we should encourage each other to stand up. (M)

Second Theme: Empathy and Altruism

After the stressful life experience, 66 percent of the participants (8 out of 12) reported that they have become more considerate and aware of the impact of their actions on other people and how other people feel when facing difficult situations. Half of these participants also reported their desire to help others who are facing life challenges. Based on the PTG study on Asian communities, Yang (2003) found that the way to actualize in collectivist cultures, such as in some Asian cultures, may be via self-correction and self-examination to develop such qualities as altruism, kindness, and conscientiousness, to uphold the ultimate goal, personal-social harmony. The findings of this study support the notion that factors related to growth among this Cambodian sample may be related to the collectivistic aspect of self and relationships with others.

Quotes from participants to illustrate this theme include:

> I mean, sometimes because actually I room with others, and sometimes they know about my problems and I am not the only one—[xxx] people are having harder lives than me and they can still do it, and then some people will just come out and talk about their difficulties too, and it makes me feel better—people have difficult things in life. (M)

> I think I learn I learn how to know what the other people are thinking when I'm with them. Instead of just doing what I want and not really taking into consideration how the other people may felt by it. Yeah. (M)

> You don't want other people to feel the same thing [*hopeless and fearful*]. I learned to give people advice and help, so they don't have to feel the same thing that I went through. (F)

Category 3: Transitions that Facilitate Growth

Transactions that facilitate growth refer to factors that are significant in helping them grow from trauma. There are three emerging themes in this category (i.e., moving from fear to courage, modifying priorities, and opening to new experiences).

First Theme: Moving from Fear to Courage

Sixty-six percent of participants (8 out of 12) reported this change. Fear is a prime emotion involved in trauma and traumatic experience, and it plays a role in PTSD by triggering mind and body to avoid certain feared situations/ persons that are a reminder of the trauma (Morey et al., 2015). This theme suggests that the increased personal strength in one's ability to overcome future adversity may stem from the conscious shift from fear to courage among this sample. This shift appears to be highly relevant to the Cambodian population and the PTSD-idiom of broken courage (*baksbat*; Chhim, 2013). Some relevant quotes from the qualitative sample include:

> It made me more brave after the loss. (F)

> I learned that even I'm look stronger, but once in a fear events or frightened events, *I'm a bit of a coward.* But, with the encouragement of my friends and family, I'll *evolve to stand up, to be strong.* (M)

> Actually when I first encountered that event, I felt very frightened, covered, and just, *scared* (laughs). I didn't move anything, but after that it taught me a lot about being courageous. (F)

> I am not fearful now, but I'm just more cautious with what I do. (F)

> I became more courageous. I mean, it didn't really impact my goal, it just made me more conscious about something that happened. (F)

Second Theme: Modifying Priorities

Fifty-eight percent of the participants (7 out of 12) stated that the way they value things in life has been different from before the stressful event. This shifting in priorities has been documented as an important change after trauma among those who experience growth. Changed philosophy of life, however small, is a highlighted element in Calhoun and Tedeschi's (1996) model. Shifts in priorities are often considered the outcome of trauma that facilitates growth in PTG among cancer patients (Cordova, Cunningham, Carlson, & Andrykowski, 2001; Sears, Stanton, & Danoff-Burg, 2003; Widows, Jacobsen, Booth-Jones, & Fields, 2005). This seems to be congruent with this present study's participants, who reported that after the stressful life experience, they realized what is more important and meaningful in life that they had before taken for granted. With regards to the modifying priorities theme, some illustrative quotes from the qualitative sample include:

> at first I wanted to go as far as possible, but right now when I learned about problems with my parents I don't want to go that far, I want to be with them more, and before, all it means to me to be successful in life was to be successful

> academically and with my career, but right now it comes to both- family and career. (M)

> Before, I focused on other people and what they think, but now I'm focusing on my goals and on what I want to accomplish. (F)

Third Theme: Opening to New Experiences

Ninety-nine percent of the participants (11 out of 12) reported that they became more open to new experiences in life. A study of the Big Five personality traits and PTG found that people who are more open to new experiences appear to be more likely to benefit from PTG (Almedon, 2005; Tedeschi & Calhoun, 2004). These studies suggest that the openness to new experiences may enable people to be more likely to seek social support, search for necessary and adaptive information, and cognitively process the information in helping them cope, find meaning, and thrive after trauma.

This speculation was supported by a more recent study on PTG and coping, which found that the appreciation of life and the new possibilities of PTGI subscales showed positive associations with six adaptive coping strategies (active coping, planning, positive reframing, turning to religion, using emotional and instrumental support) (Alexander & Oesterreich, 2013). Quotes that relate to the opening to new experience theme include the following examples from the qualitative sample:

> Because I see things differently, before…I used to be really closed minded about things, but after that, I actually see things more wide and clear. (F)

> More cautious to new experiences with new people but more open to new experiences in general. Yeah. (F)

> It helped me be more open to people and new things. (F)

In sum, three emerging themes that support the category of transitions that facilitate growth after trauma in terms of Tedeschi and Calhoun's (1996, 2004) model were: (1) moving from fear to courage, (2) modifying priorities, and (3) opening to new experiences.

Category 4: The Role of Religion/Spirituality

This category entails responses that detail the role of religion and spirituality on positive changes as a result of trauma. Two themes emerged to support this category: (1) a shift in religious/spiritual understanding and (2) a change in the role of karma.

First Theme: Shift in Religious and Spiritual Understanding

Seventy-five percent of participants (9 out of 12) reported that their religious beliefs decreased after trauma and/or played no role in their trauma and recovery to begin with. Sixty-six percent of participants' responses (8 out of 12) may potentially be understood within the realm of increased spirituality through feeling more connected with others and increasing personal faith in accepting and overcoming life stress.

Religion and spirituality have played a significant role since the conception of the term "PTG" (Shaw, Joseph, & Linley, 2005). Research, however, has shown different results when it comes to its negative or positive role on PTG. While religious coping may help explain increased PTG after trauma (Schultz, Tallman, & Altmaier, 2010), there are also studies suggesting poor mental health outcomes associated with negative religious coping and with religious rigidity (Chan & Rhodes, 2013; Harrison et al., 2001; Pargament, Smith, Koenig, & Perez, 1998). These findings suggest that it may not be religion itself, but rather it is the positive use of religion and openness to changes in a person's religious belief and spirituality that matter more in terms of PTG (Calhoun, Cann, Tedeschi, & McMillan, 2000). One study described spiritual growth as stronger spiritual orientation related to worldview, goals, relationships with others, and sense of self, dimensions which are positively related to PTG (Cole et al., 2008). Exemplary quotes for this theme include:

> Having good friends and family of course, and yeah being able to spend time with them, you know, especially after a long and tiring day at school you know, go grab something to eat. (M)

> Just that you know sometimes things do happen for a reason and maybe in the long run things will play out the you know the way they are meant to play out so. You don't always get what you want but that's for a reason. (F)

> But my faith in religion has been decreasing ever, ever...the older I get the lesser faith I have in religion," "I learned that myself is pretty strong. Like that I'm gonna face in life, that's a way for me. After that event, when I also experience like harsh things in life after that I'm not as devastated as the first time cause I know it's just something that I can overcome. (M)

Second Theme: Change in the Role of Karma

The majority of the participants (75 percent) reported that they did not believe that karma played a role in their suffering and/or their recovery. A few of the participants (33 percent or 3 out of 12) shared that they now see karma as a guide for their future actions by believing that their future is determined by their own actions. When discussing karma, one participant stated, "If I want to succeed or do something, I can do it myself." Others also expressed complex views of karma:

> I try my best to do good, but I mean, like, it doesn't necessarily mean you get any good. So ... yeah. But I keep on doing it anyway; maybe there's a part of me that believes it. (F)

> I don't know if it will or not, but if I have a choice, I wouldn't want it to because I want to make my own choices in life. I don't want something that has already been set up by, uh super natural something like that, that will gonna happen even if I don't want it to happen; I don't believe in that. I believe I always have a choice. (M)

> I don't really believe in karma. No, I mean I believe in karma, but when I'm in my hard times, I don't really think about karma or anything because I am thinking about ways to solve it. (F)

The concept of karma is an essential one to explore, as it is a central component in Khmer Buddhism, referring to the cause-effect of one's actions, and that one deserves things that happen to them because of one's past actions, including in past lives (Smith-Hefner, 1999). After the atrocities of the Khmer Rouge, many studies have attempted to understand the role of karma in individuals' healing and explanations for life events (e.g., Coggan, 2015; Harris, 2008; Ratliff, 1997). Some found that Khmer people stray from using the traditional way of understanding karma in their healing journey (Ledgerwood, Ebihara, & Mortland, 1994). The finding of this theme may suggest that an example of these shifts is a shift of the focus of Khmer Karma from past actions to present actions to determine future results.

CONCLUSION

In conclusion, data reveal that participants developed a maturing perspective, including a sense of increased personal strength, and a shifting from a powerless to an empowered sense of identity. In addition, data indicate increased and enriched connections with others, and an activated desire to help others. Finally, connection to an ability to find meaning in suffering in a future-oriented manner aided PTG after life hardships. Such data help evaluate assumptions from the existing cross-cultural literature on PTG—such as the assumption that PTG is universally experienced—that have been difficult to evaluate, given the preexisting state of information, notably the lack of data on this issue with a Cambodian sample. In particular, the Cambodian data show that many features of the PTG model described with Western samples are confirmed by the Cambodian data. These data are also important as help-seeking behaviors and options for most Cambodians differ from behaviors and options of many needing similar help in the United States and other Western nations. For instance, when seeking help for mental health issues, 50 percent of a national Cambodian sample approached family, 28 percent monks, 24 percent a medium, and 21 percent traditional healers, but only 3.9 percent approached doctors and 24 percent a pharmacy (RUPP, 2012). In addition, psychiatric medications, even when and where available, are very expensive, a year's supply often costing more than the annual salary of the average Cambodian (Rich, 2015). Understanding coping styles and PTG experiences in this sample thus may suggest interventions that are effective and feasible, given current local financial and service provider realities, and may serve as a caution to well-intentioned international groups who plan to simply attempt to apply Western models to the current situation in Cambodia.

The Cambodia data do largely support the model of PTG proposed by Tedeschi and Calhoun (1996; 2004) and which was examined in a number of studies with Western samples. The model and results carry potential significance for development of clinical interventions and applications. The findings help to enrich understanding of these issues by revealing more in-depth points of view than offered through use of only numeric questionnaires developed originally for use in Western nations. Such results provide particularly valuable information, given the extensive prevalence of exposure to traumatic events both in those who experienced the civil war in Cambodia and in younger participants in the contemporary Cambodia of today (RUPP, 2012). Unfortunately, the RUPP study (2012) did not examine PTG, but it did examine PTSD and trauma, finding similar scores between urban and rural populations.

One specifically local issue that merits detailed future study is the role of religion and spirituality (including karma) with respect to PTG in the Cambodian context. Given the tragic history of Buddhism during the Khmer Rouge era, when most of the monks were killed or driven out of the country, and many temples and libraries destroyed, it is likely that there are many unique features to the experience of religion and spirituality today in Cambodia, especially as religious and educational institutions reemerge. Since the present research utilized an urban sample, future research also should explore how PTG may manifest itself in rural Cambodian samples as well as nonstudent samples, as social support systems, financial and intellectual resources, and worldviews may differ in such groups. The present data may serve both current and future researchers well in terms of providing data on various contemporary subgroups in Cambodia (college students, employed, urban) that may be utilized to help evaluate why subgroups may vary or not vary with respect to traumatic experiences. Additionally, the present study is particularly valuable as it examines a subgroup of Cambodians that were born after the end of the Pol Pot era, yet who experienced traumatic events at similar rates as those who directly experienced the civil war in the 1970s (97 percent in the current sample of students, 92.3 percent for the RUPP (2012) sample that personally experienced the civil war). Future researchers may find it valuable to examine what is universal, or at least held in common by several groups, in the trauma experiences of these subgroups, and what may be more specific to a certain cohort and historical context.

REFERENCES

Agger, I. (2015). Calming the mind: Healing after mass atrocity in Cambodia. *Transcultural Psychiatry*, 1–18. doi: 10.1177/1363461514568336t.

Alexander, T., & Oesterreich, R. (2013). Development and evaluation of the Posttraumatic Growth Status Inventory. *Psychology, 4*, 831–844.

Almedon, A. M. (2005). Resilience, hardiness, sense of coherence, and posttraumatic growth: All paths leading to "light at the end of the tunnel?" *Journal of Loss & Trauma, 10*, 253–265.

Bandura, A. (1986). The explanatory and predictive scope of self-efficacy theory. *Journal of Clinical and Social Psychology, 4*, 359–373.

Becker, G., Beyene, Y., & Ken, P. (2000). Memory, trauma, and embodied distress: The management of disruption in the stories of Cambodians in exile. *Ethos, 28*(3), 320–345.

Boehnlein, J. K. (1987). Clinical relevance of grief and mourning among Cambodian refugees, *Social Science & Medicine, 25*(7), 765–772.

Bonanno, G. A. (2005). Resilience in the face of potential trauma. *Current Directions in Psychological Science, 14*(3), 135–138.

Calhoun, L. G., Cann, A., Tedeschi, R. G., & McMillan, J. (2000). A correlational test of the relationship between posttraumatic growth, religion, and cognitive processing. *Journal of Traumatic Stress, 13*(3), 521–527.

Calhoun, L. G., & Tedeschi, R. G. (Eds.). (2006). *The handbook of posttraumatic growth: Research and practice.* Mahwah, NJ: Lawrence Erlbaum Associates Publishers.

Chandler, D. (2007). *A history of Cambodia* (4th ed.). Philadelphia, PA: Westview.

Chhim, S. (2013). Baksbat (broken courage): A trauma-based cultural syndrome in Cambodia. *Medical Anthropology, 32*(2), 160–173.

Coggan, P. (2015). *Spirit worlds: Cambodia, the Buddha, and the Naga.* Oxford, England: John Beaufoy Publishing Limited.

Cole, B. S., Hopkins, C. M., Tisak, J., Steel, J. L., & Carr, B. I. (2008). Assessing spiritual growth and spiritual decline following a diagnosis of cancer: Reliability and validity of the Spiritual Transformation Scale. *Psycho-Oncology, 17*, 112–121.

Cordova, M. J., Cunningham, L. L. C., Carlson, C. R., & Androykowski, M. A. (2001). Posttraumatic growth following breast cancer: A controlled comparison study. *Health Psychology, 20*, 176–185.

Dass-Brailsford, P. (2007). A *practical approach to trauma: Empowering interventions*. Thousand Oaks, CA: Sage Publications.

Diaz, M., Cordova, M. J., & Spiegel, D. (2012). Posttraumatic growth in cancer patients across cultures. In L. Grassi & M. Riba (Eds.), *Clinical Psycho-Oncology: An International Perspective* (pp. 211–222). New York: John Wiley & Sons.

Field, N. P., Muong, S., & Sochanvimean, V. (2013). Parental styles in the intergenerational transmission of trauma stemming from the Khmer Rouge regime in Cambodia. *American Journal of Orthopsychiatry, 83*(4), 483–494.

George, F. R., & Sar, V. (Eds.). (2006). *Trauma and dissociation in a cross-cultural perspective: Not just a North American phenomenon*. New York: Routledge.

Glaser, B., & Strauss, A. (1967). *The discovery of grounded theory: Strategies for Qualitative research*. Chicago, IL: Aldine.

Gray, M., Litz, B., Hsu, J., & Lombardo, T. (2004). Psychometric properties of the Life Events Checklist. *Assessment, 11*, 330–341. doi: 10.1177/1073191104269954 PILOTS ID: 26825.

Hansen, L. (2014). *Mental health trauma among Cambodians and Cambodian refugees after the Pol Pot Regime conflict: A literature review*. Institute for Global and International Studies. Washington, D. C: The George Washington University.

Harris, I. (2008). *Cambodian Buddhism: History and practice*. Honolulu, HI: University of Hawai'i Press.

Harrison, M. O., Koenig, H. G., Hays, J. C., Eme-Akwari, A. G., & Pargament, K. I. (2001). The epidemiology of religious coping: A review of recent literature. *International Review of Psychiatry, 13*, 86–93.

Hauff, E. (2001). Kyol Goeu in Cambodia. *Transcultural Psychiatry, 38*, 468–473.

Helgeson V. S., Reynolds K. A., & Tomich, P. L. (2006). A meta-analytic review of benefit finding and growth. *Journal of Consulting and Clinical Psychology, 74*, 797–816.

Heylighen, F. (1992). A cognitive-systemic reconstruction of Maslow's theory of self-actualization. *Behavioral Science, 37*, 39–57.

Hinton, A. L. (2002). *Annihilating difference: The anthropology of genocide*. Berkeley: University of California Press.

Hinton, A. L. (2004). *Why did they kill?: Cambodia in the shadow of genocide*. Berkeley, CA: University of California Press.

Hinton, D. E., Hinton, A. L., Pich, V., Loeum, J. R., & Pollack, M. H. (2009). Nightmares among Cambodian refugees: The breaching of concentric ontological security. *Cultural Medical Psychiatry, 33*(2), 219–265.

Hinton, D. E., Howes, D., & Kirmayer, L. J. (2008). Toward a medical anthropology of sensations: Definitions and research agenda. *Transcultural Psychiatry, 45*(2), 142–162.

Hinton, D. E., Pich, V., Chhean, D., & Pollack, M. H. (2005). "The ghost pushes you down": Sleep paralysis-type panic attacks in a Khmer refugee population. *Transcultural Psychiatry, 42*(1), 46–77.

Ho, S. M., Law, L. S., Wang, G. L., Shih, S. M., Hsu, S. H., & Hou, Y. C. (2013). Psychometric analysis of the Chinese version of the Posttraumatic Growth Inventory with cancer patients in Hong Kong and Taiwan. *Psycho-Oncology, 22*, 157–179.

Jarl, J., Cantor-Graae, E., Chak, T., Sunbaunat, K., & Larsson, C. A. (2015). Trauma and poor mental health in relation to economic status: The case of Cambodia 35 years later. *PLoS ONE, 10* (8): e0136410. doi:10.1371/journal.pone.0136410.

Joseph, S., & Linley, P. A. (2005). Positive adjustment to threatening events: An organismic valuing theory of growth through adversity. *Review of General Psychology, 9*(3), 262–280.

Kierman, B. (2008). *The Pol Pot regime: Race, power, and genocide in Cambodia under the Khmer Rouge, 1975–1979* (3rd ed.). New Haven, CT: Yale University Press.

Ledgerwood, J., Ebihara, M. M., & Mortland, C. (1994). Introduction. In M. M. Ebihara, C. A. Morland, & J. Ledgerwood (Eds.), *Cambodian culture since 1975: Homeland and exile* (pp. 1–26). Ithaca, NY: Cornell University Press.

Lincoln, Y. S., & Guba, E. G. (1985). *Naturalistic inquiry*. Beverly Hills, CA: Sage.

Maykut, P., & Morehouse, R. (1994). *Beginning qualitative research: A philosophical and practical guide*. London: The Falmer Press.

Morey, R. A., Dunsmoor, J. E., Haswell, C. C., Brown, V. M. Vora, A., Weiner, J., Stjepanovic, D., Wagner, H. R., Brancu, M., Marx, C. E., Naylor, C. J., Voorhees, E. V., Taber, K. H., Beckham, J. C., Calhoun, P. S., Fairbank, J. A., Szabo, S. T., & LaBar, K. S. (2015). Fear learning circuitry is biased toward generalization of fear associations in posttraumatic stress disorder. *Translational Psychiatry, 5*(12).

Pargament, K. I., Smith, B., Koenig, H., & Perez, L. (1998). Patterns of positive and negative religious coping with major life stressors. *Journal for the Scientific Study of Religion, 37*, 710–724.

Powell, S., Rosner, R., Butollo, W., Tedeschi, R. G., & Calhoun, L. G. (2003). Posttraumatic growth after war: A study with former refugees and displaced people in Sarajevo. *Journal of Clinical Psychology, 59*, 71–83.

Ratliff, S. R. (1997). *Caring for Cambodian-Americans: A multidisciplinary resource for the helping professions*. New York: Garland Publishing.

Rich, G. (2015). *Internationalizing psychology in Cambodia: Lessons learned and future directions.* Paper presented at the annual meeting of the American Psychological Association. Toronto, Canada.

RUPP (Royal University of Phnom Penh) (2012). *Cambodia Mental Health Survey*. Phnom Penh: RUPP Department of Psychology.

Schroevers, M. J., Helgeson, V. S., Sanderman, R., & Ranchor, A. V. (2010). Type of social support matters for prediction of posttraumatic growth among cancer survivors. *Psychooncology, 199*(1), 46–53.

Sears, S. R., Stanton, A. L., & Danoff-Burg, S. (2003). The yellow brick road and the emerald city: Benefit-finding, positive reapparaisal coping, and posttraumatic growth in women with early-stage breast cancer. *Health Psychology, 22*, 487–497.

Schultz, J. M., Tallman, B. A., & Altmaier, E. M. (2010). Pathways to posttraumatic growth: The contributions of forgiveness and importance of religion and spirituality. *Psychology of Religion and Spirituality, 2*, 104–114.

Shakespeare-Finch, J. E., & Copping, A. (2006). A grounded theory approach to understanding cultural differences in posttraumatic growth. *Journal of Loss and Trauma, 11*, 355–371.

Shaw, A., Joseph, S., & Linley, P. A. (2005). Religion, spiritually, and posttraumatic growth: A systematic review. *Mental Health, Religion, & Culture, 8*, 1–11.

Siqveland, J., Nygaard, E., Hussain, A., Tedeschi, R. G., & Heir, T. (2015). Posttraumatic growth, depression and posttraumatic stress in relation to quality of life in tsunami survivors: A longitudinal study. *Health and Quality of Life Outcomes, 13*(18). doi: 10.1186/s12955-014-0202-4.

Sirikantraporn, J., Rich, G., Jafari, N., & Chandhok, S. (2016). Resilience and posttraumatic growth in Cambodians: Quantitative and qualitative approaches. In L. Sundararajan (Chair), *Indigenous psychology: New developments in theory and research.* Paper presented at the annual meeting of the American Psychological Association, Denver.

Smith-Hefner, N. J. (1999). *Khmer Americans: Identity and moral education in a diasporic community.* Berkeley, CA: University of California Press.

Taku, K., Calhoun, L. G., Tedeschi, R. G., Gil-Rivas, V., Kilmer, R. P., & Cann, A. (2007). Examining posttraumatic growth among Japanese university students. *Anxiety Stress Coping, 20*(4), 353–367.

Tedeschi, R. G., & Calhoun, L. G. (1996). The posttraumatic growth inventory: Measuring the positive legacy of trauma. *Journal of Traumatic Stress, 9,* 455–471.

Tedeschi, R. G., & Calhoun, L. G. (2004). Posttraumatic growth: Conceptual foundations and empirical evidence. *Psychological Inquiry, 15*(1), 1–18.

Tedeschi, R. G., & McNally, R. J. (2011). Can we facilitate posttraumatic growth in combat veterans? *American Psychologist, 66*(1), 19–24.

Van Schaack, B., Reicherter, D., & Chhang, Y. (Eds.). (2011). *Cambodia's hidden scars: Trauma psychology in the wake of the Khmer Rouge.* Phnom Penh, Cambodia: Documentation Center of Cambodia.

Widows, M. R., Jacobsen, P. B., Booth-Jones, M., & Fields, K. K. (2005). Predictors of posttraumatic growth following bone marrow transplantation for cancer. *Health Psychology, 24,* 266–273.

Woodward, C., & Joseph, S. (2003). Positive change processes and posttraumatic growth in people who have experienced childhood abuse: Understanding vehicles of change. *Psychology and Psychotherapy, 76*(3), 267–283.

Yang, K. S. (2003). Beyond Maslow's culture-bound linear theory: A preliminary statement of the double-Y model of basic human needs. *Nebraska Symposium on Motivation, 49,* 175–255.

Chapter 4

Resilience in Guatemala

Contextual Overview with Future Perspectives

Tannia de Castañeda and María del Pilar Grazioso

OVERVIEW OF GUATEMALA

Guatemala in the World

To understand the complexity of resilience processes, it is critical to understand the context in which it is being addressed. As Sothwick, Bonano, Masten, Panter-Brick and Yehuda (2014) point out, resilience can be framed from individual, family, organizational, social and cultural perspectives; and it also must be approached from a multilevel analysis that includes demographic, cultural, economic and social factors, among others (Sothwick et al., 2014). From this perspective, it is important to highlight Guatemala's stand within the world, Latin and Central America. Guatemala is no stranger to the global challenges of our time; nevertheless, the degree and way these affect issues locally are determined by unique characteristics. Among these characteristics, it can be mentioned that Guatemala has a multicultural richness represented by its four ethnic groups (Ladino, Mayan, Xinca and Garifuna), its 25 languages (Spanish, 22 Mayan languages, Xinca and Garífuna) and its predominantly young population (66.5 percent out of 16,703,000 people) (Instituto Nacional de Estadística [INE], 2014; Comisión Económica para América Latina y el Caribe [CEPAL], 2016). Guatemala's abundant natural resources are being identified as one of the most biologically diverse places on the planet (United States Agency for International Development [USAID], 2002). It's located in the Central American isthmus, bordered to the west and north by Mexico, to the east by Belize and the Honduras Gulf, to the southeast by Honduras and El Salvador and to the south by the Pacific Ocean (Programa de las Naciones Unidas para el Desarrollo en Guatemala [PNUD], 2017).

This uniqueness provides a fascinating journey to understanding resilience processes from a local lens. For a deeper understanding of resilience, the authors of this chapter consider resilience from an ecological perspective, influenced by human and contextual interactions. They base their resilience approach on Ungar's (2008) conceptualization: "In the presence of significant adversity, resilience is the capacity of individuals to navigate their way to the psychological, social, cultural and physical resources that sustain their well-being, and their capacity to individually and collectively negotiate for these resources to be provided in culturally meaningful ways" (p. 225).

Economics

Guatemala is the largest economy in Central America, and the nation has had one of the best economic performances in Latin America in recent years; despite this, it has high levels of inequality and poverty (Banco Mundial, 2017). The 2008–2009 international economic crisis had local effects; this global crisis affected the labor market, limiting social development, and deepening poverty and exclusion (Secretaría de Planificación y Programación de la Presidencia [SEGEPLAN], 2015a). As Bristow and Healy (2015) note, this economic crisis highlighted the vulnerability of many economies, emphasizing the importance of economic resilience, and suggesting changes by policymakers as well as adaptive and transformative responses in these processes. From the resilience perspective, poverty is a risk factor (Bristow & Healy, 2015), and unfortunately in Guatemala, average poverty levels reach 62.4 percent of the population, with 29.6 percent of the people living in extreme poverty conditions (PNUD, 2017).

The most important economic activities of the country are the following: industry (gross domestic product's (GDP's) 17.6 percent), agriculture (GDP's 13.6 percent) and private services (GDP's 15.8 percent). The greatest economic activities take place in Guatemala City, and 90 percent of the country's economic structure is represented by micro, small and medium-sized enterprises (SEGEPLAN, 2015b). Family remittances play a key role in Guatemala's economy, due to international migration. These migrations are influenced by the lack of job opportunities, violence and family reunification, among others (INE, 2016). Remittances represent 11 percent of Guatemala's GDP. These money transfers impact consumption spending, intermediate consumption (raw materials for manufacturing and contracting services), savings, investment, and health and education expenses (Organización Internacional para las Migraciones [OIM], 2017).

As Ferraté (2017) points out, the lack of development and access to appropriate infrastructure and access to basic services (food, nutrition, water, clothing, mobility and environmental quality) has an impact on the country's economy. One example initiative, "The Sustainable Economic Observatory Project," was recently launched at the Universidad del Valle de Guatemala (UVG) in conjunction with USAID. This project aims to contribute to the development of Guatemalans by providing a space for society to participate to promote sustainable policies and programs through discussion and consensus in which academia plays a key role. It aims to strengthen the Sustainable Development Goals in four main aspects: (1) rural development and food security, (2) agricultural sector growth, (3) environment, climate change resilience and biodiversity conservation, and (4) competitiveness and trade promotion (UVG, 2017).

Health

Another major challenge for Guatemala is health coverage. Guatemalans face high levels of malnutrition; chronic malnutrition in the rural areas is 53 percent and in the urban areas it is 34.6 percent. The indigenous population is the more affected population (61.2 percent) compared to the nonindigenous population (34.5 percent) (SEGEPLAN, 2015a). Investment in mental health reaches only 1 percent of the national health budget (Organización Mundial de la Salud [OMS], 2011) with only 11 mental health professionals per 100,000 inhabitants (OMS, 2012). The challenge today is to anticipate health problems from a prevention perspective. Under this paradigm, prevention is seen from a broad approach and must be comprehensive. Guzmán (2005) points out the importance of promoting interventions and political designs that include resilience focused interventions as a prevention approach to manage vulnerability, increase levels of resilience, and promote human development and mental health, thus reducing pathologies related to situations of risk and stress (Guzmán, 2005).

Security

Citizen security is one of the greatest concerns faced by the Guatemalan population (Banco Mundial, 2017), and it influences population resilience levels. From a developmental perspective, exposure to stress, trauma and chronic adversity has an impact on child and adolescent mental health (Wu, Feder, Cohen, Kim, Calderon, Charney, & Mathé, 2013). The primary security issues are the high levels of crime, violence, homicide, extortion and drug trafficking (SEGEPLAN, 2015b). Sadly, Guatemala is one of the most violent countries in Latin America and in the world (Interpeace, 2016).

New programs like the "Guatemalan MPP Project," funded by RTI International, are being implemented in different areas of the country, aiming toward training human capacity and providing equipment and services to enhance security, citizenship safety and foster prevention; this work is conducted in close collaboration with local authorities and national police (Gobernación de Alta Verapaz, 2017). As Pitts (2016), a criminology expert, points out, it is a fundamental issue to develop a coordinated effort between police, community leaders, district attorneys and social services providers. Furthermore, the interventions promote self-worth and enhance self-esteem in individuals, who become aware of their behaviors and their responsibilities, so that they are not misled through social cohesion into delinquent acts (Pitts, 2016). Thus, the promotion of citizenship security can be approached from a community resilience perspective that contributes to fostering changes in social structures while increasing the sense of trust in institutions and authorities (Lykes, 2013).

Education

In Guatemala, the number of average schooling years is 5.6 (INE, 2016). Investment in education is only 3 percent of the country's GDP (USAID, 2016). The National Survey of Living Conditions [ENCOVI, 2014] estimates that four million Guatemalans under 20 years of age do not have access to education. These statistics indicate that 9 out of 10 children attend primary school, 7 out of 10 adolescents between the ages of 13 and 15 are enrolled in middle school, 4 out of 10 between 16 and 19 years are in high school, and only 1 in 10 between the ages of 20 and 29 are enrolled in university (INE, 2016). As will be discussed later in this chapter, this reality of coverage and educational quality make scholarship programs central in the promotion of resilience. Masten (2015) argues that school context and settings nurture resilience, having great influence in persons' lives when schools are effective.

Climate Change

Guatemala is one of the 19 countries declared as megadiverse in the planet, and the one with the greatest biological and cultural diversity in Central America (Ferraté, 2016). It occupies the first place in Central America's ecoregional diversity with 14 ecoregions. It has 6 lakes, 37 volcanoes, 7,754 registered plant species and almost 1970 fauna species (USAID, 2002). However, Guatemala is currently among the ten countries most affected by climate change with serious consequences for the country, such as a drought caused by "El Niño" climate phenomenon, which causes a decline in agricultural production, and the formation of "La Niña," which, on the other hand, results in excessive rainfall that causes natural disasters, affecting the most vulnerable populations (Food and Agriculture Organization [FAO], 2016).

Almost 1.5 million Guatemalans live in vulnerability to the extent of requiring humanitarian assistance (FAO, 2016).

According to Ferraté (2016), deforestation and water pollution "represent vulnerabilities and risks to maintain the ecological balance and harmony between the natural and human orders" (p. 301). Undoubtedly, the effects of neglect and abuse of Guatemalan natural resources have and will influence future generations. Ferraté (2016) also points out that bio-environmental resilience processes would contribute to "a healthy, safe, enduring and dynamic environment" (p. 303).

Political Stand

Historically, Guatemala has been confronted with adversities such as an internal armed conflict that lasted for more than 30 years (1960–1997) and that still has repercussions on the country's social and political dynamics with postwar effects (PNUD, 2017). It was in 1985 that a transition to democracy was made with the military power transfer to a civilian government. In 1996, the Peace Agreement Firm was signed (PNUD, 2017).

Although the peace agreement took place more than 20 years ago, the State of Guatemala is considered weak and continues to face conflictive dynamics that became evident in the political crisis of 2015 (Interpeace, 2016). According to Castillo (2016), the task in the Guatemalan political arena is to restore the public institutions' credibility, improve the governance climate and increase political will. The author warns that political instability is risky for the country, and it represents a vulnerability that may endanger the constitutional order (Castillo, 2016).

RESILIENCE IN GUATEMALA: RESEARCH AND APPROACHES

Interpeaces (2016), in the study "Resilience and peacebuilding: Frames of analysis for resilience in Guatemala," presents what is called "resilient responses" to different problems identified in 11 departments of Guatemala. Here, several community coping strategies (resilient responses) that address these problems may be mentioned: lobbying with greater representation of women, interinstitutional networks, social auditing, support and counseling, prevention programs on security issues, social protest, diffusion of information, consultation and deliberation processes and development of various forms of economic activity. At an individual level, the work suggests focusing on three capacities to cope with conflicts: (1) absorption: referring to persistence and stability in reaction capacity, (2) adaptation: referring to increased flexibility to make changes in behavior adjusting to problematic situations, and (3) transformative capacity: entailing changing the situation. The study highlights "resistance" as the Guatemalans' capacity to cope with conflicts, conceptualized as their resilience capacity expression (Interpeace, 2016).

Radan (2007) highlights resilience expressions of refugee women from El Salvador and Guatemala who suffered and survived violence and trauma after the Guatemalan Civil War. These women presented higher level of resilience when compared with other refugee women in the United States. Despite significant challenges, such as extreme poverty, lack of educational opportunities, abuse and trauma, most of these women overcame adversity and could adjust to their new life context, where they found safety and opportunities that allowed them to use their inner strengths (Radan, 2007).

During the past decade, several studies and interventions from a resilience perspective have been conducted in Guatemala, promoting a preventive, transformative and promotive approach, with the understanding that school and educational opportunity settings represent a protective factor that prevent mental health problems for the youth (Dray, Bowman, Wolfenden, Campbell, Freund, Hodder & Wiggers, 2015). The following Guatemalan studies are focused on educational contexts and represent protective factors that help to foster coping skills and positive mental health, as well as provide change and transformational opportunities in the face of adversity.

First, the authors present the socioemotional intervention conducted within the Violence Prevention Program (VPP) (2012–2014), where youth coming from identified red zones were enrolled in university-level technical training scholarships offered by UVG, USAID, RTI-International and Centro de Estudios para la Cooperación Internacional (CECI), 2012. The students were high school graduates from private or public schools, living in conditions of economic disadvantage in the rural and urban areas of the country. This program was facilitated in three of UVG's external campuses, located in Guatemala City, the Southern Coast and the Western Highlands.

Castañeda, Saz and Grazioso (2015) present the results of the socioemotional intervention program developed as one of the VPP components. The authors utilized a Covitality Scale (Quintero, 2010; Jones, You & Furlong, 2012) as a pretest and posttest intervention. The participants were 122 Violence Prevention Program students, 61 percent men and 39 percent women (16–24 years old). The socioemotional intervention consisted of workshops based in positive psychology to promote self-awareness, improve interpersonal relationships, cooperation and coping skills development. It also included individual counseling with the students and workshops with parents, furthermore strengthening parenting skills. The assessment instrument examined eight psychological well-being constructs: self-efficacy, optimism, subjective life satisfaction, gratitude, subjective happiness, hope, persistence and passion for long-term goals, and personal adjustment. There was a higher reliability at posttest (α =.901) than at pretest (α = .807). There was a positive change in seven constructs of well-being in the Covitality Scale (self-efficacy, life satisfaction, gratitude, happiness, hope, persistence and personal adjustment); no change was reflected in the optimism construct. A *t*-test showed a significant statistical difference in the personal adjustment construct (p = .028). There was a statistically strong positive correlation between gratitude and life satisfaction constructs (r = .607, p < 0.00). The Covitality full-scale average was 442.69 units for pretest and 459.50 units for posttest indicating a significant statistical difference (p = 0.024). The personal adjustment construct had the highest statistical significance reflecting an increased capacity to manage anger, hostility and aggression. This confirms the positive influence of educational opportunities that incorporate psychological interventions to prevent violence. The socioemotional intervention also helped decrease the dropout rate from the educational program, from 22 percent to 11 percent; however, this decrease could also be attributed by many other personal and contextual factors besides the intervention. The strength of the study is that it could demonstrate that comprehensive programs incorporating educational opportunities and a psychological approach positively influence attitudes such as the ability to handle anger, hostility and aggression in youth coming from contexts of adversity. This approach can assist in preventing violence, navigating risks and negotiating with resources in a relevant way. Nevertheless, the challenge for this study is to identify other contextual factors that helped decrease desertion levels, such as the role of teachers and staff.

To deepen the youth Violence Prevention Program experience in the Western Highlands campus, Mónico, Grazioso, Castañeda, Saz and Cardona (2017) carried out a study called "Transformative Assessment of Educational Opportunities for At-Risk Youth in Guatemala." This is a transformative program evaluation. The authors are from two different universities, Elon University, the United States, and UVG. This is a study that aims for a multidisciplinary and interinstitutional collaboration to develop research based on ethical standards from both universities' Institutional Review Boards (IRBs). The research intends to establish the contributions and limitations of Violence Prevention Program promoting violence prevention in Guatemala. It also explores the program's potential and improvements to serve vulnerable youth originally excluded from the program. The participants were eight graduates from violence-stricken areas (19–23 years old), and case studies for comparison were included. These programs benefit youth (13–24 years old) from poverty-stricken and disaster-prone regions in Guatemala and high migration areas. A combination of sampling types was used for the selection of the case studies (purposive, maximum variation, critical cases and sensitive cases). Five seminars were developed to understand context and relevant best practices, engage local actors, recruit gatekeeper organizations, collect data, share preliminary findings and do member check. The preliminary results related to youth risks are: (1) violence is multidimensional: (a) physiological: organized crime; physical, sexual, emotional and psychological abuse, (b) structural: systematic denial of basic rights and lack of opportunities, and (c) inequality of gender and ethnicity; (2) forced migration: internal displacement and migration between countries. The study identified the program key elements: (a) involvement of leaders in design, (b) youth direct involvement, (c) community empowerment, (d) strengthening community ties, (e) interinstitutional collaboration, (f) institutional strengthening, (g) periodic program evaluation, (h) establishing national and local alliances, (i) staff awareness and training, (j) at-risk youth typification to generate relevant programs, (k) comprehensive support and (l) coordination with families. The study's strength lies in the inclusion of the different actors involved in the process of supporting the youth, the interconnection that can be developed between different institutions as a space to share lessons learned and future perspectives were evidenced in the five workshops that were organized by the researchers and stakeholders. One of the challenges is to include the perspective of youth who have deserted from these programs to understand the circumstances and/or difficulties that prevent them from completing their educational process in these programs.

To address the perspectives of both the students who pursue the Violence Prevention Program scholarship and are able to finish it and the ones who dropped out, Castañeda (2017) is conducting her doctoral dissertation on the topic. It is entitled "Guatemalan youth in adverse contexts: Resilience processes underlying educational opportunities." The author seeks to understand, from a transformative paradigm, the experience of Guatemalan at-risk youth who chose to participate in Violence Prevention Program. This type of knowledge would help as a follow-up for the youth who participated in the program, to understand the resilience processes of those who graduated and of those who dropped out, to deepen our understanding of their complex contexts. As previously mentioned, Castañeda and colleagues found that a socioemotional intervention to promote well-being positively influenced this cohort and helped decrease the dropout rate in the technical scholarship (Castañeda, Saz, & Grazioso, 2015).

Castañeda (2017) also seeks to identify the risks, protective and promotive factors that influence the resilience processes of the students who participated in VVP. Also, it seeks to explore their life course before, during and after the program, as well as their personal, family and work changes, and meaningful ways to influence policy and support positive changes in the community to increase youth resilience. This was a mixed-method research (Mertens, 2007) based on the Social Ecology Resilience Theory (Ungar, 2012). Fourteen people participated (average age: 26 years; 11 male and 3 female). The participants lived in conditions of economic disadvantage, coming from identified red zones. In the qualitative phase preliminary results show, two focus groups were held—graduates and dropouts—and eight in-depth individual interviews were conducted with both. Visual methods were used to elicit participants' narratives.

As a quantitative measure, the Resilience Research Centre-Adult Resilience Measure-28 (RRC-ARM-28) has been completed by the participants as a pilot to adapt the RRC-ARM-28 to the Guatemalan context, which will further incorporate a contextual section in the scale. In a next phase of the ongoing research, the RRC-ARM-28 measure will be sent online to the 151 young people who participated in Violence Prevention Program (graduates and dropouts). The qualitative phase preliminary results found are the following: (1) promotive and protective factors: family support, mothers' key role, significant adults (teachers, spiritual leaders), peers' and friends' support, educational opportunities, sports practice, socioemotional support, community service activities, job opportunities; (2) youth's personal strengths: positive, curious, creative, love of learning, capacity to dream, entrepreneurial characteristics, goal setting, self-determination, finance awareness, money saving concept, consciousness of giving back to their families, opportunity seizing, listening and looking for advice, social awareness, giving back to their communities and country; (3) challenges that youth face: unemployment, low-paid jobs, exclusion, violence, fear, poverty, the need to work at young age to pay school or for supporting their families, stigma, discrimination, judgment (physical appearance, ethnicity, neighborhood), drugs, alcoholism, lack of services and marginalization; (4) scholarship meaning for the youth: an exit of community challenges, hope for future generations, possibility to help their communities, experience and job stability, increase income, independence, setting new goals.

Castañeda (2017) emphasizes the lessons learned so far: the Local Advisor Committee's key role in getting access to the participants, researchers' long-term engagement to gain trust, the importance of follow-up and looking forward to generating new opportunities (networking, jobs, training) through the dissemination of relevant results. The study's strength is that it includes participants who deserted from the scholarship program; this allows exploring of the contextual aspects that influenced the program's dropouts. This is a contribution to understanding resilience processes, and not just focusing on young people who graduated, which allows a comprehensive approach. The challenges of the study are that the participants in the qualitative phase of the study were mostly men. There was no equitable gender participation, which could have an influence on the understanding of these young persons' resilience processes. Another challenge faced is to contact the participants due to changes of contact information.

The study conducted by Stevenson, Oldfield and Ortiz (2017) points to the exploration of educational projects and their impact on Guatemala's children at risk. In their study, "Streets of Resilience: Exploring the role of educational outreach with street connected children in Guatemala City" (Stevenson, Oldfield, & Ortiz, 2017), the authors explored resilience among Street-Connected Young People (SCYP) in Guatemala City. The researchers identified how community education projects facilitate the construction of Third Spaces of aspiration for at-risk young people. The focus was on resilience-building elements of risk-bearing environments, rather than the dangers inherent in street-connected living. They worked at three different sites, two of them were volunteer-run educational outreach projects (one in a residential house and the other one in a church building) and the third one was in a fieldwork site of the city, well known for wholesale and retail markets where young people lived and worked. Ethnographic and visual methods were used with SCYP, who attend volunteer-run community education projects. There were 12 participants in the research, 8 SCYP (ranging from 11 to 16 years; 4 male and 4 female) and 4 adults (volunteers from each outreach project). Ethnographic interviews were conducted, and the use of participatory photography and image elicitation allowed exploration of constructions of meaning in relation to versatile spaces of learning which nurture well-being and resilience.

Participatory photographic records with disposable cameras, smartphones and drawings were used as elicitation tools during interviews. The research findings highlight three main themes: (1) spaces, which are conceptualized as safe physical locations that can be offered to young people to keep them away from risks; (2) rifts, which refer to the dissonance that is found among voluntary projects where learning spaces are offered to the young people, and their families, who demand the help of their children in their work activities, distracting from educational opportunities; and (3) repair, in which it is suggested that to support the resilience processes of young people, support for them needs to be more holistic, encompassing the whole person, that is, it goes beyond the educational aspects of food, excursions, health care and spiritual guidance. It highlights the fundamental role of family support to avoid possible conflicts of interest between the educational agencies/projects and the families. The research highlights the importance of incorporating parents, especially mothers, into the scope of the programs. Finally, the aspirational aspect is highlighted as a form of empowerment for the future, through the development of skills and SCYP networking. The authors found the following: (1) resilience is not only a personal characteristic, but is also embedded in the people and places surrounding them (resilience is promoted with human and material resources); (2) the value of a holistic approach (health, nutritional, spiritual and advisory support) is facilitated by educational outreach agencies; (3) utility in understanding resilience is an ecological concept that involves agencies, educators and families; and (4) integrating visual methods is beneficial to elicit narratives to access meanings and aspirations of the participants through SCYP eyes. The strength of this study is the richness of its participatory methods that allow one to have a broad understanding of the experience and data collection that will allow the researchers to return the results to participants. A challenge for this study is to have the Guatemalan academic counterpart. Progress is being made in this area, including planning for research dissemination and future collaboration between researchers and UVG.

Oldfield (August 14, 2017, personal consultation) shared his experience and involvement in volunteering while living in Guatemala with the authors of this chapter. This approach to "Street Connected Children in Guatemala City" allowed him to stay in contact with agencies that work with these young people with whom he has led research on resilience with Stevenson and Ortiz. Another approach to the experience of these young people is found in their study, "Promoting or suppressing resilience to mental health outcomes in at-risk young people in Guatemala: The role of school connectedness and peer attachment" (Oldfield, Stevenson, & Ortiz, 2017). In this study, the authors seek to better understand at risk youth parental attachment relating to positive mental health as well as peer attachment and school connectedness that promote or suppress resilience and mental health. The participants of the study were 90 young people (Ages 11 to 18 years; 49 percent female, 51 percent male) attending two community-based schooling projects in Guatemala (urban and rural areas). These young people were considered at high risk for drug abuse, homelessness, poverty and neglect. Participants completed self-report measures of parental and peer attachment (Inventory of Parental & Peer Attachment; Gullone & Robinson, 2005), school connectedness (Psychological Sense of School Membership; Goodenow, 1993) and the Strength and Difficulties Questionnaire (Goodman, 2001). Multiple regression data analysis found that more insecure parental attachment relationships predicted poorer mental health outcomes. The study considered poor parental attachment as a risk for young people. This relationship was moderated by more secure school connectedness, although not by peer attachment. School connectedness is a predictor of higher levels of resilience. The strength of this study is that it opens a line of research related to attachment among peers, emphasizing that it is important not only to promote strong positive relationships between peers but also to ensure that they are effective; otherwise it may have a negative impact in their levels of resilience. A major challenge is the use of scales that have not been adapted to the Guatemalan context.

DEVELOPING COUNTRY: PROMISES FOR THE FUTURE

Guatemala's resilience has enormous potential from different dimensions and at different levels. As an emerging economy, and largely in response to the global economic crisis, many youth have resorted to the use of entrepreneurship and innovation as responses to current challenges. The Global Entrepreneurship Monitor (GEM) (2016) points out results from 2015 that position Guatemala at a level of potential entrepreneurship greater than the average reached in Latin America and economies based on efficiency (GEM, 2016). The report highlights key aspects to foster entrepreneurship: financial resources availability; government policies and programs that encourage entrepreneurship, education and training; transfer of research and development; access to commercial, professional and physical infrastructure; and social and cultural perceptions that stimulate entrepreneurship (GEM, 2012).

With respect to innovation, Guatemala has talented professionals that have influenced the nation at different levels, all relevant to contributing to the country's development, and therefore its resilience. In the technology field, one may mention "Duolingo," a free language learning app launched by Luis von Ahn, which has more than 170 million users around the world (Roberts, 2017). Also, one may also mention Phillip Wilson, a social entrepreneur who founded "Ecofiltro" (water filters), a company that aims to solve the growing water crisis in an efficient, sustainable manner and which has directly benefited 500,000 people (Schwab Foundation for Social Entrepreneurship, 2007). In mental health and psychology, one can mention Conecta-Tec's team app proposal, developed by three Guatemalan Applied Psychology professionals (Tannia de Castañeda, Ana Alicia Cóbar, and Marco Saz), who won third prize in the National Prize for Educational Innovation (2016). This app seeks to contribute to the adolescents' well-being and help them to improve their academic performance (Universidad del Valle de Guatemala, 2016). As one can see, Guatemala has the potential to creatively address different social problems that can have an impact not only at national level, but also worldwide.

FINAL REMARKS

To promote resilience in Guatemala, the approach must be comprehensive, contextual and culturally pertinent. It is essential to improve educational opportunities, as well as to address the population's basic needs, such as good nutrition, access to clean water, health services, security, recreation and mental health support, among others. The studies analyzed found that other factors such as spiritual guidance, family, friends and key community members (e.g., teachers and program volunteers) are key promotive and protective factors. In research and interventions, long-term involvement to gain access and trust with participants and stakeholders is critical. High levels of connection between school and peers are predictors of positive adjustment, which can, at the same time, contribute to academic success. In addition, socioemotional interventions contribute to positive adjustment, which helps to prevent young persons' violence and risk behaviors.

To conclude, more contextualized resilience studies are desired to further understanding of how Guatemalans' resilience processes are influenced by the dimensions embedded into its diverse cultural context.

REFERENCES

Banco Mundial. (2017). *Guatemala Panorama General*. Retrieved from http://www.bancomundial.org/es/country/guatemala/overview#1

Bristow, G., & Healy, A. (2015). Crisis response, choice and resilience: Insights from complexity thinking. *Cambridge Journal of Regions, Economy and Society*. 8, 241–256. doi:10.1093/cjres/rsv002.

Castañeda, T. (2017). *La experiencia de jóvenes guatemaltecos en contextos de adversidad: Procesos de resiliencia subyacentes en oportunidades educativas*. [Guatemalan youth in adverse contexts: Resilience processes underlying educational opportunities]. (Doctoral dissertation, not published). Guatemala: Universidad del Valle de Guatemala.

Castañeda, T., Saz, M. A., & Grazioso, M. P. (2015). *Violence prevention program for at risk youth in Guatemala*. Guatemala: Universidad del Valle de Guatemala. Unpublished manuscript.

Castillo, C. (2016). La reforma política. *Revista Análisis de la Realidad Nacional. Instituto de Problemas Nacionales*. Universidad de San Carlos de Guatemala: Guatemala. IPNUSAC. 5(18), 54–64.

Comisión Económica para América Latina y El Caribe [CEPAL]. (2016). *Guatemala: Perfil Nacional Socio-Demográfico*. Retrieved from http://interwp.cepal.org/cepalsat/Perfil_Nacional_Social.html?pais=GTM&idioma=spanish

Dray, J., Bowman, Wolfende, L., Campbell, E., Freund, M., Hodder, R., & Wiggers, J. (2013). Systematic review of universal resilience interventions targeting child and adolescent mental health in the school setting: Review protocol. *Systematic Review Journal*. 4, 186. doi 10.1186/s13643-015-0172-6

Ferraté, L. (2016). El derecho a un ambiente sano. *Revista Análisis de la Realidad Nacional. Instituto de Problemas Nacionales*. Universidad de San Carlos de Guatemala: Guatemala. IPNUSAC. 5(18), 273–320.

Food and Agriculture Organization [FAO]. (2017). *Corredor Seco América Central: Informe de Situación*. Retrieved from http://www.fao.org/3/a-br092s.pdf

Figueroa, D. (2005). La resiliencia: Una alternativa de prevención. *Revista de Psiquiatría y Salud Mental Hermilio Valdizán*. 6(2), 81–88. Retrieved from http://www.hhv.gob.pe/revista/2005II/5%20LA%20RESILIENCIA.pdf

Global Entrepreneurship Monitor Guatemala 2011–2012 [GEM]. (2012). *Monitor Global de Emprendimiento Guatemala 2011–2012.* Universidad Francisco Marroquín, 1ª ed. Retrieved from http://gem.ufm.edu/wp-content/uploads/2014/09/Reporte_Final_2011.pdf

Global Entrepreneurship Monitor Guatemala 2015–2016 [GEM]. (2016). *Monitor Global de Emprendimiento Guatemala 2015–2016.* Universidad Francisco Marroquín, 1ª ed. Retrieved from http://gem.ufm.edu/wp-content/uploads/2016/10/Reporte-Nacional-2015-2016.pdf

Gobernación de Alta Verapaz (2017). *Proyecto MPP de Guatemala.* Gobierno de Guatemala. Retrieved from http://gobernacionaltaverapaz.gob.gt/sitio/?p=842

Instituto Nacional de Estadística de Guatemala [INE]. (2014). *Encuesta Nacional de Condiciones de Vida 2014.* Retrieved from https://www.ine.gob.gt/sistema/uploads/2014/02/26/L5pNHMXzxy5FFWmk9NHCrK9x7E5Qqvvy.pdf

Interpeace. (2016). *Resiliencia y construcción de paz: Marcos de análsis para la resiliencia en Guatemala.* Retrieved from http://3n589z370e6o2eata9wahfl4.wpengine.netdna-cdn.com/latinoamerica/wpcontent/uploads/sites/7/2016/04/Resiliencia_y_construcción_de_paz-en_Guatemala-br.pdf

Lykes, B. (2013). Participatory and action research as a transformative praxis: Responding to humanitarian crises from the margins. *American Psychologist.* 68(8), 774–783. Retrieved from http://dx.doi.org/10.1037/a0034360

Masten, A. S. (2014). *Ordinary magic. Resilience in development.* New York: The Guilford Press.

Mónico, C., Grazioso, M. P., Castañeda, T., Saz, M. A., & Cardona, S. (2017). *Transformative assessment of educational opportunities for at-risk youth in Guatemala.* Elon University, USA—Universidad del Valle de Guatemala. Unpublished manuscript.

Oldfield, J., Stevenson, A., & Ortiz, E. (2017). *Promoting or suppressing resilience to mental health outcomes in at risk young people in Guatemala: The role of school connectedness and peer attachment.* Manchester Metropolitan University: United Kingdom. Manuscript submitted for publication.

Organización Internacional del Trabajo [OIT]. (2016). *Panorama Laboral 2016 América Latina y el Caribe.* Oficina Regional para América Latina y el Caribe. http://www.ilo.org/wcmsp5/groups/public/---americas/---ro-lima/documents/publication/wcms_537803.pdf

Organización International para las Migraciones [OIM]. (2017). *Encuesta sobre migración internacional internacional de personas guatemaltecas y remesas 2016.* Organismo de las Naciones Unidas para la Migración. Retrieved from http://onu.org.gt/wp-content/uploads/2017/02/Encuesta-sobre-MigraciOn-y-Remesas-Guatemala-2016.pdf

Organización Mundial de la Salud [OMS]. (2011). *Informe sobre el sistema de salud mental en Guatemala.* Recuperado de: http://www.who.int/mental_health/who_aims_country_reports/guatemala_who_aims_report_spanish.pdf

Organización Mundial de la Salud [OMS]. (2012). *Salud Mental. Prevención del Suicidio.* Recuperado de: http://www.who.int/mental_health/prevention/suicide/suicideprevent/es/

Pitts, W. J. (2016). *Criminología en Guatemala ¿hacia dónde vamos desde aquí?* [diapositivas de PowerPoint]. Programa de Crimen Transnacional e Investigaciones de Justicia RTI Internaional.

Programa de las Naciones Unidas para el Desarrollo [PNUD, 2017). *Guatemala en breve.* Retrieved from http://www.gt.undp.org/content/guatemala/es/home/countryinfo/

Radan, A. (2007). Exposure to violence and expressions of resilience in Central American women survivor of war. *Journal of Aggression, Maltreatment & Trauma.* (14)1–2, 147–164. Doi: 10.1300/J146v14n01_08.

Roberts, N. (2017). *He sold two companies to Google won a MacArthur "Genius Grant" and launched free Duolingo App. Forbes.com* Entrepreneurs NewTEch. Retrieved from https://www.forbes.com/sites/ninaroberts/2017/05/24/he-sold-two-companies-to-google-won-a-macarthur-genius-grant-and-launched-free-duolingo-app/2

Schwab Foundation for Social Entrepreneurship. (2017). *Philip Wilson.* Retrieved from http://www.schwabfound.org/content/philip-wilson

Secretaría de Planificación y Programación de la Presidencia [SEGEPLAN]. (2015a). *Informe final de cumplimiento de los Objetivos de Desarrollo del Milenio.* Guatemala. Retrieved from https://planes.cepal.org/bitstream/handle/123456789/554/ODM_Informe_final.pdf?sequence=1&isAllowed=y

Secretaría de Planificación y Programación de la Presidencia [SEGEPLAN]. (2015b). *Política General de Gobierno 2016–2020.* Gobierno de la República de Guatemala. Retrieved from http://www.segeplan.gob.gt/downloads/2016/PGG2016-2020.pdf

Southwick, S., Bonano, G., Masten, A., Panter-Brick, C., & Yehuda, R. (2014). Resilience definitions, theory, and challenges: Interdisciplinary perspectives. *European Journal of Psychotraumatology.* 5, 25338. Retrieved from http://dx.doi.org/10.3402/ejpt.v5.25338

Stevenson, A., Oldfield, J., & Ortiz, E. (2017). *Streets of Resilience: Exploring the role of educational outreach with street connected children in Guatemala City.* Manchester Metropolitan University: United Kingdom. Manuscript submitted for publication.

Ungar, M. (2008). Resilience across cultures. *British Journal of Social Work.* 38, 218–235. doi:101093/bjsw/bcl343.

United States Agency for International Development [USAID]. (2002). *Análisis de la Biodiversidad en Guatemala.* Retrieved from http://pdf.usaid.gov/pdf_docs/pnacx118.pdf

United States Agency for International Development [USAID]. (2016). *La educación técnica universitaria y su vinculación al mercado laboral en Guatemala.* Retrieved from https://www.usaid.gov/sites/default/files/documents/1862/FHI360-inter-Guatemala-anaalisis-del-mercado-laboral-FINAL.pdf

Universidad del Valle de Guatemala (2016). *Premio Nacional de Innovación Educativa.* www.uvg.edu.gt/ie

Universidad del Valle de Guatemala. (2017). *Observatorio Económico Sostenible. UVG Hoy* 2(4). Guatemala.

Wu, G., Feder, A., Cohen, H., Kim, J., Calderon, S., Charney, D., & Mathé, A. (2013). Understanding resilience. *Frontiers in Behavioral Neuroscience.* 7(10). doi:10.3389/fnbeh.2013.00010.

Chapter 5

Resilience in Taiwan

The Shaping Forces of its Diverse Cultural Context and Beliefs about Adversity

Ching-Yu Huang

INTRODUCTION

Although the definition of resilience in psychological research differs throughout the literature, it can be generally defined as the process of, capacity for, or outcome of successful adaptation from threatening circumstances or adverse events (Cassidy, 2015). Adversity is inevitable throughout one's lifetime; however, adverse events do not guarantee negative developmental outcomes. Abundant research evidence has suggested that people are usually not disturbed by things themselves (i.e., adversity per se) but by their interpretations of them (i.e., meaning and interpretation of adversity). In different cultures, adversity may be conceptualized differently, thus influencing how individuals endure, interpret, tolerate, and react to adversity. If adversity were regarded as a chance for personal development that is eventually beneficial to the individual concerned (e.g., constructing benefits from adversity; Affleck & Tennen, 2001), tolerance of the threat would be easier. On the other hand, if adversity were seen as punishment from God, retribution, or transmigration, it would be more difficult for the person concerned to accept it. Cultural beliefs may shape the coping resources and behavior of the individual concerned (Rokach, 1999) by providing the basis upon which people experiencing adversity make sense of their experience and develop their coping (Shek, 2004). In this chapter, I will first provide an overview of Taiwan, including a very brief history and its natural environment, which influences people's beliefs. This will provide the readers the historical and geographical contexts within which Taiwanese culture was established. Thereafter, the cultural contexts and beliefs related to resilience and adversity will be presented in the next section. As cultural contexts and beliefs are important factors impacting people's behavior and coping when faced with adversity, learning about the cultural context will enable the readers to contextualize and better understand how Taiwanese people see and cope with adversity. Finally, the chapter will conclude with some discussion about how these cultural beliefs regarding resilience and adversities affect mental health in Taiwanese and immigrant Taiwanese, to shed light on more effective ways of action for helping professions who work with Taiwanese and immigrant Taiwanese populations. Let us first start with the historical and geographical profiles of Taiwan.

TAIWAN: BRIEF HISTORY, ETHNIC AND NATURAL ENVIRONMENT

Historically, inhabitants lived in Taiwan for over 50,000 years, thus people usually identify themselves as Taiwanese, not Chinese. In 1624, the Dutch invaded southern Taiwan but then were expelled by the Zheng Dynasty in 1662, and then the Qing Dynasty took over Taiwan in 1683. During this time (1662–1895), increased numbers of Fujianese, Hakka, and Cantonese migrated to Taiwan from the southeastern part of Mainland China. It is also during this time (1662–1895) that Taiwanese society became heavily influenced by the Chinese culture. In 1985, the Qing Empire lost the First Sino-Japan War (1895), thus having to cede the province of Taiwan to Japan. For the following 50 years (1985–1945), Taiwan was a part of Japan and engaged in the Japanese culture and celebrated Japanese history. The Japanese contributed to Taiwan's modernization in various significant ways, through the electrification of the island, creating massive infrastructure of roads and railways, improving agricultural development, establishing compulsory elementary education, and improving public health and hygiene. In 1945, Japan was defeated in World War II and Taiwan was "returned" to China. At this time, China had been governed by the Chinese nationalists (i.e., Republic of China, ROC) after the downfall of the Qing Empire, under Chiang Kai-Shek's command. In 1949, the nationalists eventually fully retreated to Taiwan after losing the war against Chinese Communists, who then proclaimed government in Mainland China (the People's Republic of China, PRC). During this time (1945–1949), a significant amount of Chinese people from all over Mainland China immigrated to Taiwan. After this shift in political leadership, and with the support and assistance of other countries, especially the United States, Taiwan slowly emerged as a democratic society by 1995 (Gregor, 1995).

Ethnically, Taiwan is home to 23.4 million people, with more than 16 officially recognized indigenous tribes. The majority of the population has both Han Chinese ethnic heritage (mostly Fujianese and Hakka people) and indigenous heritage, because during the Qing governance, intermarriage between the Chinese settlers and the indigenous people residing in the western plain of Taiwan was very common (Brown, 2004). Moreover, during the Qing governance, only single men from Mainland China were allowed to cross the Taiwan Strait to settle in Taiwan, resulting in the complete acculturation of the western plain aborigines to Han Chinese culture. During the Japanese colonial time, intermarriage between Japanese and Taiwanese people also was common; hence, the Japanese education during this period resulted in the strong influence Japanese culture has on Taiwanese society even today. Therefore, although Taiwan is strongly influenced by Chinese culture, with its history of Dutch and Japanese colonial rules and ethnic diversity, it may be more diverse than commonly recognized.

Geographically, Taiwan is situated between the Philippines and Japan on the subtropic Pacific Ocean. As a result, there are a lot of typhoons (hurricanes) during summer and early autumn, which sometimes cause serious damage. Geologically, Taiwan is at the corner of Manila Trench and Ryukyu Trench; therefore, earthquakes are frequently occurring natural disasters in Taiwan. The Ministry of the Interior of Taiwan reported 113 natural disasters (including 57 typhoons, 42 floods, 9 damaging earthquakes, and 5 other disasters) occurring in Taiwan between 2006 and 2016, causing over 5950 deaths or injuries (MOI, 2017). Due to the frequent occurrence of natural disasters such as typhoons, flood, and earthquakes, Taiwanese people generally consider natural disasters the will of gods, and therefore people do not try to control nature but strive to live with nature harmoniously (Jordan, 1999). Such belief about coexistence harmoniously with nature is incorporated into a set of cultural beliefs that are supportive during a crisis and that mutually align the will of gods and natural events (Jang & LaMendola, 2007). After learning about the diverse historical, ethnic, and geographical backgrounds of Taiwan, we will next turn our focus to the prominent cultural beliefs related to adversity in Taiwan.

CHINESE CULTURAL CONTEXT AND BELIEFS ABOUT ADVERSITY

Culture has an important role to play in how people cope with adversity. First of all, culture offers the survivors meanings of disaster, which contributes to their psychological well-being (Webster, McDonald, Lewin & Carr, 1995). Cultural factors, by virtue of their influence on the healing process and ameliorating emotional distress, positively affect the nature and quality of recovery from disasters (Al-Naser & Sandman, 2000). Moreover, cultural beliefs may shape the degree of optimism and coping patterns of a person experiencing hardship. As mentioned in the previous section, Taiwan has long and complicated relations with China, and thus shares cultural roots with the Chinese. Although Taiwan is generally considered a technologically and economically advanced country, its sociocultural context is still heavily influenced by the Chinese-Confucian tradition. The Confucian tradition emphasizes inner strength and virtues such as perseverance and tolerance of individuals, and maintains that such qualities in people can be cultivated through education (Yip, 1998). Therefore, there are many traditional adages which convey the belief that hardships make people grow wiser and stronger.

For instance, with 1519 adolescents (age = 11–18 years; 50 percent female) in Hong Kong, Shek (2004) developed the Chinese Beliefs about Adversity Scale (CBAS), categorizing Chinese cultural beliefs about adversity into two categories: positive and negative beliefs about adversity. The first category emphasizes the positive values of adversity and people's capacity to overcome adversity. Such cultural beliefs are rooted in the Confucian beliefs aforementioned. Some commonly seen or heard sayings which reflect such values are "吃得苦中苦，方為人上人 (chi de ku zhong ku, fang wei ren shang ren—hardship increases stature)" and "人定勝天 (ren ding sheng tian—man is the master of his own life)." The second category, negative beliefs about adversity, stems from the influence of Buddhism and Taoism and the emphasis on fate are intrinsic to the traditional Chinese culture (Yang, 1981). Therefore, there are some cultural beliefs that emphasize people's inability to change adversity (such as fate) and the negative impact of adversity. Examples of such beliefs are "生死由命，富貴在天 (sheng si you ming, fu gue zai tian—Life and death are inevitable; fame and wealth are preordained)" and "人窮志短 (ren qong zhi duan—poverty stifles ambition)." These two seemingly contradicting views reflect the diverse belief systems in Chinese culture, with Confucianism, Taoism, and Buddhism at the same time. In particular, the positive Chinese cultural beliefs about adversity had a mitigating effect on adolescents' adjustment problems and psychological well-being in Hong Kong (Shek, 2004, 2005). Stronger endorsement of positive Chinese cultural beliefs about adversity was associated with better mental health and school adjustment, and fewer problematic behaviors, and the mitigating effect was even stronger for economically disadvantaged adolescents (Shek, 2004, 2005). Moreover, in a longitudinal study with 843 pupils from Hong Kong, Lee and colleagues (2010) reported that it is the children's Chinese culture-related beliefs about adversity (measured by CBAS, Shek, 2004), rather than any items from their resilience measure (measured by Child and Youth Resilience Measure, Ungar, 2008; and Chinese Resilience Measure for Children and Adolescents in Hong Kong, Lee et al., 2006), that predicts their positive outcome (measured by Parental Assessment of Child's Habit, Lee et al., 2010). This also reflects the measurement issue in resilience research, underscoring the importance of cultural contexts when making sense of human well-being and development.

Other than the Chinese cultural influence, the second largest ethnic group in Taiwan, the Hakka people, also contribute to the diverse cultural beliefs. The Hakka people are about 15–20 percent of the population in Taiwan. They are descendants of Hakka immigrants from Guangdong province, and are known as frugal, diligent, self-reliant, responsible, and persistent (Yang, 2004). Such characteristics as "the Hakka Spirit (Jang, 2008)" were found to contribute to their post-disaster resilience. For instance, Jang and Wang (2009) interviewed 15 Hakka survivors of the 921 Earthquake in the Tung Shih areas, where they had the highest death toll from the earthquake, and the areas were largely inhabited by Hakka people. They found that endorsing the "Hakka spirit" served as protective factor for Hakka people in facing natural disasters and contributed to their disaster resilience (Jang & LaMendola, 2006). Having a sense of responsibility (one of the traits of the Hakka spirit) toward their families and/or communities encouraged the survivor to apply a problem-focused coping style in times of crisis (Jang & Wang, 2009), which enhances disaster resilience. The Hakka people learn to accept disasters as part of life experience and live harmoniously with nature, and normalization and living with disasters are traits of disaster resilience.

Cultural beliefs regarding adversity and coping strategies can also be transmitted via parental socialization toward children, especially in Chinese-Confucian culture, where children are expected to pledge reverence to their parents (Ho, 1996). Parents can foster children's resilience by being their positive role model, providing them motivational and informational support in coping with adversity. Resilient children frequently reported being grateful for family members (especially mothers) who provided positive role modeling, consistent caring, and motivational support, which are the essence of authoritative parenting (Smokowski, Reynolds, & Bezruczko, 1999). Positive, as well as negative, role modeling is available in the family environment, and resilient adolescents are able to learn and grow from both. Positive role modeling provided the adolescents with adaptive coping strategies, and they learned risk-taking consequences from negative role modeling without experiencing it firsthand. Less-resilient adolescents seemed to have a more negative response to familial role modeling, and did not learn from the negative risk-taking role modeling (Smokowski et al., 1999).

Generally speaking, past research findings with Euro-American populations reveal positive relations between authoritative parenting and child resilience (e.g., Kritzas & Grobler, 2005), whereas authoritarian parenting is associated with maladaptive coping styles, psychological disturbances, and lower resilience (Kritzas & Grobler, 2005; Wagner et al., 1996). At the core of authoritative parenting are consistent discipline/control and high warmth/emotional support. Consistent discipline and control is essential in promoting the development of children's social processing skills and a sense of coherence. An individual's sense of coherence is defined as his/her global orientation to life as comprehensible, manageable, and meaningful (Antonovsky, 1987). Given the stress-producing and ever-changing nature of the human environment, our "normal" state is chaos and disorder, rather than stability. Sense of coherence is believed to be a factor in promoting stability and health in the face of disruption and change (Walsh, 1998). This sense of coherence fosters healthy adaptation to unexpected events that affect our lives and bring about transformations; thus, a high sense of coherence is an important coping resource in times of crisis and can be considered an integral part of resilience. The other important component of authoritative parenting, warmth/emotional support, enhances psychological resources (e.g., self-esteem) and therefore enables adolescents to cope effectively with stressful situations. Also, it gives the individual emotional support in times of adversity, and the perceived emotional and social support from family and friends are important parts of resilience. However, with non-Caucasian populations, the associations between parenting style and child resilience are still inconclusive, as research remains scarce. The only piece of research, to the author's knowledge, with Chinese populations regarding parenting and child resilience was Eisenberg et al. (2009)'s work. With a sample of 691 elementary school children (44.5 percent girls), they found a similar trend of associations between parenting and children's ego resilience in Chinese (People's Republic of China, PRC) and Caucasian children: authoritative parenting was associated with higher child ego resilience scores, whereas authoritarian parenting, particularly the use of physical punishment, was associated with lower ego resilience. Moreover, such associations were mediated by children's temperament (effortful control/EC and impulsivity, specifically). Socialization goals and processes differ from culture to culture; what is acceptable in one culture may not be deemed appropriate in another. Therefore, children in other cultures may interpret stricter and controlling parenting practices positively. In Chinese cultures, as mentioned in previous paragraphs in this section, children are required to pledge reverence to their parents, and parents take the major responsibility to govern, teach, and discipline their children. Within such cultural context, the use of scolding, criticism, and even physical discipline in attempts to control and correct children's behavior is usually deemed acceptable. As a result, Chinese children may interpret harsh parental discipline to be the demonstration of parental care and involvement, because the parents are intending to train and teach the children. However, how Chinese cultural beliefs related to adversity influence the association between parenting practice and child resilience remains unclear, highlighting the need for more research to disentangle such associations.

As demonstrated in previous research discussed earlier (e.g., Lee et al., 2010; Shek, 2004, 2005), cultural beliefs can affect children and adolescents' well-being and adjustment. Therefore, it will be helpful for helping professionals to be familiar with these cultural beliefs in order to better work with immigrant or nonimmigrant Taiwanese population who are experiencing adversity and seeking help.

IMPLICATION FOR THE HELPING PROFESSIONS

Understanding the ethnoprofiles and relevant cultural beliefs will provide a more nuanced and accurate context for helping professionals to work with Taiwanese or immigrant Taiwanese families. For instance, although Taiwanese are generally treated as homogeneous as Chinese because of some of their shared cultural and historical links, the recent history (since 1895 when Taiwan was rendered to Japan) and social changes have also resulted in divergences between Taiwanese and Mainland Chinese cultures. Compared to Mainland China, Taiwan has not been through the Cultural Revolution brought by the Communist Party, and it arguably has retained more traditional Confucian cultural values, whereas in Mainland China, the majority of Chinese people changed their attitudes and values in many spheres of social life after the Cultural Revolution (Schoenhals, 2015). Moreover, the Japanese colonial rule period in Taiwan (1985–1945) also colored Taiwanese culture with Japanese influence. Even today, it is common to hear Japanese vocabulary in the Taiwanese language.

Such sociocultural and historical contexts do have an effect on people's coping and problem-solving styles. For example, Li, Eschenauer, and Yang (2013) compared college students across the United States (n = 177; 50.8 percent women), Mainland China (n = 166; 51.8 percent women), and Taiwan (n = 179; 52.5 percent women) on their trait resilience (measured by Resilience Scale, RS; Wagnild & Young, 1993), self-efficacy (measured by General Self-Efficacy Scale, GSS; Schwarzer & Jerusalem, 1995), and problem-solving coping styles (measured by Coping Strategy Indicator, CSI; Amirkhan, 1990) and found that there was no significant difference in applying problem-solving across US, Taiwanese, and Chinese samples. However, the effective predictors of problem-solving varied across these groups. In the US sample, self-efficacy predicted problem-solving coping style; in the Chinese samples, trait resilience was the predictor; and for the Taiwanese sample, self-efficacy and trait resilience were both significant predictors of problem-solving coping. Moreover, trait resilience was found to mediate the effect of self-efficacy on problem-solving in the Taiwanese and Chinese samples, but not in the US sample. These findings verified the need for clinicians to pay close attention to the effects of cultural differences in order to understand their client's issues and develop culturally sensitive treatments

(Roysircar, 2009). The findings suggested that individuals' tendencies to solve problems can be enhanced by promoting their task-oriented traits, such as self-efficacy and trait resilience, regardless of their cultural backgrounds. Considering cultural differences, clinicians may enhance US clients' self-efficacy to promote the clients' problem-solving, because self-efficacy directly influenced problem-solving in the US sample. When counseling Chinese and Taiwanese clients, counselors may be able to enhance self-efficacy and especially trait resilience, given the finding that trait resilience is the major pathway by which self-efficacy influenced problem-solving in the Chinese and Taiwanese samples (Li et al., 2013). Therefore, knowing these nuances in sociocultural differences enable mental health professionals working with different Chinese immigrant subgroups (e.g., immigrants from Mainland China vs. from Taiwan) to work with their clients more effectively and facilitate their treatment.

However, Chinese cultural beliefs such as "吃得苦中苦，方為人上人 (hardship increases stature)" and the Hakka spirit of endurance might act as barriers for Taiwanese or immigrant Taiwanese in seeking help, because they believe in enduring hardship, and endurance implies not reaching out for help. Moreover, past research has shown that the Chinese cultural value placed on the avoidance of shame acts as a barrier to utilization of mental health services and help-seeking process among Chinese immigrants (Tabora & Flaskerud, 1997). Since the family name and "face" are important to Chinese immigrants, they tend to seek help from family members first to avoid being viewed poorly by others (Webster & Fretz, 1978) and to be more reticent in publicly admitting problems and seeking help. Chinese immigrants, similar to other minority immigrant groups, tend to underutilize mental health services, and when treatment is sought, they terminate prematurely at a much higher rate than nonminority clients (Leong & Lau, 2001). Knowing the cultural beliefs hindering these clients' help-seeking behavior enables clinicians to anticipate better what may be helpful to overcome such barriers and formulate treatment plans more effectively and to prevent early termination.

In conclusion, adversity is inevitable throughout one's lifetime, but adversity per se may not be detrimental. It is usually one's interpretations of adversity that affect one's reaction and subsequent outcomes. How an individual endures, interprets, tolerates, and reacts to adversity is very much culturally dependent. By understanding the historical, ethnic, and geographical contexts of Taiwan and the common cultural beliefs regarding adversity in Taiwan, readers will be able to contextualize resilience within Taiwanese culture, so as to more effectively work with Taiwanese or immigrant Taiwanese clients.

REFERENCES

Affleck, G., Tennen, H., & Apter, A. (2001). Optimism, pessimism, and daily life with chronic illness. In E. C. Chang (Ed.), *Optimism and pessimism: Implications for theory, research, and practice* (pp. 172–200). Washington, DC: American Psychological Association.

Al-Naser, F., & Sandman, M. (2000). Evaluating resilience factors in the face of traumatic events in Kuwait. *SQU Journal for Scientific Research, 2,* 111–116.

Amirkhan, J. H. (1990). A factor analytically derived measure of coping: The coping strategy indicator. *Journal of Personality and Social Psychology, 59,* 1066–1074. doi:10.1037/0022-3514.59.5.1066.

Antonovsky, A. (1987). *Unravelling the mystery of health. How people manage stress and stay well.* San Francisco, CA: Jossey-Bass.

Brown, M. J. (2004). *Is Taiwan Chinese?: The Impact of culture, power, and migration on changing identities.* Oakland, CA: University of California Press.

Cassidy, S. (2015). Resilience building in students: The role of academic self-efficacy. *Frontiers in Psychology,* 6. doi:10.3389/fpsyg.2015.01781.

Eisenberg, N., Chang, L., Ma, Y., & Huang, X. (2009). Relations of parenting style to Chinese children's effortful control, ego resilience, and maladjustment. *Development and Psychopathology, 21*(2), 455–477.

Gregor, A. J. (1995). R.O.C on Taiwan: China's first democracy. *Foreign Affairs, 74.5,* S5.

Ho, D. Y. F. (1996). Filial piety and its psychological consequences. In M. H. Bond (Ed.), *The handbook of Chinese psychology* (pp. 155–165). London, UK: Oxford University Press.

Jang, L. J., & LaMendola, W. (2006). The Hakka spirit as a predictor of resilience. In D. Paton & D. Johnston (Eds.), *Disaster resilience: An integrated approach.* Springfield, IL: Charles C. Thomas.

Jang, L., & LaMendola, W. (2007). Social work in natural disasters: The case of spirituality and posttraumatic growth. *Advances in Social Work Journal, 8*(2), 67–78.

Jang, L., & Wang, J. (2009). Disaster resilience in a Hakka community in Taiwan. *Journal of Pacific Rim Psychology, 3*(2), 55–65. doi:10.1375/prp.3.2.55.

Jordan, D. K. (1999). *Gods, ghosts, & ancestors: Folk religion in a Taiwanese village* (3rd ed.). San Diego, CA: Department of Anthropology, UCSD.

Kritzas, N., & Grobler, A. A. (2005). The relationship between perceived parenting styles and resilience during adolescence. *Journal of Child & Adolescent Mental Health, 17*(1), 1–12. doi: 10.2989/17280580509486586.

Lee, T.-Y., Kwong, W.-M., Cheung, C.-K., et al. (2010). Children's resilience-related beliefs as a predictor of positive child development in the face of adversities: Implication for interventions to enhance children's quality of life. *Social Indicators Research, 95,* 437–453.

Lee, T. Y., Kwong, W. M., Ungar, M., & Cheung, M. (2006). *Psychometric properties of the Chinese resilience measures for children and adolescents in Hong Kong.*

Paper presented at the 5th international conference on social work in health and mental health, HKSAR, China.

Leong, F. T. D., & Lau, A. S. L. (2001). Barriers to providing effective mental health services to Asian Americans. *Mental Health Services Research, 3*, 201–214. doi: 10.1023/A:1013177014788.

Li, M.-H., Eschenauer, R., & Yang. Y. (2013). Influence of efficacy and resilience on problem solving in the United States, Taiwan, and China. *Journal of Multicultural Counseling and Development, 41*, 144–157. doi: 10.1002/j.2161-1912.2013.00033.x.

Ministry of the Interior (MOI). (2017). *Natural disaster statistics from 1958 to 2016.* Retrieved from http://www.nfa.gov.tw/main/Content.aspx?ID=&MenuID=873

Rokach, A. (1999). Cultural background and coping with loneliness. *Journal of Psychology, 133,* 217–29.

Roysircar, G. (2009). Evidence-based practice and its implications for culturally sensitive treatment. *Journal of Multicultural Counseling and Development, 37*, 66–82.

Schoenhals, M. (2015). *China's Cultural Revolution, 1966–69: Not a dinner party.* New York: Routledge.

Schwarzer, R., & Jerusalem, M. (1995). Generalized Self-Efficacy Scale. In J. Weinman, S. Wright, & M. Johnston (Eds.), *Measures in health psychology: A user's portfolio. Causal and control beliefs* (pp. 35–37). Windsor, England: NFER-Nelson.

Shek, D. T. L. (2004). Chinese cultural beliefs about adversity: Its relationship to psychological well-being, school adjustment and problem behavior in Hong Kong adolescents with and without economic disadvantage. *Childhood, 11,* 63–80.

Shek, D. T. L. (2005). A longitudinal study of Chinese cultural beliefs about adversity, psychological wellbeing, delinquency and substance abuse. *Social Indicators Research, 71,* 385–409.

Smokowski, P. R., Reynolds, A. J., & Bezruczko, N. (1999). Resilience and protective factors in adolescence. *Journal of School Psychology, 37,* 425–448.

Tabora, B. L., & Flaskerud, J. H. (1997). Mental health beliefs, practices, and knowledge of Chinese-American immigrant women. *Residential Group Care and Treatment, 18,* 173–189. doi: 10.3109/01612849709012488.

Ungar, M. (2008). Resilience across cultures. *British Journal of Social Work, 38,* 218–235.

Wagner, B. M., Cohen, P., & Brook, J. S. (1996). Parent/adolescent relationships. Moderators of the effect of stressful life events. *Journal of Adolescent Research, 11,* 347–374.

Wagnild, G. M., & Young, H. M. (1993). Development and psychometric evaluation of the Resilience Scale. *Journal of Nursing Measurement, 1*, 165–178.

Walsh, F. (1998). *Strengthening family resilience.* New York: Guilford Press.

Webster, D. W., & Fretz, B. R. (1978). Asian-American, black and white college student's preference for helping services. *Journal of Counseling Psychology, 25,* 124–130.

Webster, R. A., McDonald, R., Lewin, T. J., & Carr, V. J. (1995). Effects of a natural disaster on immigrants and host population. *The Journal of Nervous and Mental Disease, 183*(6), 390–397.

Yang, K. S. (1981). The formation and change of Chinese personality: A cultural-ecological perspective. *Acta Psychologica Taiwanica, 23*, 39–55.

Yang, W. S. (2004). *A census of the Hakka population in Taiwan.* Taipei, Taiwan: Council for Hakka Affairs, Executive Yuan, R. O. C. [in Chinese].

Yip, K. S. (1998). Mental health concepts in Confucian thoughts. *Hong Kong Journal of Social Work, 32*, 151–165.

Chapter 6

Contextual Risks and Resilience Enablers in South Africa

The Case of Precious

Sadiyya Haffejee and Linda Theron

INTRODUCTION

The ubiquity of sexual violence in South Africa means that only the most gruesome incidents make headlines. Details of vicious sexual violence perpetrated against children resulting in severe, permanent internal injury, incidents of girls being abducted, raped, mutilated and murdered, as well as incidents of the so-called corrective rape against lesbian women tend to create a national uproar. The brutal violence that accompanies the murder and sexual assault in cases such as these serves as a catalyst, prompting calls for swift and immediate action by government and civil society alike (Buiten & Naidoo, 2016).

The normalization and perhaps fatigue that accompanies the everyday violence against women and girls does not however suggest that issues on sexual violence are ignored. South Africa has a vociferous nongovernmental and academic sector that routinely advocates for greater protection through more comprehensive legislation and increased awareness and intervention such as Thoyondou Victim Empowerment Programme, Shukumisa, Tswaranang Legal Advocacy Centre and Women's Legal Centre. Practically however, this activism and the existence of comprehensive laws, such as the Sexual Offences Act, the Children Act and the Children's Amendment Act, have not been effective in curbing sexual violence in South Africa (Artz et al., 2016). Disparity is still apparent in the child protection strategy and limited resources available to support its implementation (Mathews, Loots, Sikweyiya, & Jewkes, 2012).

In South Africa, national police statistics for the 2013/2014 period suggest that 51 cases of child sexual abuse (CSA) are reported per day. However, given that only one in nine cases of sexual abuse are reported, this number is likely significantly higher. Corroborating this assertion are findings from a national population survey by Artz et al. (2016), which revealed a sexual abuse prevalence rate of one in three. Although South African crime statistics for 2016/2017 suggest a 6.5 percent decrease in the number of sexual violence incidents, activists are angrily dismissive of this finding, stating that lower statistics are reflective of a drop in the *reported* number of sexual violence incidents rather than an actual drop in incidents, and point to a declining faith in the justice system instead (Mapumulo, 2017).

Both globally and in South Africa, sexual violence has been attributed to patriarchal constructions of masculinities and gendered power relations (Dartnell & Jewkes, 2013; Seedat, van Niekerk, Jewkes, Suffla, & Ratele, 2009). Given that constructions of gender are informed by cultural and social contexts (Morrell, Jewkes, Lindgegger, & Hamlall, 2013), greater cognizance needs to be given to the way patriarchy manifests itself within different social and cultural contexts (Buiten & Naidoo, 2016). In South Africa, the current scholarship of sexual violence has thus adopted a more nuanced view on the role of patriarchy with an appreciation of the impact that racial and economic marginalization, first under colonialism, then apartheid, and now under a democratic constitution that espouses gender equality, has on the way that patriarchy manifests (Buiten & Naidoo, 2016). The concept of hegemonic masculinity, which refers to hierarchies of masculine power over both women and other men, has been adapted in South Africa to explain high levels of violence resulting from these structural changes (Morrell et al., 2013). Ratele and Suffla (2011) note that in contexts where individual and social upliftment is curtailed or where masculine identity is challenged, violence becomes central to men's desire to be seen as successful and is used to maintain male dominance over women. While hegemonic masculinities are not necessarily violent, violence is legitimated when it is viewed as a tolerable or desirable sign of masculinity (Morrell et al., 2013). Not surprisingly then, Jewkes, Sekweyiya, Morrell and Dunkle (2010) found that in South Africa prevalent motivations for sexual violence against women stems from a sense of sexual entitlement and hierarchies of gender power; boys and men are socialized into believing in their right to assert their dominance and power through sex.

Additional social and cultural issues, like traditional leadership, the position of elders in a community, and substance abuse add to the vulnerability of girls in South Africa (Mathews et al., 2012; Seedat et al., 2009). Phasha (2010) adds that structural challenges, such as limited or absent trauma, medicolegal, police and child protection services, continue to plague black South Africans postapartheid, with these challenges more pronounced in rural areas and townships. All of these challenges heighten the vulnerability of women and girls.

Although a small number of international studies have focused attention on resilience processes of sexually abused adolescents, the particular political, cultural and social landscape mentioned above potentially results in resilience manifesting in different, more context-specific ways in South Africa (Theron & Phasha, 2015). However, a review of studies focused on resilience processes in sexually abused adolescents identified only three South African studies, only one of which focused specifically on black African adolescent girls (Haffejee & Theron, 2017). In this chapter, we add to this nascent field of enquiry by looking at the resilience processes of sexually abused adolescent African girls, framing our discussion with a particular focus on the way in which traditional African paradigms impact on such processes (Phasha, 2010; Theron & Theron, 2013). We consider that while traditional African culture may promote resilience, it also has the potential to be burdensome and not facilitative of resilience processes (Theron, 2013).

SOCIAL ECOLOGICAL RESILIENCE

Though early research on resilience overlooked the role of cultural factors, this area of enquiry within resilience studies is rapidly growing (Wright & Masten, 2015). Ungar's social ecological theory of resilience (SERT; see Ungar, 2011, 2012, 2015) has paid particular attention to the role of context and culture in resilience processes. Within this perspective, resilience is considered through the observation, examination and analysis of the wider socioecological environment within specific cultural contexts (Ungar, 2011). Resilience is thus understood as the ability of individuals, in partnership with their social ecologies, to move toward culturally relevant resources they need to thrive and the ability of individuals and their social ecologies to collectively negotiate for these resources to be made available in a meaningful way (Ungar, 2015).

From this perspective, cultural relativity and complexity are key principles that define resilience processes (Ungar, 2011). These principles emphasize contextual factors as antecedents of positive adaptation; resilience is considered a culturally embedded, dynamic process that is subject to change across time and dependent on context (Ungar, 2012). This complexity stems from both the availability of resilience promotive resources and the meaning that the individual attaches to resources (Ungar, 2011). Meaning, in turn, is determined by the given context and culture (Jefferis, 2016; Panter-Brick, 2015). Culture thus impacts meaning systems and the value apportioned to different expressions of resilience, and this in turn has an impact on the resources that are made available to children (Ungar, 2015). So while universal markers of resilience have been identified, how these manifest differs across cultures.

RESILIENCE IN SOUTH AFRICA

This increased awareness of the ways in which complex environments interact to nurture positive adaptation in culturally diverse contexts has resulted in a growing body of resilience studies in South Africa (Malindi, 2014; Phasha, 2010; Theron & Malindi, 2010; Theron & Theron, 2013; Ungar, 2011; Van Rensburg, Theron, & Rothman, 2015). A handful of these studies have focused on girls' pathways of resilience. In a study that explored the resilience promoting mechanisms of rural Sesotho-speaking girls, Jefferis (2016) noted the salience of supportive relationships with other women and girls, pragmatic support from communities, future-oriented beliefs, individual agency as well as faith. Similarly, in Malindi's (2014) exploration of resilience processes in female street youth in South Africa, faith, self-regulation and active support systems, as well as access to community-based support, facilitated positive adaptation. In her exploration of educational resilience in sexually abused African girls, Phasha (2010) found that meaning-making, determination to succeed together with faith and supportive networks nurtured the resilience of her participants and allowed them to focus on their education.

Theron and Phasha (2015) note that within South Africa, processes of resilience may be influenced by traditional African values of interdependence, spiritual beliefs and responsibility to family. This traditional way of being is captured in the philosophy of Ubuntu. Ubuntu broadly refers to the African philosophical way of being which favors "humanness, personhood and morality" (Letseka, 2012, p. 48). Within this worldview an individual's ability to flourish and reach their full potential and their eventual well-being is dependent on how one treats others (Manda, 2007; Murove, 2009). Values such as kindness, empathy, benevolence, compassion, a sense of responsibility toward others, respect and care are expected and promoted (Letseka, 2012; Manda, 2007; Murove, 2009). These values also extend to demonstrating forgiveness to those who have transgressed, with the belief that people have the ability to improve if they are supported (Phasha, 2010). In resilience studies, these values of relationality and interdependence are manifested in the presence of supportive extended family networks and pragmatically supportive community members (Jefferis, 2016). Theron, Theron and Malindi (2013) found that for black youth from rural backgrounds, attachment to extended networks, respect and adherence to traditional, ancestral values are indicative of resilience.

SEXUAL VIOLENCE AND RESILIENCE

A plethora of research examines the negative short- and long-term impact that CSA has on the individual. Mental, psychological, interpersonal and behavioral problems have all been associated with a history of CSA (Boney-McCoy & Finkelhor, 1995; Cashmore & Shackel, 2013; Collishaw et al., 2007; Finkelhor, 1994, 2009; Kilpatrick & Acierno, 2003; Maniglio, 2009; Resnick, Guille, McCauley, & Kilpatrick, 2011; Steel, Sanna, Hammond, Whipple, & Cross, 2004). Researchers working in South Africa add that outcomes nationally are further complicated by poverty, high rates of HIV/AIDS and limited or inefficient judicial, legal and mental health assistance (Meink, Cluver, Beyes, & Loening-Voysey, 2016). Some of these same studies have however noted that negative outcomes are not necessarily a given. In Domhardt, Münzer, Fegert and Lutz's (2014) systematic review of resilience in CSA survivors, a variation of between 10 and 53 percent of survivors not exhibiting any harmful symptoms was noted. A review of studies with adolescent girls (Haffejee & Theron, 2017) found that resilience-enabling factors in this group were closely aligned to universal protective systems described by Masten and Wright (2010). These included agency and motivational mastery, opportunities for meaning-making, self-regulation and self-efficacy, optimistic future perspectives, attachment relationships, cultural and religious traditions and social, community and educational systems (Haffejee & Theron, 2017; Masten & Wright, 2010). Though limited, studies on sexual violence and resilience conducted with black South African girls closely parallel findings described above. However, they also reference the protective value of traditional African ways of being, which includes extended networks of support, duty of care to others and a greater focus on education (Phasha, 2010). In doing so, they echo Theron and Theron's (2013) reminder that while resilience processes are universal, the way they operate is dependent on the cultural context.

METHODOLOGY

To illustrate the impact of macrosystems on the resilience processes of adolescent African girls, we report the case of Precious (a pseudonym). This case was drawn from a qualitative multiple, instrumental case study that included seven participants from two urban child and youth care centers (CYCC). All seven participants were legally placed in care at the time of the study.

Selection of Participants for the Study

Participants were purposefully selected through the assistance of an advisory panel (AP) that had been established to guide the execution of the multiple case studies. The benefits of having an AP has been discussed in previous resilience studies (see Theron et al., 2013); in this study, the AP provided advisory oversight and offered advice in terms of selection and identification of participants as well as feedback of findings. The AP consisted of social and child care workers. Their daily interaction with vulnerable young people and their professional training supported their effectiveness as AP members.

The AP recommended all seven cases for inclusion in the study. Across all seven cases, the earliest age of first sexual abuse was 6 and the oldest 11. Of the seven participants, three participants reported single episodes of sexual abuse, with a single perpetrator. One participant experienced chronic sexual abuse over an extended period of time. Four of the participants were perpetrated against multiple times. In six of the seven cases, the perpetrator was a known male and in four of these six cases the perpetrator was a family member.

All participants experienced other forms of adversity, which included death of one or both parents, death of other caregivers, abandonment by mother, physical and verbal abuse, neglect and poverty. The summary of risk factors that all participants in our study were exposed to is consistent with a recent national survey conducted in South Africa, which suggests that sexual violence does not happen in isolation and is often accompanied by other forms of violence (Artz et al., 2016). However, the age of first sexual abuse reported by our participants is younger than that reported in the abovementioned national survey, which suggested an average age of 14 years. Similar to the survey, perpetrators were in most cases known males.

Methods of Data Collection

In this multiple case study, we adhered to calls from both gender and resilience researchers that advocate for the use of creative, innovative research methods (Cameron et al., 2013; Mitchell, 2011; Theron, 2012). To this end, we made use of a range of participatory approaches that included participatory diagramming, digital stories and participatory video. Visual participatory approaches with youth have been credited with democratizing the research process and privileging youth voices, creating opportunities for participant reflexivity and psychosocial growth, activism and social change (Didkowsky, Ungar, & Liebenberg, 2010; Liebenberg, 2009; Mitchell, de Lange, Stuart, Moletsane, & Buthelezi, 2007; Theron, 2016). The first author engaged participants in this participatory process, meeting each one a minimum of three times individually and three times as a group. Data collection began in January 2016 and concluded in November 2016.

Data Analysis

For the purposes of this chapter, we conducted secondary data analysis (Creswell, 2012). The existing dataset from which Precious' case was drawn did not focus specifically on the ways in which sociocultural contextual factors enable and constrain resilience processes. In reanalyzing our existing dataset, the question that guided our enquiry was, "How do sociocultural factors enable and constrain resilience processes in sexually abused African adolescent girls?" We looked at data that best fit with this question and discarded all other data, creating an integrated dataset. Data from the individual interview with Precious, where we used participatory diagramming as well as the digital story, offered rich answers to the research question for this chapter and so constituted our dataset. Precious was invited to explain what her diagramming meant; visual data themselves were not analyzed.

Data were transcribed verbatim and coded using Atlas.ti 7.0 (2012) and were then subjected to inductive content analysis (Braun & Clarke, 2006). Using the guidelines described by Braun and Clarke (2006), the first author immersed herself in the data which resulted in identification of initial codes which were then grouped to form candidate themes and subthemes. These themes were then reviewed again and refined, and two main themes were defined (i.e., disabling sociocultural environments and enabling sociocultural environments). Trustworthiness was ensured through member checking as well as through the use of an independent coder (Creswell, 2009). The second author critically evaluated the analysis and interpretation of the findings.

Ethical Considerations

Sexually abused minors are considered a particularly vulnerable group; given this, we were very aware of our responsibility to conduct the study in an ethical manner that ensured no harm to the participants. We obtained ethical clearance from the institutional review board after a vigorous process. Detailed consent letters were given to directors at both CYCCs in their capacity as legal guardians. Potential participants identified by the AP were approached with details of the study by an independent care worker and not by the first author. The voluntary nature of the study was emphasized. Only if they expressed an interest and agreed to participate in the study were they approached by the first author and formal written assent was obtained. Participants were assured of anonymity and were informed that participation in the group processes was voluntary. Following data collection, participants were required to attend at least one debriefing session with an external mental health practitioner. Participants were able to review transcripts following the interviews and also given access to all materials produced in the study.

FINDINGS

To explore the nuanced role of context and culture, we share findings from Precious' case study.

Precious' Story: My Innocence has been Taken Away from Me

At the time of telling her story, Precious was 17 years old, and together with her two younger siblings had been in a child and youth care facility for the last two years. Her mother died when she was 11 years old. Her parents were not married, and the man she regarded as her father died shortly before her mother. Since her mother's death, she lived with her maternal family but was removed after allegations of severe physical abuse and was legally placed in a CYCC.

Below is a brief biography as recounted by Precious. This narrative provides the voice-over for a digital story produced by Precious and the primary researcher.

> When I was 11 years old I was raped and I didn't get justice. That man lived until he died on his own. I told my mother first and a teacher found out. She called the police. They came to ask me questions. They told me they will take me to a doctor to do a check-up but they never came back. The one who did it told the police he didn't know what he was doing, he wasn't thinking straight. Nothing happened to him. I hated him.
>
> In 2014, another man did the same thing again. He just disappeared.
>
> A third one did the same thing, he also disappeared. They always threaten that they will kill me or that I will die.
>
> I keep these things a secret because with the first case no one did anything and no one believed me, nothing happened. So I didn't feel like talking about the other times because nothing will happen.
>
> This thing used to hurt me. It still hurts me. When other people talk about being a virgin I don't like to talk about it. Sometimes I even say I am while I'm not. But I know it's not my fault because I didn't ask for it.
>
> I accepted that it passed. I don't know how I became ok. I think talking about it helps me. Getting advice from other people, like my friends and other adults. It makes me stronger. I am learning not to be ashamed about what happened and not to blame myself.
>
> I'm living my own life. I'm progressing at school. I believe in myself and I have confidence. I feel like I can achieve anything I want to. (Precious, 2016)

Disabling Sociocultural Contexts

In the opening line of the narrative told by Precious, we hear her legitimate anger at a system that failed her. In her narrative she mentions a teacher, who

Figure 6.1 Image of sangoma produced by Precious

takes action by calling the police. Although the police take a statement from her, they don't follow up and there appears to be no case. Later she recounts her mother asking her to forgive the perpetrator whom they shared a living space with; although she complied, she describes her intense anger at the perpetrator and the situation she was placed in. After this initial failure of the legal system to act on her behalf, Precious did not disclose any of the other incidents of sexual abuse. Her distrust of formal systems also meant that she had chosen not to formally disclose the sexual abuse to her current social worker at the CYCC.

After her mother died, Precious was sent to live with her maternal family. The second incident of sexual abuse that Precious mentioned in her narrative was perpetrated by a *sangoma* (traditional healer). Precious was taken to a sangoma by her physically abusive and mentally ill uncle as the family believed she was cursed.

> So after the sangoma told my uncle to wait outside....then he asked me questions about My Mother. I told him that my Mother died and all this stuff. Then... after that he, then closed the door then he said I must take off all my clothes then I did see he took a razor...there's small cuts here and even... here [indicating cuts on her arm] and near my womb. After that...he said I must turnaround and lay...then I was so scared that um...after then he wanted to sleep with me then I cried I asked him why then he said my Mother is talking to him I must do this thing.......I'm scared of sangomas so everything he told me to do I did it after then after doing it he said mustn't tell anyone because if I tell anyone I will die. (Precious, 2016)

Enabling Sociocultural Contexts

Precious, unable to trust her physically abusive family, and without any other support, turned to her informal support networks, which included friends and their families and school teachers. As in her first experience of sexual abuse, it was a teacher who assisted her by accessing help for her: "There was this teacher ... I told her what happened. I used to tell her about the beating ....she took me to another teacher....the teacher called ... a social worker."

Friends, and their families, offered pragmatic support in the form of shelter. "Fikile [a friend] used to offer her a place to hide from her uncles' attacks."

Later, at the CYCC she also relied on peer support to help her come to terms with the abuse and address her feelings of self-blame: "My close friends...they told me their stories last year. They used to talk about what happened to them, sometimes you know, so I thought I was the only one but only to find out I'm not the only one."

In spite of little formal support or previous therapeutic support, Precious displays a capacity for reflexivity, ascribing previous risk-taking behaviors to the trauma she experienced: "I didn't grow up in a good environment maybe that's why I get angry very, very fast because I'm angry at everything that happened. In everything that is still happening." Precious credits her positive adaptation to the fact that she hasn't allowed the abuse to alter the way she thinks and the fact that she is still hopeful about her future. She says: "It didn't affect me like here in my mind I'm doing well at school, I'm passing well and...I join programs if there are programs and if there's drama I join in." In addition to looking to peers for support, Precious has a strong sense of responsibility to her siblings and is motivated to do well so that she can care for them. Currently, Precious and her siblings have access to other family networks. Paternal family members have expressed an interest in caring for her.

DISCUSSION

This narrative gives credence to research that speaks to the complex ways in which cultural and contextual factors impact on individual's resilience processes. In this discussion, we explore how values encompassed by the philosophy of Ubuntu, which promotes family allegiance, forgiveness, interconnectedness and respect for elders, are subverted by individual actors and used to subjugate rather than protect. At the same time though, we complicate our discussion by pointing out instances where other systems within the ecology nurture resilience, drawing on the same traditional values that previously were used to cause harm, and where Precious herself actively engages with contextual variables.

The adverse potential that cultural systems hold has been mentioned previously by Panter-Brick and Eggerman (2012). Theron and Theron (2013) add that in a South African context, the changes that are apparent due to processes of acculturation as well as changes brought about by the HIV/AIDS epidemic are likely to impact the ways in which traditional African culture continues to scaffold youth. As mentioned above, forgiveness and respect for elders are encapsulated in the African practice of Ubuntu, where transgressors are not necessarily shunned and duty to those older than you is valued; allegiance to these values could account for Precious' mother's counsel to her to forgive the perpetrator as well as her own acquiescence to her mother, in spite of her own anger.

The placement of Precious and her siblings in the home of extended family is a common practice in traditional African communities. Youth typically may be cared for by "family communities" (Mkhize, 2006, p. 187), with extended family members, including grandparents, aunts and uncles, assuming responsibility for children, even when parental figures are present. Although previous studies have reported that these networks scaffold resilience processes in youth (Theron & Theron, 2013), in this case this potentially protective practice exposed Precious to a mentally unstable but authoritative male family member who physically and verbally abused her. In spite of her family's awareness of her uncle's mental condition, her grandfather, the head of the household, supports her uncle, and she is seen as the problem. In this instance, it is not a cultural practice, but rather patriarchy, that renders a young girl delinquent and voiceless. As discussed above, in traditional patriarchal societies, hegemonic masculinities are legitimized and male dominance is asserted through acts of violence. Within such contexts, girls and women are marginalized and vulnerable to abuse.

Subversion of culture is noted within a broader system in the abuse perpetrated by a traditional healer. Traditional healers are widely acknowledged in South Africa, and are seen as credible allies in addressing public health issues, such as HIV/AIDS and male circumcision, as well as a viable alternative to the treatment of a range of both health and social issues. Within traditional African culture, there are different types of traditional healers, many of whom have different areas of training and expertise and who perform different functions (Truter, 2007). Sangomas, or diviners, are seen as most senior in the traditional healer hierarchical structure (Truter, 2007). A sangoma's sphere is divination, where they operate within a traditional religious supernatural context and serve as a medium with ancestral spirits (Thornton, 2009). Traditionally they are called on to heal individuals or communities as well as to resolve conflicts and to offer solutions to problems and to provide leadership (Thornton, 2009). Belief in traditional healers and ancestral spirits is central to an Africentric worldview, which favors interconnectedness with both living and ancestral spirits. In this context, Precious' family's trust and belief in the healing and problem-solving ability of sangomas as well as her fear of ancestral spirits and sangomas resulted in her being placed in a compromising situation which resulted in sexual abuse.

In her brief narrative, Precious mentions her shame at not being a virgin and the pride in which other girls talk about being a virgin. Feelings of shame have been associated with negative outcomes for sexual abuse survivors. In traditional African culture, chastity is viewed positively, with the practice of virginity testing seeing a revival in the 1990s, primarily as a response to the HIV/AIDS epidemic in South Africa (Leclerc-Madlala, 2001). Virginity testing is a practice and process of inspecting girls to ascertain if they are still virgins; public and private functions are held, where girls are "tested" and given a certificate if found to be virgins. Virginity testing is regarded as a culturally appropriate way to reinforce cultural values like chastity before marriage, modesty, self-respect and pride and thus as a way to halt the increase in teenage pregnancy, STIs and HIV/AIDS (Leclerc-Madlala, 2001). This practice, however, is contested, and the Children's Act No. 38 of 2005 prohibits the testing of children under 16, although it permits testing of 16–18-year-olds (Behrens, 2014). While traditionalists support the practice, opposing views suggest that this practice is inherently discriminatory, entrenching patriarchal privilege, and is another form of violence against women (Behrens, 2014). Within this context, a traditional practice touted by some as being protective may result in stigmatization, further abuse and a sense of shame and guilt, thus hindering resilience.

Though much of the discussion has looked at practices that potentially could have a negative impact, enabling structures were not wholly absent. Access to social workers and placement at a CYCC, while resulting from a failure of certain contextual actors to offer protection and support resilience, created opportunities for other actors, like the state and civil society, to step in and support positive adaptation. Supportive teachers intervene after the first experience of sexual abuse and again when they notice the ongoing physical abuse. In both instances, their intervention is in the form of accessing help and offering pragmatic support to Precious. Teachers have been credited with playing an essential role in enabling resilience processes in youth (Jefferis, 2016). Jefferis (2016) found that empathetic teachers in rural African communities recognized girls who were experiencing difficulties, such as sexual abuse, and guided them through such difficulties. In the context of the CYCC, Precious realizes that she isn't the only one who has been through such circumstances; this realization alleviates her feelings of shame and guilt. Here, other girls directly support her adaptation. The role that supportive women play in facilitating resilience processes has been established in previous South African studies, with nonfamily members like teachers and girlfriends identified as enablers of this process (see Jefferis, 2016; Theron & Phasha, 2015; Theron & Theron, 2010).

While initially we discussed a subversion of traditional values and the risk that may result in shallow adherence to it, pragmatically and emotionally supportive friends, family of friends and teachers enabled Precious to embody the spirit of Ubuntu. Phasha (2010) explains this value as "the more we are, the stronger we become" (p. 1250), which allows the individual to reach out to a receptive community, creating in them a sense of belonging and security, which promotes resilience in times of adversity.

The complex way in which context impacts resilience processes is also captured in the manner in which Precious navigates toward resilience enabling resources. In her expressions of anger, her acting out behavior, and her decision to defy her grandfather, Precious rejects traditional cultural prescriptions. Instead, her choices are demonstrative of atypical resilience processes; although her adaptive behavior may be viewed as counterindicative to resilience in some contexts, in a context of abuse and an absence of control, her assertion of agency is functional (Ungar, 2011). At the same time though, her rejection of traditional values is not complete and is indicative of a more nuanced approach. In her support and sense of responsibility toward her siblings, in spite of her own difficulties, as well as her commitment to gaining an education, Precious chooses aspects of a traditional value system that are meaningful to her. This sense of duty to a collective is consistent with findings from Theron and Phasha (2015), with the young people providing both financial and motivational support to family members.

CONCLUSION AND FUTURE DIRECTIONS

Within traditional African structures, respect for elders, extended family networks and belief in the supernatural have all been credited with buffering against adversity. However, in the case presented, each of these structures is guilty of not only failing to respond to the needs of a 17-year-old girl, but also in perpetuating further abuse and harm. While the potential that these systems hold cannot be negated, we concur with resilience researchers who caution that slavish, shallow allegiance and one-dimensional interpretations of the ways in which such contexts enable resilience should be guarded against (Panter-Brick & Eggerman, 2012; Theron & Phasha, 2015). If interventions are to be meaningful and effective, we need to be conscious of both the protective value of adherence to cultural values as well as the ways that it may disadvantage positive adaptation (Ungar, 2015). Thus, practitioners seeking to facilitate resilience in sexually abused girls in culturally meaningful ways should be mindful that resilience is embedded within specific sociocultural and historical contexts, and as such these processes are impacted by changes in these systems (Ungar, 2011). In South Africa, and other westernizing African contexts, there is a need to be particularly attentive of the ways in which increasing westernization has impacted traditional African ways of living (Rampele, 2012). Similarly, it is important to consider the ways in which difficult colonial and other disabling histories (such as apartheid) have impacted gender roles and resultant assertions of power. Automatic reliance on traditional systems to buffer sexually abused girls should thus be avoided.

Pertinent as well is a recognition that atypical expressions of resilience may be found in contexts of severe adversity. What may seem maladapative in one context could be functional in another, and practitioners working with a specific population should seek to understand the usefulness of behaviour within the given cultural context (Ungar, 2011). Diverse expressions of resilience should be acknowledged and encouraged and should not be altered to fit in with mainstream ideas on what resilience looks like.

Lastly, practitioners championing resilience are encouraged to be creative when seeking potential supportive structures. Supportive external resources as we've discussed may take the form of social services, community networks or teachers. Engaging with systems at a wider level may provide access to other, untapped sources of support for sexually abused girls.

In conclusion, resilience processes are subject to changes across developmental periods and as such how the sociocultural context may continue to support or challenge girls like Precious as they mature cannot be predicted. The exploration reported in this chapter is thus constrained in its limited (i.e., yearlong) engagement with the participant. Future studies should thus adopt a longitudinal, life history approach so that the full impact of the ecology may be understood.

REFERENCES

Artz, L., Burton, P., Ward, C. L., Leoschut, L., Phyfer, J., Lloyd, S., … Le Mottee, C. (2016). *Sexual victimisation of children in South Africa. Final report of the Optimus Foundation Study: South Africa.* Cape Town, South Africa: UBS Optimus Foundation.

Atlas.ti (Version 7.0) [Computer software]. (2012). Berlin, Germany: Scientific Software Development.

Behrens, K. G. (2014). Virginity testing in South Africa: A cultural concession taken too far? *South African Journal of Philosophy, 33*(2), 177–187. doi:10.1080/02580136.2014.912471.

Boney-McCoy, S., & Finkelhor, D. (1995). Prior victimisation: A risk factor for child sexual abuse and for PTSD-related symptomatology among sexually abused youth. *Child Abuse & Neglect, 19*(12), 1401–1421. doi:10.1016/0145-2134(95)00104-9.

Braun, V., & Clarke, V. (2006). Using thematic analysis in psychology. *Qualitative Research in Psychology, 3*(2), 77–101. doi:10.1191/1478088706qp063oa.

Buiten, D., & Naidoo, K. (2016). Framing the problem of rape in South Africa: Gender, race, class and state histories. *Current Sociology, 64*(4), 535–550. doi:10.1177/0011392116638844.

Cameron, C. A., Tapanya, S., Lau, C., Theron, L., Li, C., Liebenberg, L., & Ungar, M. (2013). Visual perspectives on majority world adolescent thriving. *Journal of Research on Adolescence, 23*(1), 149–161. doi:10.1111/j.1532-7795.2012.00794.x.

Cashmore, J., & Shackel, R. (2013). The long-term effects of child sexual abuse. *Australian Institute of Family Studies, 11*, 1–29. Retrieved from http://www.aifs.org.au/cfca/pubs/papers/a143161/cfca11.pdf

Collishaw, S., Pickles, A., Messer, J., Rutter, M., Shearer, C., & Maughan, B. (2007). Resilience to adult psychopathology following childhood maltreatment: Evidence from a community sample. *Child Abuse & Neglect, 31*(3), 211–229. doi:10.1016/j.chiabu.2007.02.004.

Creswell, J. W. (2009). *Research design: Qualitative, quantitative, and mixed methods Approaches* (3rd ed.). Los Angeles, CA: Sage Publications.

Creswell, J. W. (2012). *Research design: Qualitative, quantitative, and mixed methods Approaches* (4th ed.) Thousand Oaks, CA: Sage Publications.

Dartnell, E., & Jewkes, R. (2013). Sexual violence against women: The scope of the problem. *Best Practice and Research Clinical Obstetrics and Gynaecology, 27*(1), 3–13. doi:10.1016/j.bpobgyn.2012.08.002.

Didkowsky, N., Ungar, M., & Liebenberg, L. (2010). Using visual methods to capture embedded processes of resilience for youth across cultures and contexts. *Journal of the Canadian Academy of Child and Adolescent Psychiatry, 19*(1), 12–18. Retrieved from https://www.ncbi.nlm.nih.gov/pmc/articles/PMC2809441/

Domhardt, M., Münzer, A., Fegert, J. M., & Lutz, G. (2015). Resilience in survivors of child sexual abuse: A systematic review of the literature. *Trauma, Violence & Abuse, 16*(4), 476–493. doi:10.1177/1524838014557288.

Finkelhor, D. (1994). Current information on the scope and nature of child sexual abuse. *The Future of Children, 4*(2), 31–53. doi:10.2307/1602522.

Finkelhor, D. (2009). The prevention of childhood sexual abuse. *The Future of Children, 19*(2), 169–194. doi:10.1353/foc.0.0035.

Haffejee, S., & Theron, L. (2017). *Resilience processes in sexually abused adolescent girls: A scoping review of the literature*. Manuscript submitted for publication.

Jefferis, T. (2016). *Resilient Black South African girls in contexts of adversity: A participatory visual study*. (Unpublished doctoral dissertation). North-West University, Vanderbijlpark, South Africa.

Jewkes, R., Sikweyiya, Y., Morrell, R., & Dunkle, K. (2010). Why, when and how men rape: Understanding rape perpetration in South Africa. *South African Crime Quarterly, 34*, 23–31. doi:10.17159/2413-3108/2010/v0i34a874.

Kilpatrick, D. G., & Acierno, R. (2003). Mental health needs of crime victims: Epidemiology and outcomes. *Journal of Traumatic Stress, 16*(2), 119–132. doi:10.1023/A:1022891005388.

Leclerc-Madlala, S. (2001). Virginity testing: Managing sexuality in a maturing HIV/AIDS epidemic. *Medical Anthropology Quarterly, 15*(4), 533–552. doi:10.1525/maq.2001.15.4.533.

Letseka, M. (2012). In defence of Ubuntu. *Studies in Philosophy and Education, 31*(1), 47–60. doi:10.1007/s11217-011-9267-2.

Liebenberg, L. (2009). The visual image as discussion point: Increasing validity in boundary crossing research. *Qualitative Research, 9*(4), 441–467. doi:10.1177/1468794109337877.

Malindi, M. J. (2014). Exploring the roots of resilience among female street-involved children in South Africa. *Journal of Psychology, 5*(1), 35–45.

Manda, D. L. (2007). *The importance of the African ethics of Ubuntu and traditional healing systems for Black South African women's health in the context of HIV and AIDS* (Unpublished doctoral dissertation). University of KwaZulu-Natal, Pietermaritzburg, South Africa.

Maniglio, R. (2009). The impact of child sexual abuse on health: A systematic review of reviews. *Clinical Psychology Review, 29*(7), 647–657. doi:10.1016/j.cpr.2009.08.003.

Mapumulo, Z. (2017, March). Rape is down? No way, says experts. *City Press.* Retrieved from: http://m.news24.com/news24/SouthAfrica/News/rape-is-down-no-way-say-experts-20170305-2.

Masten, A., & Wright, M. (2010). Resilience over the lifespan: Developmental perspectives on resistance, recovery and transformation. In J. W. Reich, A. J. Zautra, & J. S. Hall (Eds.), *Handbook of adult resilience* (pp. 213–237). New York: The Guilford Press.

Mathews, S., Loots, L., Sikweyiya, Y., & Jewkes, R. (2012). Sexual abuse. In A. Van Niekerk, S. Suffla, & M. Seedat (Eds.), *Crime, violence and injury in South Africa: 21st century solution for child safety* (pp. 84–96). Houghton, South Africa: Psychological Society of South Africa.

Meink, F., Cluver, L. D., Boyes, M. E., & Loening-Voysey, H. (2016). Physical, emotional and sexual adolescent abuse victimisation in South Africa: Prevalence, incidence and perpetrators. *Journal of Epidemiology and Community Health, 70*(9), 910–916. doi:10.1136/jech-2015-205860.

Mitchell, C. (2011). *Doing visual research.* London, United Kingdom: Sage Publication.

Mitchell, C., de Lange, N., Stuart, J., Moletsane, R., & Buthelezi, T. (2007). Children's provocative images of stigma, vulnerability and violence in the age of AIDS: Revisions of childhood. In N. De Lange, C. Mitchell, & J. Stuart (Eds.), *Putting people in the picture: Visual methodologies for social change* (pp. 59–71). Rotterdam, The Netherlands: Sense Publishers.

Mkhize, N. (2006). African traditions and the social, economic and moral dimensions of fatherhood. In L. Richter & R. Morrell (Eds.), *Baba: Men and fatherhood in South Africa* (pp. 183–198). Cape Town, South Africa: HSRC Press.

Morrell, R., Jewkes, R., Lindegger, G., & Hamlall, V. (2013). Hegemonic masculinity: Reviewing the gendered analysis of men's power in South Africa. *South African Review of Sociology, 44*(1), 3–21. doi:10.1080/21528586.2013.784445.

Murove, M. F. (2009). An African environmental ethic based on the concepts of Ukama and Ubuntu. In M. F. Murove (Ed.), *African ethics: An anthology of comparative and applied ethics* (pp. 315–331). Scottsville, South Africa: University of KwaZulu-Natal Press.

Panter-Brick, C. (2015). Culture and resilience: Next steps for theory and practice. In L. C. Theron, L. Liebenberg, & M. Ungar (Eds.), *Youth resilience and culture: Commonalities and complexities* (pp. 233–244). Dordrecht, The Netherlands: Springer.

Panter-Brick, C., & Eggerman, M. (2012). Understanding culture, resilience and mental health: The production of hope. In M. Ungar (Ed.), *The social ecology of resilience. A handbook of theory and practice* (pp. 369–386). New York: Springer.

Phasha, N. T. (2010). Educational resilience among African survivors of child sexual abuse in South Africa. *Journal of Black Studies, 40*(6), 1234–1253. doi:10.1177/0021934708327693.

Rampele, M. (2012). *Conversations with my sons and daughters.* Johannesburg, South Africa: Penguin.

Ratele, K., & Suffla, S. (2011). Violence, masculinity and well-being in Africa. In K. Kondlo & C. Ejioku (Eds.), *Africa in focus: Governance in the 21st century* (pp. 259–281). Pretoria, South Africa: HSRC Press.

Resnick, H. S., Guille, C., McCauley, J. L., & Kilpatrick, D. G. (2011). Rape and other sexual assault. In S. M. Southwick, B. M. Litz, D. Charney, & M. J. Friedman (Eds.), *Resilience and mental health: Challenges across a lifespan* (pp. 218–237). New York: Cambridge University Press.

Seedat, M., van Niekerk, A., Jewkes, R., Suffla, S., & Ratele, K. (2009). Violence and injuries in South Africa: Prioritising an agenda for prevention. *The Lancet, 374*(9694), 1011–1022. doi:10.1016/S0140-6736(09)60948-X.

Steel, J., Sanna, L., Hammond, B., Whipple, J., & Cross, H. (2004). Psychological sequelae of childhood sexual abuse: Abuse related characteristics, coping strategies, and attributional style. *Child Abuse & Neglect, 28*(7), 785–801. doi:10.1016/j.chiabu.2003.12.004.

Theron, L. C. (2012). Resilience research with South African youth: Caveats and ethical complexities. *South African Journal of Psychology, 42*(3), 333–345. doi:10.1177/008124631204200305.

Theron, L. C. (2013). Black students' recollection of pathways to resilience: Lessons for school psychologists. *School Psychology International, 34*(5), 527–539. doi:10.1177/0143034312472762.

Theron, L. C. (2016). Researching resilience: Lessons learned from working with rural, Sesotho speaking South African young people. *Qualitative Research, 16*(6), 720–737. doi:10.1177/1468794116652451.

Theron, L. C., & Malindi, M. J. (2010). Resilient street youth: A qualitative South African study. *Journal of Youth Studies, 13*(6), 717–736. doi:10.1080/13676261003801796.

Theron, L. C., & Phasha, N. (2015). Cultural pathways to resilience: Opportunities and obstacles as recalled by Black South African students. In L. C. Theron, L. Liebenberg, & M. Ungar (Eds.), *Youth resilience and culture: Commonalities and complexities* (pp. 51–65). Dordrecht, The Netherlands: Springer.

Theron, L. C., & Theron, A. M. C. (2010). A critical review of studies of South African youth resilience, 1990–2008. *South African Journal of Science, 106*(7/8), 1–8. doi.org/10.4102/sajs.v106i7/8.252.

Theron, L. C., & Theron, A. (2013). Positive adjustment to poverty: How family communities encourage resilience in traditional African contexts. *Culture and Psychology, 19*(3), 391–413. doi:10.1177/1354067X13489318.

Theron, L. C., Theron, A. M. C., & Malindi, M. J. (2013). Toward an African definition of resilience: A rural South African community's view of resilient Besotho youth. *Journal of Black Psychology, 39*(1), 63–87. doi:10.1177/0095798412454675.

Thornton, R. (2009). The transmission of knowledge in South African traditional healing. *Africa, 79*(1), 17–33. doi:10.3366/E0001972008000582.

Truter, I. (2007). African traditional healers: Cultural and religious beliefs intertwined in a holistic way. *South African Pharmaceutical Journal, 74*(8), 56–60. Retrieved from http://www.sapj.co.za/index.php/SAPJ/article/view/239/231

Ungar, M. (2011). The social ecology of resilience: Addressing contextual and cultural ambiguity of a nascent construct. *American Journal of Orthopsychiatry, 81*(1), 1–17. doi:10.1111/j.1939-0025.2010.01067.x.

Ungar, M. (2012). Social ecologies and their contribution to resilience. In M. Ungar (Ed.), *The social ecology of resilience. A handbook of theory and practice* (pp. 13–31). New York: Springer.

Ungar, M. (2015). Resilience and culture: The diversity of protective processes and positive adaptation. In L. C. Theron, L. Liebenberg, & M. Ungar (Eds.), *Youth resilience and culture: Commonalities and complexities* (pp. 37–50). Dordrecht, The Netherlands: Springer.

Van Rensburg, A., Theron, L. C., & Rothman, S. (2015). A review of quantitative studies of South African youth resilience: Some gaps. *South African Journal of Science, 111*(7/8), 1–9. doi:10.17159/SAJS.2015/20140164.

Wright, M. O., & Masten, A. C. (2015). Pathways to resilience in context. In L. C. Theron, L. Liebenberg, & M. Ungar (Eds.), *Youth resilience and culture: Commonalities and complexities* (pp. 3–22). Dordrecht, The Netherlands: Springer.

Chapter 7

Trauma, Coping, and Resiliency among Syrian Refugees in Lebanon and Beyond

A Profile of the Syrian Nation at War

Naji Abi-Hashem

INTRODUCTION

How are the Syrian refugees coping and surviving? And how are they handling the many losses, displacements, traumas, psycho-emotional struggles and sociocultural obstacles? What motivates them to keep facing hardships and to thrive in the face of adversities in constructive ways? This chapter will attempt to highlight the abilities of many deeply affected Syrians to transform their tragedy and misery into a trajectory of purpose, a mission of survival, and a path toward resiliency. They are willing to work extremely hard, live in tight places or on tiny budgets, and keep a grateful attitude in order to preserve their dignity, basic survival, and safety of their loved ones. Syrian refugees are proving to be quite industrious and able to utilize any available resource, opportunity, facility, and support to their benefit and family welfare. All the while they carry with them many scars of war, torn memories, and strong longings for *home*, from where they were suddenly uprooted and unwillingly left behind. In spite of all their misfortunes, they seem to keep the hope alive.

As the author of this chapter, and a Lebanese-American clinical and cultural psychologist, I have been living and functioning in two geographic regions, the United States in North America and the Middle East, almost dividing my time between the two. In both places, I am involved in teaching, counseling, training, lecturing, networking, writing, and cross cultural service. While in Lebanon, I normally spend time consulting with health care providers, counselors, educators, pastors, and community leaders. One of my passions is to care for the caregivers, especially those who are working under stress, serving underprivileged populations, or operating in danger and on the front lines. Often I am called upon to conduct training seminars or debriefing sessions for those teachers, caregivers, and volunteers who are helping some of the multitude of refugees in their area. Therefore, I have observed firsthand the related struggles, stress, agonies, and persisting symptoms. Also, I had the opportunity to work with hundreds of Syrians from all walks of life and social backgrounds, formally and informally, as we see them and interact with them on a daily basis everywhere we go in town.

Personally, I grew up in a mountain town in Lebanon called Aley, went to a Catholic school there, and initially pursued technical college in Beirut for training in Electronics. My first job was at the American University Hospital. So, I lived in Beirut in late 1970s and early 1980s, during what known as the civil armed conflicts and other people's wars on our land. While enduring the long bloody troubles and trying to help others through their dark times, I continued my education in the general area of liberal arts, covering social and cultural studies, psychology, pastoral care, philosophy, counseling, and theology. At age 30, I traveled to the United States in 1984, to focus more on graduate studies in pastoral counseling and clinical psychology, respectively earning an MDiv, an MA, and a PhD in these fields. Then, I became fully licensed as a psychologist in the State of Washington in 1995. While in the States I served as a consultant to a number of agencies that deal with Arab Americans and with Middle Eastern congregations. So, I have had a long educational journey and community service heritage both in Lebanon and the United States. In terms of my spiritual practice and religious preference, although it is within the Protestant tradition, I really consider myself as interdenominational, relating to all churches and faith traditions. I have been involved in many interfaith conferences and been part of several ongoing in-depth Christian-Muslim dialogues, especially in Beirut, Lebanon.

Therefore, my academic background and outlook on human service are varied, broad, intercultural, and interdisciplinary in nature. Often, I am invited to speak in public, teach an intense course, or present at conventions on subjects related to the Middle East, cross-cultural counseling, migration and refugees, Arab Americans, the impact of globalization, psychology of religion and spirituality, fundamentalism and radicalism, tragic loss and grief, and war stress and coping. Now, that personal background overview will lead us to explore the topics and themes of this particular chapter.

As of today, it is estimated that the Syrian crisis is one of the worst humanitarian disasters in our modern times. The armed conflicts in Syria are still raging, and it seems that there is no end in sight for its calamities. These intense wars and fighting have been going on nonstop since 2011, tearing apart the land and its people. The reality is that nobody knows exactly how many people have escaped, relocated, or been forced out; how many have been hurt and injured; and how many have totally disappeared or tragically lost their lives (Almoshmosh, 2015; James et al., 2014; Quosh, Eloul, & Ajlani, 2013).

Many political observers and social analysts are truly concerned about such a crisis of such a magnitude (Carpenter, 2013; Geha, 2016; Laub & Masters, 2013; OCHA, 2017). It has the potential to heavily burden and destabilize, not only neighboring countries, which is already happening, but also faraway societies, countries, and governments. It is affecting political establishments, geographical borders, the global economy, and world powers. Iraq came first and now Syria. The combined effects of both misfortunes are causing a substantial increase in negative discourses, hostile sentiments, religious fundamentalism, and political radicalism in the Near East and beyond.

Since 2011, it is estimated that the death toll of Syrian people has reached about 500,000 of all ages and backgrounds. Some reports predicted that about 400,000 victims died as a direct result of the bombing and fighting, and about 100,000 died as a result of the military sieges, lack of basic living necessities and care, and break down of the infrastructure. In addition, five to six million have become refugees outside Syria and six to seven million have been displaced within Syria. Between 50,000 and 100,000 are reported detainees or missing. Millions are injured, and thousands have been drafted, persecuted, starved, or tortured. Presently, between 13 and 14 million are in need of essential humanitarian aid and improved basic living conditions (Boghani, 2016; Mercy Corps, 2017; OCHA, 2017; UNICEF, n.d.; World Vision, 2017).

Background and National Profile

The country of Syria is located on the eastern side of the Mediterranean Sea in southwestern Asia, with a population of approximately 22 million. It is surrounded by Iraq to the east, Lebanon and seashore to the west, Turkey to the north, and Jordan to the south. In addition, Syria has a small section border with Israel/Palestine, mainly the Golan Heights, which is located in the southwest. Syria is about 71,500 square miles and most of it is positioned at the western end of a rich farmland, called the Fertile Crescent.

The nation is officially known as "The Syrian Arab Republic" or "The Arab Republic of Syria" (In Arabic, *Al-Jamhooriyyah el-Arabia Assouriyah*). Its landscape consists of many fertile plains, a few mountain ranges, and widespread deserts. Its borders do not match with Ancient Syria and Damascus Land (*Souriyyah al-Koubra wa bilaad el-Shaam*). The country has been the home to many diverse ethnic, sociocultural, and religious populations. Lifestyles are mixed, reflecting the urban, complex, and modern styles and the rural, simple, and traditional styles. The majority population is Arab Muslim of the Sunni branch. Other minority groups include the Kurds, the Armenians, the Assyrians, the Alawites, the Shiites, the Arab Christians, and the Arab Druze (cf. Abi-Hashem, 2003, 2008a; Hourani et al., 2016; Lawson, 1992; Nation Master, 2013).

Syria is an extremely ancient country, and has a rich cultural heritage. Many old civilizations have passed through, invaded, and ruled the whole area, leaving clear and deep marks. Once, *Greater Syria* was the hub for the ethnic Arab Kingdoms, long before the Arab-Muslims came to the scene. Later, Greater Syria became a center for the Islamic Empire. Thus, it has a history of being the guardian of *Arab Nationalism* and, at some point, of the Muslim heritage, thought, and culture.

In 1946, Syria became a fully independent nation, ceding from the French Mandate. Prior to that, it was part of the Ottoman Empire, similar to the fate of many nearby countries. Since then, Syria has been a member of the Arab League, the United Nations, and the Organization of the Islamic Conference (OIC), as well as many other global organizations. Modern Syria has also a history of political unrest and coups. One of these coups brought Havez el-Assad to power, the father of the current president, Bashar el-Assad. Since then, Syria has been a very stable and cohesive society, because Assad established a one-party rule, a secular ideology (with a thin cover of religion), and an authoritarian regime in the style of a police state. The 1973 constitution gave the president major executive powers, including the commander in chief of the armed forces and the secretary general of the ruling party, which is known as *El-Baath Party* (Hourani, et al., 2016).

Along with other concentration areas of cultures in the Near East, like Mesopotamia, Egypt, and Phoenicia, *Ancient Syria* was also part of the cradle of civilizations, where some of the greatest human achievements were established. Language, philosophy, astronomy, religious thought, human trade, systems of agriculture, governing models, cultural exchanges and other fields of inquiry had their roots there. Damascus has been the longtime capital and is the largest city in Syria. Damascus, along with Aleppo and Hama, pride themselves on being among the oldest continuously inhabited cities in the world (Abi-Hashem, 2003, 2008a; Abul-Fadil, 1998; Haddad, 1994).

Rural Syria is extremely traditional. Nomadic and seminomadic tribes are still roaming the countryside. There are also several racial-ethnic people-groups who settled there through the generations, and some of them are integrated within their region. Historically, the location of villages was usually determined by the availability of water, fertile land, and safe fortification. Community living is in very close proximity, and streets are very narrow. A mosque, a shrine, or a church normally stands in the middle of the community, or built on higher grounds nearby, so that it can be seen from afar and provide a landmark for the surroundings. Even within cities, several families (usually related) live in one large dwelling place, around an enclosed major entrance, with a garden and a water fountain inside the compound. The families often gather there daily to eat, visit, stay abreast of current events, and discuss important social affairs. However, this type of high-density living proved to have both advantages and disadvantages on the structure of Syrian marriages, families, and communities. Life is normally characterized by a strong sense of collectivism and social bonding, but leaves little space for personal maneuver and privacy (Hourani, et al., 2016; Mulaika, 1979; Sfeir, 2000).

Because work is seasonal and opportunities are very limited in rural-desert areas, many families and younger generations have been migrating to larger towns and cities, thus facing extra challenges for mental and sociocultural adjustments and placing extra demands and pressures on the limited social institutions. The country's rich natural resources and agriculture supplies have been subject to internal feuds and commercial exploitations. The industrialization of many areas has caused pollution of already-overstretched water resources. Inefficient irrigation methods and misuse of fertilizers have compounded this phenomenon creating further competition and wider gaps between the haves and the have nots. Many observers see these trends as the genesis of the current unrest and popular uprising, which has triggered civil turmoil, and therefore dragging the country into localized fighting, open borders, and multiple battles and leading it into deeper divisions and widespread wars.

Syrians, like other Middle Easterners, are a very hospitable people and easily welcome friends and strangers into their homes. Aleppo is the second largest city and the economic-industrial center of the country. It is also the home of the Armenian population, about 400,000 people, who became well integrated and prosperous in that region. The Arabic language is strongly emphasized in Syria, at the expense of other foreign languages. All school and university curricula are transliterated and taught in Arabic. Syria has prided itself as the protector of *Arabism*.

The following facts reflect some vital statistics about the country (cf. Hourani, et al. 2016; Lawson, 1992; Nation Master, 2013; UN Data, 2017; UNHCR, 2015a, 2015b): The gender distribution in Syria is 51.3 percent for males and 48.7 percent for females. The distribution of population is 54 percent urban and 46 percent rural. The literacy rate in Syria for those 15 years of age and over in 1995 was 75 percent as the government requires six years of compulsory primary education for all. The average life expectancy in 2012 was 75 years. The annual growth rate was 6.2 in 2005, 3.4 in 2010, and 0.4 in 2014. The ethnicity of Syria is composed of: Arabs, 75 percent; Bedouins Arab, 7.5 percent; Kurds, 7.3 percent; Palestinians, 4 percent; Armenians, 2.8 percent; and Others 3.4 percent. The distribution of religious affiliations as of 1992 was: Muslim Sunni, 74 percent; Alawites and Shiites, 11 percent; Christians, 10 percent; Druze, 3.0 percent; and Others (like Yezidis), 2.0 percent. Before the current extended conflict, Syria hosted a number of refugees and asylum seekers from Iraq, Sudan, Somalia, and Afghanistan in addition to the Palestinian refugees settlers, who have been in Syria since 1948. Many of those had to flee and relocate multiple times in recent years, both inside and outside Syria.

Trauma Through Cultural Lenses

What is considered tragic or traumatic in one place is not exactly considered the same everywhere. The concept of trauma is very broad and has many layers and dimensions. There is a variety of terminology to describe any *traumatic event*, like tragedy, disaster, adversity, calamity, destruction, catastrophe, terrifying event, severe crisis, devastating loss, threatening danger, horrific violence, etc. Although there are some technical differences among some of these terms, they have often been used interchangeably in the literature as well as in the mass media, due to their perceived similarities and impact on human nature. There are many aspects to the notion and experience of trauma; among them are the mental-emotional, interpersonal-behavioral, physical-physiological, tribal-communal, religious-spiritual, social-national, existential-philosophical, and traditional-cultural.

How people perceive, label, experience, or express trauma, or any other event, concept, notion, or feeling for that matter, is quite different. All depends on many vital aspects and wide influences. These include ethnic, social, emotional, religious, cultural, psychological, and existential factors. Experiences of acute stress and tragic occurrences affect people regardless of age, location, mentality, or status, yet each in their own way. Traumatic experiences can have equally deep influences on both the personal-individual and the collective-communal levels. Cultural background, emotional capital, life wisdom, psychological awareness, communal cohesiveness, mental outlook, social support, and religious faith all are essential dynamics in responding to crises and tragedies. Interestingly, communities, societies, and nations tend to react, process, struggle, and cope with adversities and disasters in a similar way to an individual person or a private self (Abi-Hashem, 2011a, 2012, 2014b, in press; Ellis & Abdi, 2017; Kleber, Figley, & Gersons, 1995; Mitschke et al., 2017; UNHCR, 2015a, 2015b).

In contrast to most Western views and models, life experiences, in general, and traumatic stressors, in particular, extend beyond the individual person or one human soul. They reach a broader level and scope to the large social context. People's understanding and reactions to life's events are significantly informed by their worldview, subcultures, and values, and are guided by their collective bonds and family sustenance, which typically are provided generously within their group, tribe, or community. In most poor, low-income, and developing countries, people expect hardships in life and seem to have a higher tolerance to pain. According to Kleber, Figley, and Gersons (1995), trauma does not occur to us in a vacuum; rather, it is shaped and approved by our surroundings, our value system, and our cultural heritage. Societal and cultural dimensions of traumatic stress are organic and fundamental. Thus, trauma is not only an individual matter but also a collective and communal matter, and that fact should necessitate a careful approach to all labeling and clinical diagnosing, like the posttraumatic stress disorder (PTSD), acute stress disorder (ASD), and related *Diagnostic and Statistical Manual of Mental Disorders* (DSM) classifications. Many international educators and clinical caregivers believe that mental health criteria cannot be applied everywhere in the world equally or blindly. In addition, some of these experts observed that certain diagnoses, like the PTSD, have been overly used and mechanically applied, not only in the general West, but also elsewhere across the world (Abi-Hashem, 2008b, 2014a, 2015, 2016a; Arkowitz & Lilienfeld, 2009; Kleber, Figley, & Gersons, 1995; Marsella, 1982).

For typical Syrian evacuees and refugees, losing their sense of stability, basic life functions, rootedness in the land, most of their physical possessions, and sense of national pride are considered major and significant losses. Moreover, experiencing suddenly and for the first time intense fighting, the outbreak of war, and severe destruction, accompanied with blood, death, horrific images, and disabling fear were too tragic and traumatic for them to bear. Most Syrians have expressed that after growing up in an extremely safe, secure, and controlled environment (as in a police state) along with plenty of almost free services, like education and medical care, (provided by the government), now trying to settle in a totally new location, learn new ways of life, and dealing with a new set of rules and authorities made them go through a serious mental shock and stressful reorientation process (adjustment disorders), some of which have been traumatic in nature, since many relocated from rural areas into dense urban settings. Although they stated that they were not easily shaken by mini-traumas and regular hardships of life, at the same time they described the tearing apart of their tightknit families and community bonds, the total disappearance of close friends and relatives, and the disturbing sounds and smells of heavy fighting hitting home as a real tragedy (*ma'saat*) and a deep trauma (*fajiaah*) (Abi-Hashem, 1999a; Almoshmosh, 2015; Arkowitz & Lilienfeld, 2009; Clinic Psychology, 2016; Hassan et al., 2016; James et al., 2014; Mitschke et al., 2017; Quosh, Eloul, & Ajlani, 2013).

The Syrian Crisis

Syria was once a very stable country and its people were nicely settled in their communities, rooted in their land, embedded in their routines, and tranquil in their generational living. Suddenly, they were caught up in a devastating war, totally unprepared and terribly unequipped to face such a calamity of such magnitude. Like the Iraqis before them, Syrians quickly became destabilized, traumatized, and victimized, with no time to process their disorientation, bind their wounds, sort their options, or say goodbye to their homes, community, and way of life. Many had to flee with minimum belongings (if any) and with no sense of awareness or direction as where to go or what to do next. They were caught off guard, were ill prepared, and quickly began to manage serious disillusionments and endure multiple losses, injuries, and huge uncertainties. Some decided to stay "home" regardless of the dire situation, choosing the known for the unknown.

In the Middle East, *home* is precious, and symbolic of a family's heritage. Also, such decisions depend on the circumstances of the violence, on the windows of cease-fire, and on the mental-physical ability of the survivors. Not everyone could pack a few things and run. So, many anxious people stayed behind not knowing what would happen to them or their neighborhood. Those who remained soon came under siege of brutal militias or military, enduring heavy bombardment and trying to survive among the rubble. In other developed countries, immediately following any major accident, tragedy, crime, mass shooting, or natural disaster, scores of first responders, counselors, social workers, pastors, volunteers, etc., hurry to the scene to offer their therapeutic attention and service. Then, the survivors would continue to receive guidance, treatment, and supportive care. In contrast, Syrian victims have been largely left alone to help each other and, at times, to suffer in silence and obscurity. They lean on and uplift each other. When one falls or collapses emotionally, the others rally around him or her to support and encourage. They take turn in containing the pressures, intervening when needs are urgent, and morally elevating each other in dark times. Obviously, the most difficult aspect of any crisis or tragedy is its consistency and unpredictability. In times of war, when the agony keeps unfolding, the uncertainty is prolonged, the stress becomes chronic with no end in sight, and the ability to survive and the tolerance to endure all drop down significantly (Abi-Hashem, 2006, 2011a, 2014b; Hobfoll et al., 1991; OCHA, 2017; Wong & Wong, 2006).

In 2011, what appeared to be a regular uprising and police confrontation, in one small corner of Syria, developed quickly into a widespread armed conflict that engulfed various regions. The Syrian crisis became so complex that no analyst is able to understand it completely. It grew rather fast, shifted numerous times, ignited so many fronts, involved many inner and outer players, penetrated into all the sociopolitical layers, and put the nation on a serious downhill spiral. What used to be a very stable land, ruled by a strict regime with heavy security apparatus, quickly slipped into major disorder and dangerous turmoil. Mini wars and social chaos became the norms. Cities were divided and militias ruled the streets. Black markets, arms dealing, and trafficking youngsters flourished overnight. "Green lines" (a term used to describe the dividing line or limit between two warring factions in urban civil wars) were formed on the ground, and many cities and towns were transformed into mini battlefields. Fierce fighting raged heavily with the use of conventional weapons and war machines to inflict unbelievable physical destruction and mental-emotional pain and horror.

Of course, there are some regions and city areas that are still intact within Syria and life is going on naturally there. Other areas are restricted and require passes and maneuvers to go around (with plenty of check points). But there are way too many other areas and places that are highly dangerous, utterly devastated, and completely destroyed. Even seasoned caregivers and reporters, at times, don't have words to describe the scenes they are observing. A reporter described a town, which was once a hub of activities and livelihood, as a *ghost city* (Masters & Kourdi, 2016). Another, a veteran of war coverage, shares her intense *eerie feeling*, when walking through some of the neighborhoods in Aleppo and sensing the *deafening silence* and the dark shadows of death. Another said, "This is Hell!" Others declared that there would be no real *winners* in these compound wars, only and certainly *losers* (Ward, 2016). Although the news media still relay powerful images, five years into the troubles, unfortunately most of the viewers around the world have become numb to the realities of war, distancing themselves from that agony, to protect themselves consciously or unconsciously, or justifying their passive attitude by considering the tragedy as a Syrian problem and part of the Middle East's chronic troubles. However, scores of volunteers, caregivers, and humanitarian aid workers are still working tirelessly on the ground in refugee centers, neighborhoods, and camps. They are bringing much needed help, hope, and healing and a new zest for life to the desperate and destitute (Abi-Hashem, 2004, 2016a, in press; Boghani, 2016; Ko-Din, 2017; Uechi, 2016; Ward, 2016; World Vision, 2017).

War Migrants and Sociocultural Adaptation

Since the beginning of the armed conflict and bloody war, the Syrian society has plunged into dark living conditions and communal disasters. According to a number of sources and statistics (cf. Mercy Corps, 2017; Norton, 2014; SCPR, 2015; UNHCR, 2015a, 2015b; WHO, 2017), almost half of the existing population in Syria (about 11 million) has shifted or relocated to another place or region, at least once; two-thirds of the population is now considered living in low socioeconomic conditions, in tangible scarcity, or in extreme poverty; life expectancy has decreased from 75.8 in 2010 to 55.6 years in

2014 and it continues to drop lower due to the significant impacts of the war; the destruction has endangered all resources and infrastructures in the country affecting family life, individual well-being, and social welfare; the unemployment rate has increased from 15 percent in 2010 to 28 percent in 2014, and is expected to reach about 50 percent at the end of this year; half of Syria's children have dropped out of school or never had any academic training at all, due to the collapse of the schools and educational systems; 60 out of 90 public hospitals are damaged or malfunctioning and about 40 hospitals are completely out of service; most people remaining inside Syria are forced to live under some kind of security siege, social alienation, internal subordination, or terrible estrangement; 90 percent of the displaced and refugees actually remain in the Middle East (Lebanon, Turkey, Jordan, Iraq, Egypt, Iran, Gulf area, etc.), and 10 percent only are trying to migrate to other continents, mostly Western Europe. Finally, Syrians now constitute the single largest migrant, displaced, or transplant population and humanitarian crisis in the world. More than half of these refugees are children and teenagers.

Mental-Emotional Agonies

Among Syrians today, few have escaped the effects of the tragic events or war insecurities. Symptoms of acute stress and psychological disturbances are elevated among survivors of all groups and ages, each one exhibiting psycho-emotional troubles in their own way (Alpak et al., 2015; Hassan et al., 2016; James et al., 2014; Quosh, Eloul, & Ajlani, 2013).

Unfortunately, the most difficult type of stress is the one that is inherently prolonged in nature. Many sociopolitical observers predict that the Syrian armed conflict and multiple-militia fighting will continue to drag on in the country for a long time (Carpenter, 2013; Laub & Masters, 2013). Sadly, there is no global or regional political will to end the disaster… and even if there is a clear resolve, there is no simple solution available at the moment for this enormous crisis (Abi-Hashem, 2006, 2016a; Hobfoll et al., 1991; WHO, 2017).

Besides the major disorientation and disillusionment many people experienced, those who were directly exposed to war atrocities were affected the most. The more severe the traumas, the more serious were the symptoms, at least at first. Thus, the degree of impact depended on the degree of exposure. Most people neither had words to describe their agonies nor were aware of their serious psychological conditions. Right after evacuation, most individuals and families began to display symptoms and shared their internal suffering. Here is a sample of such cases and statements (James et al., 2014; News, 2016; Personal communication, 2016; UNHCR, 2015a, 2015b; Ward, 2016; WHO, 2017): a young girl looking weak and pale, keeps hiding, barely talking or smiling, and is regularly withdrawn; a mother, exhausted and depressed, easily cries with anguish every time there is a mention of her previous life and present refugee status; an elderly man cannot stop thinking of his home, garden, and neighborhood, memories that plunge him into unspeakable sadness; a boy, acting out during the day and wetting his tiny mat at night; a teenage girl cannot sleep more than two hours without waking up afraid, at times screaming from nightmares; another young lady cannot hide the hurt and shame of being sexually assaulted and raped during a militia invasion, yet she tries to help a boy whose body is full of shrapnel after a nearby explosion; a young man cannot erase bloody images of his best friend and cousin who went into pieces in front of his eyes, due to a shell bomb hitting their small street; an older man refuses to eat much, or mix with others, after witnessing his own building collapse and kill all his family members; a young woman, who was a schoolteacher, now shares a tent with relatives, and deeply grieves the loss of many family members and students as she saw her own school hit repeatedly, destroyed, and burned with fire; a child, when still under siege and bombardment, kept seeing a dream of a fountain running of fresh water and a basket of fresh fruits; and an older lady kept wondering whether she would ever again see and smell a fresh rose, before she dies.

Psychosocial Effect and Adjustment

In the aftermath of any natural disaster, major tragedy, or war violence, survivors often experience a wide range of mental-emotional disturbances. Besides the horror of wars, people carry the scars of loss and grief, memories of shattered communities, and the lack of stability and security. The pressures of uprooting and escaping, and then squeezing everybody in tiny living places so as to share the quarters with other families (e.g., kitchenette, one entrance, small bathroom, a drinking tab), have created tremendous mental stressors and relational tensions among the people involved.

Six years of intense wars have torn the country apart. Young families, along with children and elderly, have borne the weight and disastrous consequences of this conflict. Helpers from humanitarian, media, religious, and volunteer organizations working in Aleppo, reported that the situation there was the direst ever seen, and the victims of that urban war have endured hardships that would last for several lifetimes (Ward, 2017; World Vision, 2017).

Those who were less exposed to war traumas and atrocities still suffer from significant anxieties, apprehensions, mourning, and existential questioning. Many Syrians feel they have lost their social identity, life savings, sense of belonging, communal lifestyle, unique heritage, and national pride. When everything seems collapsing, people are forced to redefine their lives and outlook on existence. Some find new meaning and purpose, others fall into despair and apathy, yet others mobilize their spare energy and passion to help those less fortunate, and with that they help themselves in return. That is the resilient art of *meaning making* (cf. Wong, 2013).

Unlike medical and humanitarian aid, psychological caregiving and mental health services are not as prominent, available, or urgent as the physical and medical needs. Limited psycho-emotional care started very late in the process, well after the war events unfolded and intensified. Assessment and therapeutic interventions were scarcely offered or even accessible to Syrians, both inside and outside Syria. There is still a major shortage of trained personnel, social workers, and therapy counselors. Some serious mental health problems were actually discovered by default or chance, while other health care providers and volunteers attended to pressing needs of the affected and displaced. In the last couple of years, psychiatric/psychological caregiving and trauma counseling have been more available to some of the needy, who have responded very well. They show enthusiasm and gratitude to any therapeutic activities, clinical intervention, educational programs, or pastoral care, especially among the children and young generation (cf. Abi-Hashem, in press; Mercy Corps, 2016, 2017; News, 2016).

The multiple concerns and agonies of Syrians include their ongoing grief over the collapse of their country along with excessive worry over their safety and means of survival. The unknown destiny of their properties and fate of family members, the uncertainties of having enough income, and a lack of information about their own future all add to their marked disorientation and acute anxiety. They are constantly facing challenges, like adapting to new environments and tight living surroundings, receiving mixed messages from the hosting societies, trying to manage their cultural shock, and binding their wounds while relearning to survive again (UNHCR, 2015a, 2015b).

Intercultural adjustment and cross-cultural adaptation place extra pressure on any displaced people or refugees. In a new setting, some remain isolated and aloof (alienation), others mingle and melt within the setting (fusion), while others assimilate well and achieve a healthy adaptation (integration). Therefore, *acculturation stress* can be a significant burden for those vulnerable, drained, distressed, and demoralized (Abi-Hashem & Brown, 2013; Chan, Young, & Sharif, 2016; Mitschke et al., 2017; Wong & Wong, 2006).

Mutual Impact on the Countries of Lebanon and Syria

Lebanon has the largest refugee population in the world compared to its size and population (Caryl, 2016; Karam, 2015; Marsi, 2015; Refaat & Mohanna, 2013; Sobelman, 2015). It is roughly the size of Rhode Island in the United States or the Island of Cyprus in the Mediterranean Sea. Although Lebanon was caught by surprise with the magnitude of the Syrian turmoil and displacement, it has done great favors to host far more Syrians per capita than any other country in the world. There are no sanctioned camps or refugee concentrations in Lebanon (except a few with loose security apparatus), unlike in Jordan and Turkey, where guards closely check the camp entrances and activities. At first, the Lebanese accommodated the Syrians realizing this may be just for a short time before they return home, once the troubles subside. Instead, the Syrian troubles escalated further and spread wider, making Lebanon one of the easiest and best choices for escape and resettlement. In the last couple of years the Lebanese authorities woke up to the fact that this may be a long and chronic crisis and began to put requirements and restrictions on Syrians in order to regulate their influx and intense presence (e.g., criteria for entrance into the country, need to have a Lebanese sponsor in order to work, and short but renewable residence).

Evidently, the majority of Syrians coming to Lebanon have experienced immense hardships, yet they are decent, hard-working, law abiding, and god-fearing people. They qualify to be labeled as refugees. Those able to work are quite willing to provide cheap labor, which eventually helps the Lebanese economy. However, other Syrian civilians, not directly affected by the war and who do not consider themselves as refugees, are also drawn to Lebanon due to its open policy, safety, and opportunities for livelihood. These come in and go out as they wish (no visa required, just minimal paper work), get benefits similar to the refugees, compete with the Lebanese for jobs, and take the money back home, yet are only considered regular workers or visitors. This has been confusing as to "who is who?" A tiny Syrian elite came to Beirut from Damascus and Aleppo early on, and brought their wealth; but a vast majority of Syrian evacuees are now extremely poor and depending on Lebanese welfare, menial jobs, and private donations. The sudden migration from Syria and constant influx through the wide borders into Lebanon has absolutely overwhelmed this tiny country's infrastructure and limited resources.

Due to previous friendly agreements between the two countries, people could move easily between them. Therefore, it is difficult to know exactly how many Syrians are in Lebanon as they have literally infiltrated almost every street, corner, and town in Lebanon, from up the mountains to the seashores. Many Lebanese are apprehensive about such migrant density and even begin to feel as strangers in their own land (Geha, 2016; Marsi, 2015; Refaat & Mohanna, 2013).

According to several analyses and reports (Aljazeera, 2017; Geha, 2016; UNHCR, 2015a, 2015b), Lebanon has been drained and devastated for paying such a high price and is currently at risk. The refugees' presence has created a number of social dilemmas, including housing shortages, serious competition for jobs, an educational and medical crisis, an unprecedented street children problem, major safety and security concerns, higher unemployment, and ethno-demographic shift. There are plenty of mixed marriages and unwanted out-of-wedlock children. The childbirth rate among the Syrians in Lebanon is double that of the Lebanese themselves (Aljazeera, 2017; Geha, 2016; Marsi, 2015; Refaat & Mohanna, 2013; UNHCR, 2015a, 2015b).

In addition, there has been an increase in using or abusing public services and private donations, drug dealing, money laundering, prostitution, child exploitation and trafficking, gang and crime activity, secret arms selling, and black market activities. Lebanese observers fear that some fighters, criminals, and radical militants, freely roaming in Syria, may have already infiltrated the border into Lebanon and may create dangerous cells and draw followers. The Lebanese security forces are strong and alert but the task of keeping up security is enormous and is stretching their capabilities. Thus, there are some serious threats to the cohesiveness, survival, and integrity of the Lebanese themselves. Such negative consequences and social disorders normally follow any major armed conflict, population displacement, and forced migration.

In spite of all the disadvantages and tangible or existential threats, Lebanon has so far shown extreme resiliency, containment, and adaptability as a tiny nation, which already has its share of problems. Lebanon continues to mobilize its limited resources and highly motivated service personnel to help and accommodate the huge social demands of Syrian refugees, visitors, and migrants. The market place, housing, schools, factories, shops, labor forces, construction sites, homes, etc., still are welcoming Syrians openly. This was unexpected, due to the negative way the Syrian regime and its army treated the Lebanese in the past, when they ruled Lebanon with an iron fist for almost 20 years (Akoury-Dirani et al., 2015; Aljazeera, 2017; Geha, 2016; UNHCR, 2015a, 2015b).

According to Karam (2015), Lebanon has been the recipient of more than a million Syrian evacuees and migrants (those registered back then prior to 2015), even without having a major say in the matter. Although struggling and overwhelmed, Lebanon as a hosting country is surviving and helping the Syrians to survive as well. With that, it is setting an example for the international community, especially Europe, that accommodating refugees is possible and doable, of course with a price but also with an advantage of having industrious people on its land—very hard working and highly family-community oriented (see also Caryl, 2015; Sobelman, 2015).

A few hundred thousand Syrians used Lebanon temporarily as a stepping-stone to apply, via the local United Nations offices, for political asylum or full immigration to a Western nation of their choice. The rest have settled in and built their lives locally, until further notice. Some of them express a strong desire to return home to their beloved country. Others seem very happy in Lebanon and have no intention of leaving again (Caryl, 2016; Karam, 2015; Marsi, 2015; Refaat & Mohanna, 2013; Sobelman, 2015).

The very fact that Lebanon does not require that Syrian refugees and war victims be grouped in reservation camps, is by itself an empowering fact that offers a major psychological boost to their morale. Syrians love Lebanon due to its open policy and freedom of moving, working, living, mingling, and enjoying its diversity, leisure, and beauty (with no need to learn a new language). These aspects and ample commodities and the availability of social services are greatly contributing to the Syrian refugees' sense of personal dignity, restoration of some stability, emotional recovery, and general empowerment. However, as with every sudden population influx and relocation, such huge numbers coming from Syria, a neighboring and sister country, has created serious implications on this hosting society of Lebanon. Therefore, anxiety, fear, and resentment are rising among locals and nationals. The Lebanese government, social institutions, and private sectors were never ready for this demographic flooding, so they became at loss what to do and how to handle this unplanned migration. After a year or so, when it became evident that there was no solution in sight, and the flood of Syrians into Lebanon continued, reports of discrimination cases, refusal of service, and tightening of privileges and freedoms increased. Still, the Lebanese in general are accommodating, employing, facilitating life, and providing for the Syrians, young and old, with generous hospitality, trust, and solidarity. Thus, what was a Syrian struggle for survival and recovery has now become a duel Lebanese-Syrian struggle for survival, recovery, and resiliency (Akoury-Dirani et al., 2015; Carta, Moro, & Bass, 2015; Caryl, 2016; Karam, 2015; Marsi, 2015; Refaat & Mohanna, 2013; Sobelman, 2015).

Thus, in many ways, the country of Lebanon and its people can be presently considered as co-partners in the coping process of the Syrian crisis and as co-survivors alongside the Syrian people in enduring and thriving toward better tenacity, mastery, and resiliency, all in the face of an unprecedented communal, national, and regional war disaster and adversity of such magnitude.

Healthy and Unhealthy Coping Styles

As in any major crisis and disaster, people, often labeled as victims or survivors, try to find ways to soothe the pain and cope with the anxieties and acute stresses. They usually develop coping strategies that range from the healthy-constructive to the unhealthy-destructive ones.

Some of the unhealthy, risky, and damaging modes of coping include withdrawing, isolating, becoming cynical, falling into apathy and pessimism, perpetually moving and relocating, acting out behaviors, resorting to aggression and domestic violence, engaging in addictions, resorting to occult/ black magic practices, gambling and overspending, using/abusing drugs and alcohol, overworking, oversexualizing, etc. However, in terms of healthy coping strategies, the following are a sample of those that survivors usually employ during and after tragedies. Syrians are displaying many of these skills and others as well, reflecting their unique ways and subcultures in handling stress and striving toward restoration (cf. Abi-Hashem, 2006, 2008b, 2011b, 2013, 2014b, 2016a; Chan, Young, & Sharif, 2016; Clinic Psychology, 2016; Hassan et al., 2016; Mercy Corps, 2016, 2017; Mitschke et al., 2017): Syrians are bonding and adopting each other as friends and relatives, especially those who lost family members. They are becoming creative in finding innovative ways to work and survive financially. Even young children and teenagers are becoming little entrepreneurs and market smart (unfortunately at times in black markets) as many are cleaning cars, working as bag boys in grocery stores, trading in vegetables, collecting any good items for recycling from stores, garbage, or trash, are willing to work in anything and with any capacity, even selling items on the streets and among cars or begging there for long hours, just to raise small funds to help mother or grandmother or siblings with food and rent and the basics. They are bravely enduring the hardships of street life—the hot sun, dust, dirt, and harassment by others, young and old, even competition among themselves, just to make enough at the end of day, if at all possible.

Traditionally, Syrians tend to socialize with each other closely and celebrate all social events and feasts together, with hosting families or communities around them. Often that includes having music and singing and, at times, folk dancing. This proves to be therapeutic in many ways, which provides beautiful communal strength and restoration. Often, they gather in small circles, ladies for morning coffee, and older men in the afternoon for playing cards or table games, smoking water pipes, and discussing current worries, events, and politics. Children are found playing ball in the tiny corner of their street or shelter building. All of these have become very healing activities. When gathering around food, which is an engrained habit in the Middle East psyche since ancient times, normally people have a great opportunity to nurture and support each other, bond closer, and show solidarity with each other. Many Syrians are becoming spiritually more active and finding strength in faith. Although the majority of people in the Middle East are religious by affiliation, if not by practice (religious affiliation/celebrations are part of social identity and culture), many are now seeking genuine faith and new spiritual experiences for deeper meaning, comfort, commitment, camaraderie, and contentment.

Others are volunteering to help fellow refugees and evacuees who are less fortunate than themselves, both in Lebanon and back home in Syria. Many are cultivating passions and future inspirations even among children who are begging on the streets of Beirut. I usually stop and talk with many of them. They gather around me eagerly and love the attention. I get to meet them by name and inquire about their lives. Where do they come from? Are they alone or with any family members? How long have they been begging on the streets? When did they eat last? Were they ever at any school in their lifetime? In response, I hear sad stories. But when asking what would they like to become when growing up and why, without hesitation, and with a spark in their eyes, they answer: nurse, to help treat my sick family and all victims of this ugly war; teacher, to educate children so they will not miss school like us; farmer, to help my aging father work in our good land; etc. Unfortunately, many children have lost their childhood and have not played, studied, or laughed much, yet they have not lost their ability to dream and set worthy and bright goals for the future.

Promoting Further Resiliency and Strength

Resiliency refers to the human individual potential and the collective communal spirit to effectively and positively face adversity, tolerate ambiguity, handle pressure, cope with crises, and recover from disaster or tragedy (Abi-Hashem, 2011a, 2016b; Ungar, 2008, 2013). Nevertheless, surviving usually comes with a price tag. People normally bounce back but not without a scar, a stress, a residual, or a heaviness.

Resiliency focuses on the hopeful side of life and mobilizes the positive strength in human nature. Other words are used to describe resiliency: Flexibility, hardiness, elasticity, resourcefulness, tenacity, robustness, and mastery. There are several psychological dynamics, cultural mediators, and spiritual factors at work in every aspect of surviving, coping, and thriving. However, enduring suffering constructively somehow adds to the emotional maturity and spiritual depth of people. For the sake of our discussion, *resiliency* then is more than an isolated *individual construct*. It can be best described as a *cultural competency in action* and as a *fluid concept* that is a function of the emotional resources, social identity, religious values, and cultural capitals of the group or the community (Abi-Hashem, 2011a, 2016b; Chan, Young, & Sharif, 2016; Ungar, 2008, 2013).

Syrians Respond Well to Lebanese Outreach

Government agencies, NGOs, community groups, schools, churches, mosques, and other local societies and organizations are doing all they can to help, accommodate, and empower the refugees of all walks and ages, especially the women and children. Foreign agencies often work with national Lebanese teams in joint efforts. Together, they are providing health care, social work, and medical clinics, in fixed or mobile locations. Most hospitals treat Syrians free or with minimal fees. The ministry of education established after-school tracks across Lebanon for refugee children, as the Syrian curriculum is somehow different and less rigorous than the Lebanese (still many cannot enroll because they have to work). Also, women are being trained in basic reading, writing, and entrepreneurial skills to help them start small businesses or sell products. In addition, services provide for emotional recovery, personal training, pastoral ministry, and spiritual care to help the displaced find more healing, solace, restoration, and existential hope. Sociocultural coaching helps those feeling intimidated and lost in transition.

Syrian refugees are responding amazingly well to all these initiatives and services and are asking for more. Although the majority of Lebanese caregivers are exhausted and depleted, they keep on giving enthusiastically, realizing the rewarding outcomes and sense of fulfillment. Countless Syrians are bouncing back, flourishing, and doing much better under unfavorable circumstances. They are deeply grateful to all the attention, help, and care. Many have lost almost everything to the ugly war, but maintain their imagination, resolve, affection, and hopefulness (Clinic Psychology, 2016; Geha, 2016; Mercy Corps, 2016; UNHCR, 2015a, 2015b).

Implications for Mental Health Care and Counseling

The following are hints for intervention, and practical guidelines for health care providers and mental health professionals, including key questions to ask the survivors during almost any therapeutic encounter and counseling service (cf. Abi-Hashem, 1999b, 2008b, 2011b, 2013, 2014a, 2014b, in press; Almoshmosh, 2015; Chan, Young, & Sharif, 2016; Clinic Psychology, 2016; Hassan et al., 2016; James et al., 2014; Lee, 2010; Mitschke et al., 2017; News, 2016; UNHCR, 2015a, 2015b; WHO, 2017):

- Establish a welcoming atmosphere and a warm relationship for the distressed people, so they would feel comfortable and safe (could be on a walk or over a meal).
- Gently ask about general details of what happened to them without pressing them with questions. Avoid sounding like you are interrogating them.
- Show basic empathy and provide much needed comforting statements.
- Educate the sufferers about the nature of common emotional disturbances that usually follow tragedies.
- Insure the safety and survival of each person with whom you are working by providing solidarity, reassurance, and physical provision (if needed and possible).
- In case of multiple traumas and victimizations, start with the most urgent one and gradually move to the others.

- Teach people basic ways how to reduce their anxiety, stress, and interpersonal tension.
- Help people discover the unhealthy reactions they use to protect themselves, their loved ones, or their fragile emotions.
- Introduce desensitization and encourage them to reverse any unhealthy coping modes in a gentle, yet effective manner.
- For those struggling with acute traumatic stress, teach them to reframe their thinking and responses, so their fears and calamities will not become exaggerated.
- Be careful when uncovering tragic memories, because some aspects of any recollection could expand unconsciously to become vague, and the real becomes mixed with the unreal.
- Ask them what they miss most about their previous lives before becoming refugees. Help them process and treasure good memories.
- Remember that the experience of grief, loss, trauma, and tragedy is not separate from people's mentality, worldview, culture, and spirituality. These always interact and overlap.
- Make sure to conduct grief counseling simultaneously with trauma therapy in order to facilitate the mourning process of complicated bereavement and the mastery of traumatic reactions.
- Refer severe cases to medical and psychiatric evaluation/treatment as needed.
- Investigate the challenges of social adjustment and cultural integration they are facing. "What are the most difficult aspects of you being a refugee right now?"
- Acknowledge the hardship and possible discrimination they may be facing.
- Commend them on any positive step and degree of strength they are utilizing, gaining, and demonstrating.
- Help them to constantly shift their mental focus from being *victims* to being *survivors*.
- Network with other caregivers to find out what supportive resources are available in nearby cultural centers, communities of faith, and society at large.
- Introduce experiential activities alongside talk therapy. Give them homework to do, even simple activities, and discuss the next steps of recovery to avoid any future lapses.
- Guide them to establish new relationships, set new goals, develop realistic expectations, and discover new inner potentials and aspirations.
- Inspire them to possibly get involved in helping other people who are struggling with similar agonies, so by helping others they will eventually help themselves.

- Encourage them to cultivate healthy soul care and spiritual vitality. To do that, first find out whether faith has become a part of the solution or the problem in their lives. "How can your faith and religious values inspire you at this time of life?"
- "Are there any elders, mentors, or sages in your life circle that you can seek to guide and nurture you?"
- "How would your grandparents handle and cope with a similar situation? What common sense, insight, and generational wisdom from your heritage can you use and employ?"
- "If you are a role model, what can others, young or old, see and observe in you? And learn from you?"
- Encourage them to use resources from the new environment and also make contributions into it.
- Help them navigate the challenges of adjustment and integrate well in the hosting society, without losing much of their social identity or cultural heritage, yet without isolating and becoming socially rigid, in order to blend well and function best.
- Encourage them to practice basic meditation and mindfulness.
- Promote resiliency and survival. Hopefully, these people will begin to transfer their pain into purpose, their crippling into creativity, their misery into mission, and their tragedies into treasures.
- Finally, remain available for continual support, guidance, accountability, nurture, and encouragement.

CONCLUSION

In this chapter we have discussed the agony and perseverance of the Syrian people who have been directly affected by the ongoing armed conflict and large-scale war since 2011. We have described the background of their ordeal and focused on the dynamics of their coping skills and survival abilities. We have presented an overview of the circumstances preceding the massive troubles and tribulations that hit most of their homeland along with a general profile of the country and its population, subcultures, social norms, and religious faiths, so to help us better understand the scope and seriousness of the current situation and put its acute humanitarian crisis in the right social framework and psychological perspective.

As the armed conflict and fighting continue and, at times, spread or switch from one regional area to another, scores of Syrians continue to suffer greatly. Besides their tangible losses, actual military sieges of their communities, and destruction of their homes and neighborhoods, they had to endure severe emotional horrors, multiple physical displacements, bodily injuries, and often death of a family member or loved one, and obviously accumulated levels of traumatic stress.

Some of them became refugees in their own country. Others became refugees in a nearby country across the border, like Jordan, Lebanon, Turkey, and Iraq. A few of them, relatively speaking to the millions displaced, made their way to North Africa, the Gulf region, or to the European continent. However, the majority of them settled in residential communities or large established camps near the Syrian border, indefinitely waiting and desperately hoping to return home perhaps someday.

We have found that, under the right circumstances, and with the intentional help, care, and hospitality of the hosting country or community, even the most traumatized and victimized Syrian refugees have been able to slowly (but surely) readjust, gain strength, persevere, recover, and build a new life in exile. Those who were able to return to their relatively safe towns and villages have started cleaning, repairing, and reestablishing their neighborhood again. Survival and resiliency are manifested by their ability to utilize well the resources available to them, respond well to the coaching and training provided to them, engage in the guidance and counseling given to them, and be indigenous and creative in finding solutions and new innovative ways around the many obstacles facing their restoration.

We have also seen that the welfare and survival of Syrian refugees has not been without negative consequences on the hosting communities, societies, or countries. In this chapter, I have included a Lebanese perspective about that difficult aspect and how, since the very beginning of the Syrian war, the tiny nation of Lebanon has been extremely strained, and still, as a full resolution of the crisis appears unattainable. Lebanon is now considered having the largest refugee population in the world per capita. However, and in spite of this sobering reality, the Lebanese government and people, regardless of their socioeconomic background, political persuasion, religion, or education rally behind accommodating Syrian evacuees and migrants in all areas and on all levels. Thus, the Lebanese have become partners with the Syrians in enduring their crisis and paying the heavy price of their displacement. The Lebanese people also have shown tremendous resiliency, practiced great absorption, and exhibited remarkable solidarity. And together they have displayed a great model of containing the aftermath of an ugly war and a catastrophic tragedy, which have caused a national misery, an unbelievable regional dilemma, and an unprecedented humanitarian crisis.

As the author of this chapter, I have shared many personal insights, observations, and conclusions based on my social interactions, clinical interventions, private interviews, in-depth readings, and cross-cultural works. A glimpse of what the helpers, providers, and volunteers, who are working with Syrian refugees, are facing and experiencing is also included. This perspective is to complete the psychosocial picture and provide a global view of the impact of such a war disaster on both the caregivers and care-receivers alike.

In conclusion, the whole account may serve as a testimony to the resilient human spirit which, on one hand, can endure adversities, experience various traumas, and be moved deeply by multiple calamities and, yet, on the other hand, can begin to restore the many losses, heal the profound emotional wounds, recover from the painful agonies, and chart a new path toward a future filled with hope, confidence, patience, striving, and survival.

REFERENCES

Abi-Hashem, N. (1999a). Loss of function. In D. G. Benner & P. C. Hill (Eds.), *Baker encyclopedia of psychology and counseling* (2nd ed., p. 705). Grand Rapids, MI: Baker.

Abi-Hashem, N. (1999b). Grief, loss, and bereavement: An overview. *Journal of Psychology and Christianity, 18*(4), 309–329.

Abi-Hashem, N. (2003). Syria. In B. Sherif-Trask (Ed.), *The Greenwood encyclopedia of women's issues worldwide: The Middle East and North Africa* (Vol. 4, pp. 355–380). Westport, CT: Greenwood.

Abi-Hashem, N. (2004). Peace and war in the Middle East: A psychopolitical and sociocultural perspective. In F. M. Moghaddam & A. J. Marsella (Eds.), *Understanding terrorism: Psychosocial roots, consequences, and interventions* (pp. 69–89). Washington, DC: American Psychological Association Press.

Abi-Hashem, N. (2006). The agony, silent grief, and deep frustration of many communities in the Middle East: Challenges for coping and survival. In P. T. P. Wong & L. C. J. Wong (Eds.), *Handbook of multicultural perspectives on stress and coping* (pp. 457–486). New York: Springer.

Abi-Hashem, N. (2008a). Syria. In I. Epstein & G. H. Talhami (Eds.), *The Greenwood encyclopedia of children's issues worldwide: North Africa and the Middle East* (pp. 269–292). Westport, CT: Greenwood.

Abi-Hashem, N. (2008b). Arab Americans: Understanding their challenges, needs, and struggles. In A. Marsella, P. Watson, F. Norris, J. Johnson, & J. Gryczynski (Eds.), *Ethnocultural perspectives on disasters and trauma: Foundations, issues, and applications* (pp. 115–173). New York: Springer.

Abi-Hashem, N. (2011a). On cultural resiliency. *The Australian Community Psychologist, 23*(2), 23–31. Online version https://groups.psychology.org.au/Assets/Files/Abi-Hashem-ACP-2-11.pdf

Abi-Hashem, N. (2011b). Working with Middle Eastern immigrant families. In A. Zagelbaum & J. Carlson (Eds.), *Working with immigrant families: A practical guide for counselors* (pp. 151–180). New York: Routledge.

Abi-Hashem, N. (2012). Clinical trauma psychology. In C. R. Figley (Ed.), *Encyclopedia of trauma: An interdisciplinary guide* (pp. 98–100). Thousand Oaks, CA: Sage. Online version http://knowledge.sagepub.com/view/trauma/n32.xml

Abi-Hashem, N. (2013). Religion and spirituality. In K. D. Keith (Ed.), *Encyclopedia of cross-cultural psychology* (pp. 1091–1094). Malden, MA: Wiley-Blackwell. Online version http://onlinelibrary.wiley.com/doi/10.1002/9781118339893.wbeccp299/abstract

Abi-Hashem, N. (2014a). Cross-cultural psychology and counseling: A Middle Eastern perspective. *Journal of Psychology and Christianity, 33*, 156–163.

Abi-Hashem, N. (2014b). Social support: A psychological and cultural perspective. *APA's International Psychology Bulletin, 18*, 74–77.

Abi-Hashem, N. (2015). Revisiting cultural awareness and cultural relevancy. *American Psychologist, 70*, 660–661.

Abi-Hashem, N. (2016a). Understanding and working with people from Arab and Middle Eastern backgrounds. Workshop 4-Hour Continuing Education, Online Library of the American Psychological Association. Retrieved from http://apa.bizvision.com/product/2016-ce-workshop-recordings/understandingandworkingwithpeoplefromarabandmiddleeasternbackgrounds(13904).

Abi-Hashem, N. (2016b, December 8). Promoting resiliency: Integrating mental-emotional, socio-cultural, and spiritual-existential aspects in short term care. Power point workshop presented at the meeting of the *Brief Therapy Conference* in San Diego, California.

Abi-Hashem, N. (in press). Pastoral and spiritual response to trauma and tragedy. In P. Barker (Ed.), *On trauma: A guide for pastors* [tentative title]. London, UK: Langham Partnership International.

Abi-Hashem, N., & Brown, J. R. (2013). Intercultural adjustment. In K. D. Keith (Ed.), *Encyclopedia of cross-cultural psychology* (pp. 744–746). Malden, MA: Wiley-Blackwell. Online version http://onlinelibrary.wiley.com/doi/10.1002/9781118339893.wbeccp299/abstract

Abul-Fadil, L. (1998). *Traditionalism versus modernism in Middle Eastern society* (in Arabic). Damascus, Syria: Dar al-Tibaa.

Akoury-Dirani, L., Sahakian, T. S., Hassan, F. Y., Hajjar, R. V., & Asmar, K. E. (2015). Psychological first aid training for Lebanese field workers in the emergency context of the Syrian refugees in Lebanon. *Psychological Trauma: Theory, Research, Practice, and Policy*, *7*(6), 533.

Aljazeera. (2017, April 1). Lebanon at a 'breaking point' due to refugees. Retrieved from http://www.aljazeera.com/news/2017/04/saad-al-hariri-lebanon-big-refugee-camp-170401045951087.html

Almoshmosh, N. (2015). Highlighting the mental health needs of Syrian refugees. *Intervention*, *13*(2), 178–181.

Alpak, G., Unal, A., Bulbul, F., Sagaltici, E., Bez, Y., Altindag, A., Dalkilic, A., & Savas, H. A. (2015). Post-traumatic stress disorder among Syrian refugees in Turkey: A cross-sectional study. *International Journal of Psychiatry in Clinical Practice*, *19*(1), 45–50.

Arkowitz, H., & Lilienfeld, S. O. (2009, November). Foreign afflictions: Mental disorders across country borders. *Scientific American*. Retrieved from https://www.scientificamerican.com/article/foreign-afflictions/

Boghani, P. (2016). A staggering new death toll for Syria's war—470,000. *PBS Frontline*. Retrieved from http://www.pbs.org/wgbh/frontline/article/a-staggering-new-death-toll-for-syrias-war-470000/

Carpenter, T. G. (2013). Tangled web: The Syrian civil war and its implications. *Mediterranean Quarterly, 24*(1), 1–11.

Carta, M. G., Moro, M. F., & Bass, J. (2015). War traumas in the Mediterranean area. *International Journal of Social Psychiatry, 61*(1), 33–38.

Caryl, C. (2016, February). If you think Europe has a refugee crisis, you're not looking hard enough. *Foreign Policy*. Retrieved from http://foreignpolicy.com/2016/02/02/the-weakest-links-syria-refugees-migrants-crisis-data-visualization/

Chan, K. J., Young, M. Y., & Sharif, N. (2016). Well-being after trauma: A review of posttraumatic growth among refugees. *Canadian Psychology/Psychologie Canadienne, 57*(4), 291.

Clinic Psychology. (2016). Working with refugees from Syria and surrounding Middle East countries. *Public Mental Health Initiative*. Retrieved from http://clinicpsychology.com/wp-content/uploads/2016/04/tip-sheets-final.pdf

Ellis, H. B., & Abdi, S. (2017). Building community resilience to violent extremism through genuine partnerships. *American Psychologist, 72*(3), 289–300.

Geha, C. (2016). The Syrian refugee crisis and Lebanon's endemic deadlocks: Trading reform for resilience. *Middle East Institute*. Retrieved from http://www.mei.edu/content/map/syrian-refugee-crisis-and-lebanon's-endemic-deadlocks-trading-reform-resilience

Haddad, M. R. (1994). Syria. *The world book encyclopedia* (Vol. 18, pp. 1070–1075). Chicago, IL: World Book.

Hassan, G., Ventevogel, P., Jefee-Bahloul, H., Barkil-Oteo, A., & Kirmayer, L. J. (2016). Mental health and psychosocial wellbeing of Syrians affected by armed conflict. *Epidemiology and Psychiatric Sciences, 25*, 129–141.

Hobfoll, S. E., Spielberger, C. D., Breznitz, S., Figley, C., Folkman, S., Lepper-Green, B., Meichenbaum, D., Milgram, N.A., Sandler, I., Sarason, I., & van der Kolk, B. (1991). War-related stress: Addressing the stress of war and other traumatic events. *American Psychologist, 46*(8), 848.

Hourani, A. H., et al. (2016). Syria. *Encyclopedia Britannica*. Retrieved from https://www.britannica.com/place/Syria

James, L., Sovcik, A., Garoff, F., & Abbasi, R. (2014). The mental health of Syrian refugee children and adolescents. *Forced Migration Review*, (47), 42.

Karam, M. (2015, November 14). How Lebanon is coping with more than a million Syrian refugees. *The Spectator*. Retrieved from https://www.spectator.co.uk/2015/11/how-lebanon-is-coping-with-more-than-a-million-syrian-refugees/#

Kleber, R. J., Figley, C. R., & Gersons, B. P. (Eds.). (1995). *Beyond trauma: Cultural and societal dynamics*. New York: Springer.

Ko-Din, J. (2017, February 16). After years in war zone, burnout rises among those who serve Syrians. Retrieved from http://catholicphilly.com/2017/02/news/world-news/after-years-in-war-zone-burnout-rises-among-those-who-serve-syrians/

Laub, Z., & Masters, J. (2013). Syria's crisis and the global response. *Council on Foreign Relations*. Retrieved from https://www.cfr.org/backgrounder/syrias-crisis-and-global-response

Lawson, F. (1992). Syria. *Collier's Encyclopedia* (Vol. 22, pp. 3–25). New York: Macmillan Educational.

Lee, T. Y. (2010). The loss and grief in immigration: Pastoral care for immigrants. *Pastoral Psychology, 59*, 159–169.

Marsella, A. J., & White, G. (1982). *Cultural conceptions of mental health and therapy: Culture, illness, and healing* (Vol. 4). New York: Springer.

Marsi, F. (2015, November 21). Syrian refugees overwhelm Lebanon to the breaking point. *USA Today*. Retrieved from https://www.usatoday.com/story/news/world/2015/11/19/lebanon-beirut-refugees-syria/73475896/

Masters, J., & Kourdi, M. E. (2016, September 27). Aleppo has become a 'ghost city.' *First on CNN*. Retrieved from http://edition.cnn.com/2016/09/26/middleeast/aleppo-syria-bombing-aid/index.html

Mercy Corps. (2016). Unlocking a future for Syria's youth. Retrieved from https://www.mercycorps.org/articles/syria/unlocking-future-syrias-youth

Mercy Corps. (2017). Quick facts: What you need to know about the Syrian crisis. Retrieved from https://www.mercycorps.org/articles/iraq-jordan-lebanon-syria-turkey/quick-facts-what-you-need-know-about-syria-crisis

Mitschke, D. B., Praetorius, R. T., Kelly, D. R., Small, E., & Kim, Y. K. (2017). Listening to refugees: How traditional mental health interventions may miss the mark. *International Social Work, 60*(3), 588–600.

Mulaika, L. K. (1979). Family status in Syria. *Qira'at fi Ilm-in-Nafs al-Ijtima'i fi-l-Watan el-Arabi, 3*, 125. [Readings in Social Psychology in the Arab World].

Nation Master. (2013). Syria people stats. Retrieved from http://www.nationmaster.com/country-info/profiles/Syria/People

News. (2016, January) Healing invisible wounds of the Syrian conflict. *Bulletin of the World Health Organization*. Retrieved from http://www.who.int/bulletin/volumes/94/1/16-020116/en/

Norton, B. (2014, June). The shocking statistics behind Syria's humanitarian crisis. Retrieved from https://thinkprogress.org/the-shocking-statistics-behind-syrias-humanitarian-crisis-a0cbe79a63a2

OCHA. (2017). Syrian Arab Republic. *United Nation Office for the Coordination of Humanitarian Affairs*. Retrieved from https://www.unocha.org/syria

Quosh, C., Eloul, L., & Ajlani, R. (2013). Mental health of refugees and displaced persons in Syria and surrounding countries: A systematic review. *Intervention, 11*(3), 276–294.

Refaat, M. M., & Mohanna, K. (2013). Syrian refugees in Lebanon: Facts and solutions. *The Lancet, 382*, 763–764.

Sfeir, M. (2000, Summer/Fall). Focus: Women's centers. *AL-Raida, 17-18* (90–91), 35–38.

SCPR. (2015). Syria: Alienation and violence. Retrieved from https://www.unrwa.org/sites/default/files/alienation_and_violence_impact_of_the_syria_crisis_in_2014_eng.pdf

Sobelman, B. (2015, September 8). Which countries are taking in Syrian refugees? *Los Angeles Times*. Retrieved from http://www.latimes.com/world/europe/la-fg-migrants-scorecard-20150908-story.html

Uechi, J. (2016, November 14). The heroic mental health workers helping Syrian refugees recover from the trauma of war. *National Observer*. Retrieved from http://www.nationalobserver.com/2016/11/14/news/heroic-mental-health-workers-helping-syrian-refugees-recover-trauma-war

UN Data, A World of Information. (2017). Syria Arab Republic. Retrieved from http://data.un.org/CountryProfile.aspx?crName=Syrian%20Arab%20Republic

Ungar, M. (2008). Resilience across cultures. *British Journal of Social Work, 38*, 218–235.

Ungar, M. (2013). Resilience, trauma, context, and culture. *Trauma, Violence, & Abuse, 14*(3), 255–266.

UNHCR. (2015a). Culture, context and the mental health and psychosocial wellbeing of Syrians. Retrieved from http://www.unhcr.org/55f6b90f9.pdf

UNHCR. (2015b). Refugees from Syria: Lebanon. Retrieved from https://data.unhcr.org/syrianrefugees/download.php?id=8649

UNICEF. (n.d.). Syrian crisis. Retrieved from https://www.unicef.org/emergencies/syria/

Ward, C. (2016, August 15). This is hell: There are no winners in Aleppo. *CNN International Edition*. Retrieved from http://edition.cnn.com/2016/08/12/middleeast/clarissa-ward-unsc-syria/

Wong, P. T. P., & Wong, L. C. J. (Eds.). (2006). *Handbook of multicultural perspectives on stress and coping*. New York: Springer.

Wong, P. T. (Ed.) (2013). *The human quest for meaning: Theories, research, and applications*. New York: Routledge.

WHO. (2017. March). Helping Syrians cope with depression. *World Health Organization, Europe*. Retrieved from http://www.euro.who.int/en/media-centre/events/events/2017/04/world-health-day-2017-depression-lets-talk/news/news/2017/03/helping-syrians-cope-with-depression

World Vision. (2017). Syria refugee crisis: Facts you need to know. Retrieved from https://www.worldvision.org/refugees-news-stories/syria-refugee-crisis-war-facts

Chapter 8

Meaningfulworld Trauma Outreach and Prevention across Cultures

Utilizing the 7-Step Integrative Healing Model for Resilience and Meaning-Making

Ani Kalayjian and Daria Diakonova-Curtis

INTRODUCTION

The interest in and the volume of literature about the psychological aspects of resilience, coping, and survival related to trauma and disasters have increased dramatically in recent years. Without elaborating upon this history, suffice it to say that in the past quarter century, research, theory, and broader scholarship in the psychology, sociology, and ethics of disasters and mass trauma have increased in quality and quantity to such a degree that this body of work has a compelling argument to communicate to the rest of psychology and to allied disciplines.

More than one billion people have been affected by violence and disaster throughout the world. In *Disaster & Mass Trauma* (Kalayjian, 1995), the first author speculated that disasters will be occurring with more frequency and intensity and will be causing more casualties than ever before in our history. Additionally, these disasters will be impacting a larger number of people and places and will cost a larger sum of capital to recover (1995). This chapter will share the foundation and mission of the Association for Trauma Outreach and Prevention, Meaningfulworld, and its outreach around the globe with the goal to maximize scientific, cultural, spiritual, and other meaning-making practices to reduce suffering, minimize disability, nurture unity and oneness, and increase resiliency, meaning, and healing worldwide.

We will begin by describing the overall process of Meaningfulworld's global humanitarian outreach missions. Then we will explain the 7-Step Integrative Healing Model (aka the Bio-Psychosocial and Spiritual Model), developed and used by the first author around the globe (Kalayjian, 1995).

This is a healing program that offers a transformative training experience incorporating the mind-body-eco-spirit continuum to lead communities to mental health recovery.[1] Finally, we will select a few from over 100 humanitarian outreach relief missions conducted by our teams in over 45 countries, and share firsthand accounts from survivors of disasters in the past three decades, and lessons learned, so that the reader can understand the impact of trauma in regions such as Asia, the Caucuses, the Middle East, and North America. These accounts include survivors of three natural disasters (i.e., an earthquake in Armenia, Hurricane Andrew in Florida, and the tsunami in Sri Lanka), and three human-made disasters (i.e., the 9/11 terrorist attack in NYC, the Ottoman Turkish Genocide of Armenians, and the Israel-Palestine ongoing conflict). Our hope is to share ways for disaster mitigation, coping, resilience, and prevention. More specifically, forgiveness and meaning-making will be highlighted as common denominators to bringing peace on the personal, community, and larger global levels.

HUMANITARIAN OUTREACH RELIEF MISSIONS

No matter what country or time period, Meaningfulworld's missions follow the same basic protocol, with minor adjustments to take into account the particular country's setting, culture, and feasibility. The missions use a three-prong approach: (1) to provide healing to individuals affected by trauma through discussions with participants about the ways in which trauma impacts their physical, emotional, and spiritual well-being; (2) to conduct research and collect data on the current levels of trauma symptoms, forgiveness, and meaning-making; and (3) to begin conversations and establish goals for communities regarding larger policy changes.

Before each mission, the first author begins by networking and connecting with interested organizations (e.g., universities, nonprofits, agencies affiliated with the United Nations) in the countries that sustained a trauma due to a sizeable natural disaster, war, terrorist act, etc. These organizations then agree to host the Meaningfulworld team and invite the team to provide workshops, trainings, or seminars, or to participate in conferences on the topic of trauma, healing, and resilience. For countries where English is not the main or official language, prior to the team's departure, all materials (e.g., brochures, handouts, and questionnaires) undergo a rigorous translation process into the host language. Two teams go through a back-translation process, discuss linguistic discrepancies, and agree on the most accurate wording. During the missions, participants in the host countries are asked to complete anonymous and voluntary questionnaires, whereby research data are collected. Earlier missions utilized the UCLA posttraumatic stress disorder (PTSD) Reaction

Index (Frederick, 1985) due to its brevity and clarity to measure the level of PTSD, as well as additional questions to elicit changes in survivors' personal and social lives. More recent missions have updated to using Part Four of the Harvard Trauma Questionnaire (Mollica, McDonald, Massagli, & Silove, 2004), consisting of 16 traumatic stress symptoms derived from *Diagnostic and Statistical Manual of Mental Disorders* (DSM)-IV criteria, where participants respond to each question on a four-point Likert-type scale (1 = *not at all*; 4 = *extremely*). This instrument is now used because of its good psychometric properties and over 35 translations (Harvard Program in Refugee Trauma, 2016). Forgiveness is measured using a three-item forgiveness subscale of the Brief Multidimensional Measure of Religiousness/Spirituality (Fetzer Institute, 1999), and meaning in life has been systematically measured using the Meaning in Life Questionnaire (Steger et al., 2006), which is a ten-item self-report scale designed to assess presence of, and search for, meaning in life on a seven-point Likert-type scale (1 = *absolutely untrue*; 7 = *absolutely true*). The Institutional Review Board (IRB) approval is obtained prior to each mission. The last essential component of Meaningfulworld's outreach programs is continuous follow-up, either through continued correspondence with the connections made in the host countries or, in cases where the need is great, through follow-up missions several months—to up to several years—after the disaster.

At the basis for all programming is the 7-Step Integrative Healing Model, through which various aspects of traumatic exposure are assessed, identified, explored, processed, integrated, and released with a positive meaning discovered. The model was developed by the first author based on the idea that any trauma can cause physical, emotional, and spiritual symptoms leading to a variety of illnesses. Such illnesses include PTSD, major depression, generalized anxiety disorder, phobic disorders, somatic disorders, addictions, and aggression turned inward and outward, as well as physical illnesses, such as back pain, gastrointestinal diseases, cardiovascular diseases, etc. On a spiritual level, traumas cause spiritual vacuums and loss or disillusionment of faith. The list of psychological symptoms includes nightmares, night terrors, flashbacks, regression, loss of or increase in appetite, loss of hope, loss of status, and helplessness. Also, a trauma may not only affect the survivors themselves, but it often affects families over several generations (Kupelian, Kalayjian, & Kassabian, 1998).

The model builds from the integration of multiple theories, including psychodynamic (Freud, 1910), interpersonal (Sullivan, 1953), existential and humanistic (Frankl, 1962), electromagnetic field balancing (Dubro & Lapierre, 2002), forgiveness and reconciliation (Kalayjian & Paloutzian, 2010), learning theory, flower essences, essential oils, physical release (van der Kolk, 1993) and soul-surfing (Kalayjian, 2015), prayers, and meditation. Next, each step of the model is explained.

7-STEP INTEGRATIVE HEALING MODEL FOR TRANSFORMING TRAUMA INTO RESILIENCE AND MEANING

1. *Assess Levels of Distress:* Participants are brought together at a meeting place and given the questionnaires described above in order to assess their levels of trauma, forgiveness, and meaning at the outset.
2. *Encourage Expression of Feelings:* One at a time, each member of the group is encouraged to express his or her feelings in the "here and now," in relation to the trauma, paying close attention to the following feelings commonly associated with posttraumatic stress: fear, uncertainty of the future, flashbacks, avoidance behaviors, anger at the perpetrator(s), sleep disturbances and nightmares, somatic symptoms, substance abuse, and domestic abuse.
3. *Provide Empathy and Validation:* The members of the group validate each survivor's feelings by using statements such as "It makes sense to me" and share information about how other survivors from around the world have coped. Intentional therapeutic touch, such as holding a survivor's hand, is also used. In this step, it is emphasized that the survivor's feelings of grief, fear, and anger, as well as the joy of surviving, are all natural responses to the disaster and need to be expressed. When trauma ruptures an individual's connection with a group, an intolerable sense of isolation and helplessness may ensue. Providing validation and empathy in a group setting addresses these effects by reestablishing the mutual exchange between the individual and the group, and the individual and the universe. Forgiveness is introduced as a mechanism for creating inner peace in spite of unjust acts committed against the individual and in spite of ongoing denial of injustices. It is reinforced that when someone angers us, they control us. When we feel controlled, we feel helpless. Therefore, participants are encouraged to find ways to release and transform their anger and sublimate it, or use it in a therapeutic way.
4. *Promote Discovery and Expression of Meaning:* Survivors are asked, "What lessons, meaning, or positive associations did you discover as a result of this traumatic experience?" This question is based on Frankl's (1962) logotherapeutic principles, which stipulate that a positive meaning can be discovered in the worst catastrophe, as well as on the Buddhist assertion that it takes darkness to appreciate and reconnect with light. Again, each member of the group is invited to focus on the strengths and meanings that naturally arise from any disaster situation. Following are some of the positive lessons learned and expressed by survivors from around the world: interpersonal relationships are more important than material goods; it is important to release the resentments; working through

anger and practicing forgiveness is healthy; it is possible to take charge of one's own life; and it is important for nations to come together for the purpose of peace. Once forgiveness is practiced regularly, one feels freer to move into this phase of searching for a meaning and is more likely to recognize the positive growth that can occur after a hardship.

5. *Supply Didactic Information:* Practical tools and information are given on how to gradually return to one's daily routine by using the systematic desensitization process. The importance of preparation in advance of disasters is taught and elaboration is provided on specific ways to prepare. Handouts are given to teachers and prospective group leaders on how to conduct disaster evacuation drills and create safe and accessible exits from buildings, homes, factories, and other potential disaster sites. Booklets are distributed to parents and teachers on how to understand and respond to their children's nightmares, fears, and disruptive behaviors after wars. In addition, assessment tools are given to mental health professionals. Handouts are provided on grief as well as on how to take care of oneself as a caregiver and prevent secondary traumatization.
6. *Eco-Centered Processing:* Practical tools are shared to connect with Mother Earth. Discussions and exercises are conducted around environmental connections. Ways to care for one's environment are shared, starting with one's environment and expanding to the larger globe, being mindful of systems' perspectives, how we can impact our environment and how the environment in turn impacts us. Here, Mother Earth is presented as a way to heal oneself and others. Connecting with the sunrise and sunset, connecting with trees and flowers, and merging ourselves with the ocean or sea for cleansing our body and soul. Flower remedies and essences are also used to minimize the negative impact of trauma, and help us regain our sense of self.
7. *Soul-Surfing Exercises with Deep Breaths:* Breath is used as a natural medicine and a healing tool. Since no one can have full control over nature, others, or what happens outside of one's self, survivors are assisted in learning how to control the way that they respond to traumas. A demonstration is provided of exercises that bring a sense of harmony to the mind, body, and spirit by focused and guided attention, imagery, and suggestion. It is important to note that breathing exercises may be uniquely adapted to the beliefs or customs of the people being helped. This is the experiential section of the model. Survivors are given instructions on how to dissipate fear, uncertainty, and resentments from mind, body, and spirit. In addition, survivors are instructed on how to move toward self-empowerment as well as to engender gratitude, compassion, faith, strength, and forgiveness in response to disasters, mass trauma, and denial of the trauma. Forgiveness meditation exercises are

conducted. Forgiving oneself as a first step is introduced. We end with meditation, and then our signature Heart-to-Heart-Circle of Love and Gratitude.

The next sections provide case examples from several of Meaningfulworld's humanitarian outreach missions in various parts of the world. First, the disaster and the country's cultural context are briefly described, then the lessons learned from each experience by both the country's residents and the Meaningfulworld teams are provided.

EARTHQUAKE IN ARMENIA IN 1988

On Wednesday, December 7, 1988, at 11:41 am, a devastating earthquake shook the Republic of Armenia (Soviet Armenia then) for 40 seconds. This catastrophic destruction occurred in a zone where several plates of the earth's surface converge, which occasionally results in devastating consequences when movement occurs. Although the quake did not come as a total surprise to American and Soviet experts in the field, according to Purkaru of the Geological Institute in Frankfurt (Sullivan, 1988), due to gross unpreparedness and lack of emergency and evacuation plans, the community experienced the quake as a total nightmare. "If there was a horror movie like the quake, I would have not believed it," stated Gurgen, a 32-year-old survivor from Leninakan (now Guymri). "I have Chernobyl behind me, but I have never seen anything like this," Yevgeny I. Chazov, the Soviet health minister, told the government newspaper *Izvestia* after visiting the scene with fellow physicians (Fein, 1988).

Measuring 6.9 on the Richter scale, the quake occurred in an area highly vulnerable to seismic activity. It destroyed two-thirds of Leninakan, Armenia's second-largest city (now Guymri, population 300,000), and half of Kirovakan (population 150,000), obliterated Spitak—the epicenter (a town of about 30,000), and heavily damaged some 56 of 150 villages and towns in the northwest corner of Armenia, near the Turkish border. Initial reports of casualties spoke of "thousands," which soon became "tens of thousands" and went on to climb day by day to 130,000, even though the official death toll was announced as 25,000. In the end, about 500,000 people were handicapped, approximately 500,000 children orphaned, and over half-a-million, one-sixth of Armenia's population, left homeless. The exact number of human loss was very difficult to determine for several reasons: the uncertain number of refugees from the February 1988 massacres in the Azerbaijani cities of Baku and Sumgait, the poor record-keeping procedures, and, finally, the Soviet government's covert style of operations. Therefore, the above estimates, or any estimates from this incident, are only provisional.

The first author immediately organized an outreach team of mental health professionals. Participants in Armenia consisted of earthquake survivors in Yerevan, Leninakan, Kirovakan, Spitak, and five other villages. Six follow-up trips with 40 volunteer professionals continued as teams traveled back to Armenia annually, helping over 3,500 participants in total. Now in 2017, another team of four volunteers returned to Armenia to continue the outreach, now focusing on the Syrian refugees who have settled in Armenia.

Lessons from the Earthquake in Armenia

In Armenia, those survivors who were preoccupied with the "why's?" were uninterested in the scientific explanation of the earthquake. They countered with the questions, "Why us? What have we done to deserve this tragedy?" The question "Why was my child, my parent or my school affected?" implied that trauma and disaster happens to bad, sinful, or unworthy people, attributing a negative meaning to the disaster.

Survivors who attributed a positive meaning focused instead on the present moment and the meaningful experiences they had gained by helping or receiving help from one another and from the world. As one survivor stated, "Look at how the world has come to help us (the Armenians), the closed Soviet system has opened its curtains and doors, there is more communication, caring and sharing." According to the first author's research findings (reported elsewhere; see Kalayjian, 1991), 20 percent of the survivors in Armenia were convinced that they were indomitable, echoing the words of Nietzsche, who said, "What does not destroy me makes me stronger" (1889/1998, maxim #8, p. 5).

HURRICANE ANDREW IN SOUTHERN FLORIDA

A ferocious hurricane slammed into the Bahamas Sunday afternoon on August 23, 1992, with 120 MPH winds, heavy rain, and surging tide. Four people were reported dead as a result of the storm. The damage in Louisiana, in the northwest, while severe in places, did not compare with the panorama of ruin in southern Florida. Officials reported that the storm left over 250,000 Floridians homeless. As it ended its journey across the Gulf of Mexico, Hurricane Andrew struck as far west as the major populated areas around New Orleans, moving inland over sparsely populated marshlands, and doing its worst damage in small towns along Interstate 90 from Morgan City to New Iberia. The marshes and the swamps took the brunt of the storm in Louisiana, thus causing less human loss there. One man described the situation by saying, "I spent two years in Vietnam and I have not seen anything like this."

In some areas, extensive looting took place. Therefore, there were strictly enforced curfews and helicopters patrolling overhead, along with heaps of rubble, tent cities, and overturned cars.

After a five-day journey of destruction, in southern Florida alone, over 750,000 people evacuated, 100,000 residents of Dade County left the area (about 27 percent of the total population there), 180,000 people were left homeless, 15 people were dead in Florida (for a total of 52 hurricane-related deaths in Florida, Louisiana, and the Bahamas combined), 9 public schools were destroyed and 23 suffered heavy damage, causing $18 billion in estimated insurance loss, and over 4,082 complaints of fraud were filed against contractors, licensed and unlicensed.

Hurricane Andrew caught the community by surprise. Although some people were prepared—having bought batteries, groceries, bottled water, and plywood to board their windows—most people had not taken the threat of the storm seriously. The majority reacted by saying, "We've been hearing these threats every year; nothing is going to happen; I am sure we'll deal with this," and "Not me, I think this one will blow over us. This are hasn't been hit in a long time." These attitudes, borne of familiarity and disbelief, led to greater shock immediately following the hurricane. Many members of the community intended to ride out the storm no matter what anyone said. Although the author was not there during the initial disaster relief, she was able to follow the relief process by way of radio and television announcements. Many survivors stated that they felt that it was the closest they had ever come to death. The community reacted with overwhelming fear and uncertainty.

The humanitarian team consisting of several mental health professionals arrived in Miami less than six weeks after Hurricane Andrew. Our assessment, after using the questionnaires, revealed the following initial psychological impact: shock, fear, uncertainty, and nightmares. Three months later, a follow-up assessment revealed feelings of hopelessness, helplessness, anger, and fear. Six months later, follow-up revealed more uncertainty, frustration, abusive relationships, increased fear, despair, and apathy (Kalayjian, 1995).

At our six-month follow-up, we found people were still "walking wounded," suffering emotionally from posthurricane trauma. The author conducted research to indicate the levels of PTSD, using the Reaction Index Scale. Participants consisted of 127 individuals who had survived Hurricane Andrew. Respondents were selected from several shelters in southern Florida, as well as from South Miami Hospital in Homestead.

Follow-up at six months revealed that survivors were overwhelmed by feelings of uncertainty and despair. Some began to rely on substances to alleviate or numb their pain and suffering, sharing, "There is no use; I might as well get drunk." Others became short-tempered and irritable and began physically and verbally abusing one another. Domestic violence increased, as did spousal and child abuse. Responses such as, "She irritates me so much, I can't take it anymore," were common for situations of child abuse. Those who did not have a spouse or children reported abusing their pet dogs or cats. However, those survivors who had positive meaning associated with the disaster, about 22 percent of those interviewed, coped in a healthy manner.

Lessons from Hurricane Andrew, Florida

In southern Florida, over 30 percent of the survivors interviewed indicated that they had established positive meaning in their experiences of the hurricane. Responses such as "Although I felt vulnerable to Mother Nature, talking and working with friends and fellow employees I found the most meaningful" and "Helping friends and neighbors are most important in life" were indicative of the meanings attributed to their traumatic experiences.

Respondents who found meaning in their trauma measured much lower on the PTSD instrument. They also reached acceptance, which is an essential step in the move toward resolving an existential crisis. The acceptance stage, as defined by Kubler Ross (1969), is neither happy nor sad. It is devoid of feeling, a passive acquiescence to the tragic triad of human existence: pain, guilt, and death (Frankl, 1962).

Some survivors mentioned that it was their work ethic that helped them be resilient, some indicated that it was their faith in God, and others talked about karma or destiny. Those who did not take the hurricane warnings seriously learned the importance of preparation.

TERRORISM IN NYC ON 9/11/2001

On September 11, 2001, beginning at 9:10 am horror arrived in episodic bursts in the New York City metropolitan area. This shocking incident was signified by trembling floors, cracked windows, sharp eruptions, dark smoke, loud explosive sounds, dust, and debris. The unfathomable sight of helpless bodies falling and running from flames that engulfed the World Trade Center shocked the world. Safety was nowhere to be found. At 9:30 am, an American Airline Boeing 757, carrying 58 passengers and 6 crew members, slammed into the Pentagon, the first in the history of the 58-year-old building. This set off a state of emergency in the nation's capital. These two attacks constituted the most deadly terrorist attacks on US soil in American history. Approximately 3,000 individuals were killed and several thousand were injured. Thousands of individuals were involved in rescue efforts and the cleanup continued for a year after the disaster.

According to the United Nations (2002), terrorism is the act of destroying or injuring civilian lives or destroying or damaging civilian or government property without the expressly chartered permission of a specific government, thus acting independently of governments using a group's own belief in an attempt to affect some political change.

Because Meaningfulworld is based in New York, for the first six months after the attack, team members were on the ground to provide free training to mental health professionals working in the city, as well as those residing at Ground Zero, the site of the attacks. Our questionnaires were given to mental health professionals who voluntarily attended a conference on coping methods in the wake of 9/11. Consistent with previous findings, men reported less PTSD symptoms than women. The findings revealed no apparent additional traumatization or vicarious traumatization in mental health professionals and pastoral counselors since their levels of PTSD were moderately low. Additionally, we examined cultural and religious practices that participants utilized to assist them in coping and meaning-making.

Lessons from the 9/11 Terrorist Attacks

Finding meaning and rediscovering a new purpose in the aftermath of a mass trauma is a necessary condition for healing (Frankl, 1978). For Frankl, meaning can be found in any situation, even a traumatic one. According to Frankl, each life situation is unique and the meaning of each situation must be unique. He asserts that psychotherapists can never define what is or is not meaningful for individuals; meaning is often found in a self-transcendent encounter with the world (1978).

The majority of the respondents stated that they had found new meanings in their lives. Typical statements included the following: "In the midst of terrible tragedy and suffering, compassion emerged," "I learned that our lives are of tremendous importance to ourselves and to others: No more bickering for mundane things," "This is an opportunity to examine our prejudices and learn about other cultures," and "I learned to look more within." Others echoed the wisdom of Nietzsche: "If we have our own why in life, we shall get along with almost any how" (1889/1998, maxim #12, p. 6). The following statements exemplify those kinds of beliefs: "If I survived through this, I can survive through anything," "I am now stronger and more aware of important things in life," and "I am now profoundly committed to peace."

TSUNAMI IN SRI LANKA

The Meaningfulworld team traveled to Batticaloa, Sri Lanka, in February 2005 after the tsunami devastated the country the day after Christmas. Since the tsunami occurred, various international aid organizations were providing aid for basic needs such as purified water, food, clothes, school supplies, and medical supplies. In spite of receiving mixed reports regarding the emotional and psychological needs, thousands of people who lost their loved ones, homes, and livelihood had just begun receiving psychological first aid. When the Meaningfulworld team arrived, it began working with survivors residing in shelters, schools, and camps that had the greatest need (i.e., Navalady, Zahira, and the Central Methodist College). Administrative meetings with the minister of health, the presiding psychiatrist, and the NGO coordinator provided the team the opportunity for program evaluation and to form a framework for future initiatives and collaborative efforts. Group sessions and follow-ups were conducted with men, women, and children. Together the team and participants brainstormed and problem-solved about issues related to future placement, current housing, employment, recreational activities, and community building. In response, we facilitated swimming desensitization groups, women's craft groups, art therapy groups for children, tree planting in barren camp grounds, and a chicken coop project.

Additionally, the team conducted on the spot health checks. In one instance, team volunteers distributed toothbrushes and toothpaste to group participants, including children. A majority of the camp residents were observed to have poor dentition, and, when interviewed, reported having minimal access to even the most basic cleaning supplies (i.e., bathing soap). The importance of dental hygiene was reinforced, proper tooth brushing techniques were demonstrated, and instructions were repeated until all participants expressed verbal understanding and offered an adequate return demonstration.

Our Meaningfulworld team observed that almost all survivors expressed fear: fear of the sea, fear of going back to their homes, and fear of the tsunami reoccurring. Shock and disbelief were expressed consistently. "I just could not believe that the sea was so black, the wave was so high, and I felt trapped," exemplified their feelings. As a result, there was a tremendous feeling of helplessness expressed. Guilt was expressed by almost 92 percent of participants, including guilt of surviving and guilt of not doing enough to save their children, spouses, or relatives. Therefore, most survivors were haunted by repetitive nightmares of hands of their loved ones waving in the air as the waves were taking their loved ones away to the sea of black water as they were calling out their names "father, help me" or "mother, help me please." Flashbacks, avoidance behaviors, and sleep disturbances were also expressed.

The team provided empathy and validation to the survivors in groups as well as individually. It was reinforced that they did the best they could in circumstances above and beyond their control. Many team members were sad and overwhelmed as they heard survivors, one after the other, tell stories of courage, creativity, survival, and loss. People expressed multiple losses that they could not endure. One man told our group that 48 members of his clan had died.

He was one of the two who survived. Often, the team members were perplexed as to how to provide empathy when so much loss is expressed. When trauma ruptures the individual's connection with the group, a strong sense of isolation, disarray and helplessness occurs. Providing validation and empathy in such a group helped these survivors reestablish the mutual exchange between the individual and the group, guiding them to a new and positive meaning.

Survivors were eager to tell their stories, as they expressed feelings of wanting to feel normal again. When encouraged to express lessons they learned and meanings associated with this devastation, some expressed that they learned to be united, with Buddhists, Hindus, Christians, and Muslims living collaboratively and as brothers. Many expressed that they now wanted to spend more time with their family and relatives, rather than pay attention to material goods. Others expressed that they learned to not rely on government but rather to rely on self and the spirit of unity.

There was one predominant repeated response to answer the question of why the tsunami happened: over 20 years of conflict between Tamil and Sinhalese races, ethnic strife, and civil war. Therefore, the lesson for some was to unite and to appreciate one another. Since the tsunami did not discriminate between Tamil and Sinhalese in death, they wanted to learn how to collaborate and unite in life. Of course, as one 25-year-old Christian Tamil man stated, "This unity concept is in thought only and it needs a lot to have it put in practice." Others defined the tsunami as the giant monster of the sea. Parents used this phrase to deter their unruly children: "Behave, or else the Giant (Monster) will come from the sea." Almost all described the tsunami as a "giant monster." The team members shared scientific information regarding how and why tsunamis are formed in the didactic part of our 7-Step Model. Survivors listened with great interest and with a thirst for more. Although afterward some parents expressed confusion as to what phrases to use to discipline their unruly children, we hope that they learned that provoking fear is not healthy for child development or behavior modification.

Overall, survivors were assisted in asking empowering questions rather than victimizing ones such as "Why me? Why us?" If one asks why it happened, one is transformed to the past, to the tsunami, where feelings of fear, victimization, and guilt prevail. When one asks the question "What can I do about it now?" one remains in the here and now, and remains with curiosity to find ways of coping, and to be in control of the present.

Lessons from the Tsunami in Sri Lanka

Our six-month follow up humanitarian mission revealed tremendous community healing. The following were participants' expressions that exemplify their empowerment and health: "This morning I had nothing to live for, I had no hope, but now, after your healing group, I feel so alive and so happy" and "If you can come all the way from America to help us, we can find ways to help ourselves too." Other community building and sustainable activities were offered to the survivors, including swimming classes for women, arts and crafts, men's groups, occupational therapy, chicken coup business, and sowing for women.

OTTOMAN TURKISH GENOCIDE OF ARMENIANS

Throughout the twentieth century, genocide has claimed many lives across the world. Government genocidal policies alone have resulted in over 210 million deaths—80 percent of which were civilian deaths, representing nearly four times the number of individuals killed in combat during international and domestic wars during the same period. Approximately a century ago, under the cover of World War I, Turkish armed forces systematically moved to exterminate Turkey's Armenian population.

Our research (Kalayjian, Moore, Aberson, & Kim, 2010) in the United States with Armenian Americans focused on the level of PTSD and the extent of physical symptomatology, as well as how Armenian survivors coped with the genocide, what gave them the strength to cope, and the meanings they associated with the trauma. We gathered survival accounts from 16 Armenian Americans (born before 1917) who had witnessed the Ottoman Turkish genocide of the Armenians, and other Christian minorities.

The research findings indicated that although these survivors had adjusted and prospered in the American life, some levels of PTSD persisted. Those who have found a positive meaning in their experiences have coped better and their level of PTSD and physical symptomatology was lower. This research was a follow-up to another study (Kalayjian, Shahinian, Gergerian, & Saraydarian, 1996) in which Armenian survivors were interviewed to explore their coping styles and patterns eight decades after the genocide. The study revealed that against a background of losses and atrocities beyond the realm of usual life experience, these aged survivors reflected a sense of accomplishment, tempered with anger about the perpetrators' denial (i.e., the Turkish government denial), which is the last stage of genocide.

Furthermore, this denial of the genocide has affected not only its survivors, but the entire community of Armenians in the world, and in fact, the work of Meaningfulworld itself. In 1999, the first author traveled to Istanbul, Turkey, to make a presentation on our published research on coping with the Ottoman Turkish genocide, An Exploration of the Experience of Armenian Survivors, at the Psychotraumatology and Human Rights conference of the International Society for Traumatic Stress Studies.

Being fully cognizant of the Turkish government's denial propaganda, I (this chapter's first author) entitled my abstract "Mass Human-Rights Violations: Resilience vs. Resignation." At the conference, the keynote speakers talked freely regarding the host country's more recent human rights violations against the Kurds. I felt encouraged by this and decided to distribute my original abstract on the genocide against Armenians. At this point, the threats began. First, my life was threatened by the Turkish National Intelligence Organization, to whom I responded with skepticism that I did not believe that anyone would dare kill me in front of the 600+ scholars from 48 countries who were present at the conference. The following day, I was threatened to be tortured if I talked about the genocide. On the third day, the abstracts of my presentation were snatched from my hands. On the last day of the conference, the organizers called me and the then British president of the European Association for Traumatic Stress Studies for a private meeting in Istanbul. At this meeting, I was taken to the basement, presented with an ultimatum: I must either sign the letter stating that I would agree to refrain from talking about the genocide of the Armenians or forcibly leave the conference escorted by the Turkish police (who were waiting at the door). Although I reminded the police and the president that they were attending a human rights conference and that they were in fact violating my human rights as a presenter, it was to no avail. They reiterated that because of the political situation, they were obliged to "protect the conference organizers from the government." After a difficult deliberation, I chose to sign the letter so that I would not lose the opportunity to address the conference. The audiovisual department helped me revise my transparencies by covering the controversial words with a special black marker.

When I began delivering my lecture and the first transparency was projected, I apologized for the black lines without looking at the screen, and then noticed that many of my colleagues had smirks on their faces. The Turkish audience was enraged. When I turned around to look at the screen, I saw that the censored words were showing through the black marks. I then said spontaneously, "Whoops, the light is so bright it is coming through. I guess we cannot hide it any longer." Tension grew in the audience. At that point, I told the audiovisual technician to turn off the projector, and reinforced that I was there to focus on transcending hatred and embracing forgiveness through dialogues. I focused on the importance of empowerment and moving on to the next phase of dialogue, education, and collaboration. I asserted that the admission of genocide is a very difficult task to take on, especially when children of the perpetrators have been misinformed for almost a century. I then asked the scientific community to assist the Turkish community to accept responsibility and apologize for the wrongs of their ancestors. They too need to forgive their ancestors in order to overcome denial and accept responsibility. After the lecture, numerous international colleagues came forward and hugged and congratulated me for my courage and for the depth of my message. I cried in their arms out of relief, happiness for being alive, and for having delivered that important message, and although I endured a lot of trauma, the outcome was extremely positive and enlightening for many.

Out of the research and personal experience in Turkey, and in an effort to transform conflictual relationships between Turkish and Armenian Americans, the author began a decade of dialogue groups. The more than 102-year-old conflict that exists between Armenians and Turks is based upon their differing perceptions of the killing of over 1.5 million Armenians under Ottoman rule between 1915 and 1923.

To Armenians, as well as to the majority of the international community, the mass killings constitute genocide, though the official position of the Turkish governments throughout the 102 years is one of total denial and revisionism. We organized a series of dialogue groups, community gatherings, open forums, and psycho-educational programs between the years of 2000 and 2010 to bring together members of both groups for dialogue and to work on transforming the generational transmission of trauma.

In order to move both groups in the direction of intercommunication and reconciliation, Turkish and Armenian facilitators were invited to implement our 7-Step Model with the goal of educating and generating empathy among people with disparate viewpoints. The 7-Step Model was also used with Armenian participants in processing traumatic memories and experiences while helping them to discover positive meanings in spite of the legacy of cultural dislocation and emotional trauma and the loss of nationhood.

Lessons from the Armenian-Turkish Dialogue

Cultural and religious practices were explored, including the use of spiritual healers. Assumptions were examined with regard to a sentiment of the "other" as the enemy, which is exacerbated by religious and national resentment, and misguided premises.

Recommendations resulting from the dialogues within and between groups stressed the importance of communication and education as key components of the process of reconciliation. Reciprocal compassion was called for, as well as mutual appreciation for one another's differences. As Maya Angelou states in her poem *On the Pulse of Morning*, "History, despite its wrenching pain, cannot be unlived, but if faced with courage, it need not be lived again" (1993).

Both parties, Armenian and Turkish second and third generations, had expressed the generational transmission of trauma. Among the Armenian

American members, the generational legacy was of extreme sadness, which could turn into anger at any moment of smallest challenge. The Turkish Americans, growing up in a denialist country, were oblivious to the Genocide, felt extremely humiliated and wanted to reject it, identifying and fearing their government, and often withdrew from the dialogue groups.

THE ISRAEL-PALESTINE ONGOING CONFLICT

The first author began working on the Israel-Palestine conflict in 1990, with several humanitarian missions having been conducted in the region throughout the last decades. One of the missions was organized with the help and invitation of the first author's friend, Prof. Khawla Abu-Baker, who was the only professor of Palestinian descent at her Israeli university in a small town on the Mediterranean Sea. Prof. Khawla Abu-Baker's home was directly on the sea, and three generations of her grandparents have lived in the same town.

Although it seemed like any other place—people shopping, going to and from school, or pushing their babies in a stroller—I felt an ever-present tension in the hot air that weighed heavily on the inhabitants of the town like the walls erected between Israel and Palestine. The Palestinian houses along the beach were dilapidated, and when I inquired why, my colleague told me it was because the Israeli government prohibits any renovation of "Arab homes." This is a political tactic adopted in many regions of Israel to force Palestinian families to relocate out of desperation and frustration, so the government can then take over and place families of European- or Russian-Jewish descent in the houses. We also observed that there were only 17 psychiatrists, and a handful of psychologists, in the West Bank region for close to 2 million Palestinians, while Israel had more than 1,000 psychiatrists and just as many psychologists for about 6 million Israeli Jews.

We conducted several workshops at Camp Faraa, a camp of Palestinian residents in the Israeli region, and presented the 7-Step Integrative Healing Model. Most of the participants were university students. Our healing work was very much needed after a night of traumatic experience. We were all violently woken up from our sleep at around 2 am, and a young Palestinian man was dragged out of his bed with his mother screaming and crying. The family would not know where their son was taken for at least three weeks. The major trauma discussed was the night's Israeli invasion of the camp with a bomb sound, and people were not sure what to do and kept hiding under beds. Horizontal Violence was also a topic of discussion, as participants reported that violence is often exhibited in factionalism among political groups, namely Fateh and Hammas, in the form of domestic violence and corporal punishment.

Lessons from the Israel-Palestine Conflict

Although a deep transformation took place after our workshop with Israelis and Palestinians utilizing the 7-step Integrative Healing Model in which participants began to hug one another instead of fighting, I (first author) know that it is only a drop in the ocean. We need to continue healing workshops daily in order to be able to reach out to everyone.

I (first author) learned the following: both nations see themselves as victims, acting from their fears, both are engaging in continued violence and are unable to empathize with each other; Israel continues discriminatory practices against Palestinians such as blockading Gaza, killing Palestinian leaders, forcefully confiscating Palestinian lands, and committing mass violations against human rights, while Palestinians in an attempt to defend themselves are also practicing violence via suicide bombing (which has not happened for several years) and launching rockets from Gaza. Both nations have a siege mentality, and both nations distrust each other and fear one another. Israel comes from a traumatized history of thousands of years, encompassing events such as expulsion from Egypt and the Holocaust. Although these atrocities have nothing to do with Palestine, somehow Israeli fear and trauma are consciously or unconsciously being projected onto Palestinians. Palestinians are also alone within their own Arab World and the larger world, seeing themselves as victims of Israeli oppression, Arab oppositions, and an indifferent world.

CONCLUSION

Frankl (1978) calls for developing a wider horizon, both within ourselves and out in the world, celebrating the will and choosing one's freedom of response. In practice, this means learning how to walk the walk, and how to be role models providing empathy and encouraging discovery of a new meaning for building a sustainable global community. Many of the survivors expressed their resilience in words such as the following: "I would not have chosen to go through the trauma, but now that I did I am glad, otherwise I would not have learned what I know today." They were able to integrate the past experience of trauma and shattered self with a new, stronger, and more resilient narrative of themselves.

Survivors mentioned the following factors facilitating their resilience, coping, and meaning-making post disasters in order of importance:

1. Family Support: Feeling part of a family, a unit, and enjoying supportive, empathic and compassionate relations.

2. Work Ethic: Having a grounded and solid work ethic, as well as responsibility for one's life choices and circumstances, thus taking ownership of their choices and the outcomes of those choices.
3. Participation in the larger community development: They reported their need to help others and to be of service gives them a sense of strength, recognition and importance. It seems to contribute to resilience and healing.
4. Sense of purpose and meaning: Having a very clear mission in life.

The importance of meaning in disasters has been acknowledged since the beginning of disaster research. On the one hand it, was found to be a fundamental part of suffering in disasters. On the other hand, meaning, even in the worst situations such as concentration camps, could enhance survival (Frankl, 1978). We guide survivors to be cautious of adopting maladaptive meaning as expressed in the following words: "The world shattered. There was no justice in it anymore." New, discovered meanings need to be positive values that we learn to reinforce and cultivate in ourselves, indicating that meanings are higher-level constructs of the human mind which include positive symbols of morality, values, dignity, identity, and beliefs about the universe.

NOTE

1. www.meaningfulworld.com

REFERENCES

Angelou, M. (1993). *On the pulse of morning.* Poem performed at the first inauguration of President Bill Clinton on January 20, 1993. Retrieved from http://www.nytimes.com/1993/01/21/us/the-inauguration-maya-angelou-on-the-pulse-of-morning.html

Dubro, P. P., & Lapierre, D. P. (2002). *Elegant empowerment: Evolution of consciousness.* Boca Raton, FL: Platinum Publishing House.

Fein, E. (1988, December 9). Toll put in tens of thousands from quake in Soviet Armenia. *New York Times.*

Fetzer Institute. (1999). *Multidimensional measurement of religiousness/spirituality for use in health research: A report of the Fetzer Institute/National Institute on Aging Working Group.* Kalamazoo, MI: Author.

Frankl, V. (1962). *Man's search for meaning: An introduction to logotherapy.* Boston: Beacon Press. (Original work published in 1946)

Frankl, V. (1978). Unheard cry for meaning. *Psychotherapy & Humanism.* New York: Simon & Schuster.

Frederick, C. J. (1985). Selected foci in the spectrum of posttraumatic stress disorders. In J. Laube & S. A. Murphy (Eds.), *Perspectives on disaster recovery* (pp. 110–130). East Norwalk: Appleton-Century- Crofts.

Freud, S. (1910). The origin and development of psychoanalysis. *The American Journal of Psychology, 21*(2), 181–218.

Harvard Program in Refugee Trauma. (2016). Studies. Retrieved from http://hprt-cambridge.org/research/studies/

Kalayjian, A. (1991, June). *Meaning in trauma: Impact of the earthquake in Soviet Armenia.* Paper presented at the VIII World Congress of Logotherapy, San Jose, CA.

Kalayjian, A. (1995). *Disaster & mass trauma: Global perspectives in post disaster mental health management.* Long Beach, NJ: Vista Publishing.

Kalayjian, A. (2015). 7-step integrative healing model: Biopsychosocial and eco-spiritual model for healing, transforming disputes, conflict transformation, peace building, and forgiveness. Retrieved from www.meaningfulword.com

Kalayjian, A., & Paloutzian, R. (2010). *Forgiveness & reconciliation: Psychological pathways to conflict transformation and peace building.* New York: Springer Publishing.

Kalayjian, A., Moore, N., Aberson, C., & Kim, S. (2010). Exploring long-term impact of mass trauma on physical health, coping, and meaning-making: Exploration of the Ottoman Turkish Genocide of the Armenians. In A. Kalayjian & E. Dominique (Eds.), *Mass trauma and emotional healing around the world* (pp. 287–306). New York: Praeger, ABC-CLIO, LLC.

Kalayjian, A., Shahinian, S. P., Gergerian, E. L., & Saraydarian, L. (1996). Coping with Ottoman Turkish Genocide: An exploration of the experience of Armenian survivors. *Journal of Traumatic Stress, 9*(1), 87–97.

Kubler Ross, E. (1969). *On death and dying.* New York: Macmillan Company.

Kupelian, D., Kalayjian, A. S., & Kassabian, A. (1998). The Turkish genocide of the Armenians: Continuing effects on survivors and their families eight decades after massive trauma. In Y. Danieli (Ed.), *Multigenerational transmission of trauma: An international handbook* (pp.192–210). New York: Plenum Publishing.

Mollica, R. F., McDonald, L. S., Massagli, M. P., & Silove, D. M. (2004). *Measuring trauma, measuring torture: Instructions and guidance on the utilization of the Harvard Program in Refugee Trauma's versions of the Hopkins Symptom Checklist-25 (HSCL-25) & the Harvard Trauma Questionnaire (HTQ).* Cambridge: Harvard Program in Refugee Trauma.

Nietzsche, F. (1998). *Twilight of the idols, or how to philosophize with a hammer* (D. Large, Trans.). New York: Oxford University Press. (Original work published 1889)

Steger, M. F. (2016). The meaning in life questionnaire. Retrieved from http://www.michaelfsteger.com/?page_id=13

Sullivan, G. (1988, December 9). Pressing rock masses mark center quake. *The New York Times.*

Sullivan, H. S. (1953). *The interpersonal theory of psychiatry.* New York: W. W. Norton.

United Nations. (2002). *United Nations General Assembly: Report of the Ad Hoc Committee established by General Assembly resolution 51/210 of 17 December 1996, Sixth session.* Retrieved from http://www.un.org/documents/ga/docs/57/a5737.pdf

Van Der Kolk, B. A., & Saporta, L. (1993). Biological response to psychic trauma. In J. P. Wilson & B. Raphael (Eds.), *International handbook of traumatic stress syndromes* (pp. 25–33). New York: Plenum Press.

Chapter 9

Resilience and Recovery in Natural Disasters and Epidemics

Comparisons, Challenges, and Lessons Learned from Train-the-Trainer Projects

Judy Kuriansky, Alexandra Margevich, Wismick Jean-Charles, and Russell Daisey

INTRODUCTION

Incidences of natural disasters have been prevalent in present times, generating increased interest in the impact and required response to these tragic phenomena. Recent events include those in the United States and the Caribbean Islands (Hurricanes Katrina, Harvey, Maria, Irma, and Superstorm Sandy), Haiti (the earthquake in 2010 and Hurricane Matthew in 2016), and Asia and Japan (the tsunamis of 2004 and 2011). All of these have claimed hundreds of thousands of lives and caused millions of dollars in damage and destruction to business, livelihood, infrastructure, and social cohesion.

Epidemics have also plagued the world population. The Ebola epidemic, hitting hardest in West African countries of Sierra Leone, Liberia, and Guinea, but also with some scattered cases in the Western world, caused over 11,000 deaths with over 28,000 cases (WHO, 2016a). With regard to the devastating outbreak of the Zika virus, causing birth defects, 61 countries and territories have reported continuing mosquito-borne transmission (WHO, 2016b).

Other lesser widespread epidemics in recent times include the Chikungunya virus disease, H1N1 virus, West Nile Virus, and Middle East Respiratory Syndrome coronavirus (MERS-CoV). The Severe Acute Respiratory Syndrome (SARS) devastated parts of China and Toronto and other regions, and the HIV/AIDS virus notoriously claimed thousands of lives until medications brought it under control only in recent years.

The prevalence of such disasters has escalated the need for approaches to respond to such events, especially in low-resource nations with inadequate health infrastructure. Additionally, certain issues have become salient in planning such responses, both to be adequately responsive and to be sustainable.

One such response is the application of a train-the-trainers (TTT) model, whereby experts enlist a cohort of people who can be trained in various supportive techniques, who can then administer them to others (e.g., a group of community people) in order continue the perpetuation and cascading of the helpful interventions.

The TTT programs have been implemented globally in post-disaster contexts like the 2004 tsunami in Asia and the 2010 earthquake in Haiti (Becker, 2006, 2007; James & Noel, 2013; James et al., 2012; McCabe et al., 2012; Kuriansky, Zinsou, Arunagiri, et al., 2015). These programs have similarly been implemented to address public health issues created by the spread of communicable diseases, namely HIV/AIDS (Booth-Kewley et al., 2001; Jones, Weiss, & Chitalu, 2015; Tobias et al., 2012; Weiss et al., 2014; Williams et al., 2014; Yarber et al., 2015; Yu et al., 2014). While limited, the body of research evaluating such community-based psychosocial support interventions collectively demonstrates their efficacy, sustainability, and scalability in benefiting both recipients of support and helpers themselves. Indeed, not only are trained lay mental health workers empowered in their ability to address the needs of their community through effective psychosocial care techniques, but they also experience healing indirectly through their interventions.

When applied in a large community population, this stepped training model is most useful and effective when it includes techniques that are easily learned and easily applied, with cultural acceptability (Kuriansky, Polizer, & Zinsou, 2016; Kuriansky, Zinsou, Arunagiri, et al., 2015)

This chapter describes the TTT model applied after natural disasters and also an epidemic. The discussion includes some allied trainings that are deemed useful to include in such a review as this chapter, even though they were applied under different circumstances, as they elucidate other applications of the model and further encourage empirical research. The chapter also presents preliminary outcomes based on trainee self-reports, through pre-post-structured questions as well as anecdotal reports.

RESILIENCE

Much is said about the resilience of individuals and communities after disaster, with statistics supporting this view that point to the low rates of post-traumatic syndrome (U.S. Department of Veterans Affairs National Center for PTSD, 2010). However, it must be noted that other studies point to the lingering emotional aftereffects of traumatic situations and natural disasters (e.g., Furr et al., 2010; Neria, Nandi, & Galea, 2008), thus highlighting that, given the extent of losses of life and livelihood, attention must be paid to the importance of a long-term view of resilience and ongoing attention to emotional sequealae of natural disaster or epidemics.

Research has also established the principle of posttraumatic growth (PTG) in the wake of disasters (Calhoun & Tedeschi, 1998, 2004; Tedeschi & Calhoun, 2004a, 2004b). Preliminary results of surveys reported in this chapter, based on self-reports of trainees in a training model, indeed reveal some positive outcomes. However, it is suggested that underlying emotional reactions may still be present and should be noted, in order to maintain the mental health and well-being of helpers.

Resilience is generally defined as "the process of adapting well in the face of adversity, trauma, tragedy, threats or even significant sources of stress" (American Psychological Association, 2014). A useful definition is: learning from the past, being firmly grounded in the present, and seeing ourselves in the future (Nemeth & Oliver, 2017)

TWO INSTRUMENTS THAT UNDERSCORE THE IMPORTANCE OF THIS APPROACH

The TTT projects and evaluations are relevant in the context of two global instruments that have recently been adopted by the governments of the world. Both instruments support the value of these trainings targeted at improving the mental health and well-being of affected populations.

The first is the United Nations 2030 Agenda for Sustainable Development that was agreed upon by the member governments of the United Nations (UN) in 2015 to set the global agenda for the years 2015–2030 (UNDESA, n.d., 2015). This instrument includes—for the first time in such a global agreement—the importance of mental health and well-being, which appears in the text in three places. Paragraph 7 of the Preamble envisions a world "where physical, mental, and social well-being are assured." The title of Sustainable Development Goal (SDG) 3 states: "Ensure healthy lives and promote well-being for all," and Target 3.4 states "By 2030, ... promote mental health and well-being." Additionally, paragraph 26 of the introduction states: "To promote physical and mental health and well-being, and to extend life expectancy for all, we must achieve universal health coverage and access to quality health care." The first author was instrumental in insuring this inclusion, in collaboration with the Ambassador of Palau to the UN (Kuriansky, 2016).

The second is the Sendai Framework for Disaster Risk Reduction, agreed to by governments at the Third World Conference for Disaster Risk Reduction in Sendai Japan in May 2015, which outlines agreements made by the world governments regarding disaster risk reduction (UNISDR, 2015a). Paragraph 33 (o) states the commitment: "To enhance recovery schemes to provide psychosocial support and mental health services for all people in need."

The interventions using the TTT model described here represent a means of implementation and monitoring of the above commitments. The achievement of sustainable development after a natural disaster or an epidemic requires ensuring and reinforcing the psychosocial resilience and self-efficacy of citizens and the community.

While it is well known that after a disaster there is a considerable need for psychosocial support, often just a few individuals and qualified personnel are available to provide this service. Empirical and clinical evidence increasingly reveals the value of enlisting community volunteers even without formal training to deliver simple support using preliminary techniques that not only help survivors recover but further have a positive impact on the helpers themselves.

This chapter covers clinical observations and preliminary assessments of the impact on groups of volunteers who participated in various workshops based on the TTT model, giving them skills to support others in crisis after natural disasters. The trainings consist of elementary techniques of support, stress reduction and relief, and creative arts activities to achieve recovery, resilience, and empowerment.

Results suggest the positive outcome of such trainings on dimensions including increased self-esteem and motivation for further skills building. Such trainings and mobilizations of volunteer resources are a valuable asset to build human capital especially in the context of developing countries with limited resources.

To the authors' knowledge, research is not available comparing the psychological sequelae and approaches of natural disasters and epidemics. However, an article by the first author does reflect on comparison between nature-induced versus human-induced environmental trauma (Kuriansky, 2013e).

The present chapter presents observations about these two events (i.e., natural disaster and epidemics) based on the authors' on-the-ground experiences, as well as some very preliminary research that leads to suggestions about similarities between the two events, although it is certainly acknowledged that some differences also occur in the nature of the two events and in the necessary interventions and that any suggestions must be substantiated by empirical research.

Epidemics are differentiated from natural disasters, whereby the latter results from a physical or geological force of nature and the former is caused by a biological agent. Natural disasters and epidemics have been shown to be linked, since in some situations epidemics follow natural disasters, due to environmental changes, population displacement, poor sanitation, and pathogens facilitating incidence and transmission (Kouadio et al., 2012; Spiegel et al., 2007). Consequently, for example, in the case of the 2017 mudslides in Sierra Leone as well as Hurricane Harvey in Texas and the Cajun coast of the United States (occurring at the time of this writing), advocates and media reports were on the alert for potential infectious diseases that might emerge from the extensive contaminated water.

The points addressed in this chapter include:

1. Events of natural disasters have similarities to that of epidemics.
2. A model of a stepped pyramid TTT program can be applied in both situations, with suggestions of positive outcome in terms of the trainer's personal and professional growth.
3. Psychosocial resilience is evident after such tragic events, but policies and programs must address and provide long-term recovery from psychosocial sequelae.

EVENTS ADDRESSED

The events addressed in this chapter all derive from on-the-ground firsthand experience during and after natural disasters and epidemics worldwide. The observations and discussions have also been presented by the authors in many international conferences (Jean-Charles, 2015; Jean-Charles, Kuriansky, & Margevich, 2016; Kuriansky, 2005, 2010d, 2012a, 2014, 2015, 2017a, 2017b, 2017c, 2017d; Kuriansky & Daisey, 2011, n.d.; Kuriansky & Margevich, 2017a, 2017b; Kuriansky & Nemeth, 2016; Kuriansky, Jean-Charles, & Margevich, 2017; Kuriansky, Lytle, & Chiu, 2011; Kuriansky, Polizer, & Jean-Charles, 2015; Kuriansky, Jean-Charles, Margevich, & Daisey, 2017; Kuriansky, Jean-Charles, Nemeth, & Margevich, 2017; Kuriansky, Jean-Charles, Margevich, & Nemeth, 2017; Margevich, Kuriansky, & Jean-Charles, 2017a, 2017b).

FOCUS ON CHILDREN

Interest in the resilience of children is considerable (Goldstein & Brooks, 2005; Masten, 2011; Wir, 2017). Since the trainings addressed in this chapter are meant to ultimately benefit children, it is relevant to emphasize the importance of interventions for children in natural disasters and epidemics. Children are at risk and especially suffer when it comes to such traumatic events affecting a community. The importance of providing psychosocial assistance to children to aid in their recovery from traumas of wide-ranging nature has been well established (Qian, Gao, Wu, et al., 2011; Silverman & La Greca, 2002). Reports have documented the necessity to address both immediate and long-term effects, given the long-lasting impact of traumas on children (Liu, Wang, Shi, et al., 2011).

While less research has been done on the effects on children of contagious diseases compared to the amount of research available about natural or large-scale human-made disasters, common aftereffects are apparent in the two situations from other studies and from the chapter authors' vast experiences in both circumstances (Thienkrua, Cardozo, Chakkraband, et al., 2006; Koller, Nicholas, Goldie, et al., 2004). Traditionally, interventions for children have centered on simple supervised play experiences in child-friendly spaces (UNICEF, n.d.; World Vision, 2016).

The model provided in the TTT programs described in this chapter is consistent with the basic emotional needs of children in crisis situations, ranging from safety to security. While children's needs are widely recognized, much research still needs to be done to establish best practices/gold standards for intervention with children in such emergencies.

OVERVIEW OF THE TTT TECHNIQUES ADDRESSING CHILDREN'S NEEDS

The TTT model used by the authors and colleagues is intended to build resilience and empowerment specifically for children facing serious stress from a trauma or health emergency (Kuriansky, Polizer, & Zinsou, 2016). As was mentioned, in this stepped TTT model, experts train paraprofessionals and volunteers who can then deliver the training to children and train others, thus cascading the training. The model is based on sound psychological constructs underlying the techniques. These have been applied in many diverse settings (Kuriansky, 2007, 2008; Kuriansky & Berry, 2011a, 2011b), with cultural adaptation. The psychosocial constructs reflect important issues in the process of recovery, resilience, and empowerment in immediate and follow-up stages of trauma, targeted to the following: securing safety (safe space), boosting strength (self-efficacy and self-esteem), transforming trauma/grief into empowerment and PTG, and creating connection (facilitating family and community engagement and cohesion). The specific psycho-educational techniques and cultural arts experiences involve simple, easily learned practical activities that follow established guidelines.

The specific exercises, and advice for helping children recover from disaster, have been developed and applied over many years and in varied circumstances and cultures and adapted for specific situations and cultural contexts. These include interventions after various natural disasters as well as those from the Global Kids Connect Project (GKCP) designed by the first author, that have been used to train trainers and been applied with youth post-disaster in Haiti, over many years, as well as in China, Japan, and Sri Lanka, and with youth in poverty conditions in African countries (Jean-Charles, 2011a, 2011b; Kuriansky, 2008, 2010a, 2010b, 2010c, 2011a, 2012b, 2013a, 2013b, 2013c, 2103d; Kuriansky & Berry, 2011a, 2011b; Kuriansky & Jean-Charles, 2012; Kuriansky & Nemeth, 2013; Kuriansky, Wu, Bao, et al., 2015; Kuriansky, Zinsou, & Arunagiri, et al., 2015). It also includes exercises applied by IsraAID (2014) in its many interventions worldwide. The exercises in the model are further consistent with the approach to psychosocial support identified by UNICEF (UNICEF & UNISDR, 2011) and the three approaches of psychological first aid in response to Ebola-affected communities, that is, Listen, Look, and Link (Ministry of Social Welfare, Gender and Children's Affairs, 2014; Mohdin, 2014; WHO, 2014).

The resulting training and workshop is intended to be implemented in a group setting with community individuals as trainees, who are identified as potential leaders motivated and capable to implement the workshop for children, even if they have minimal training in psychological techniques. It is further meant to be consistent with the principles of (1) psychosocial support (UNICEF, 2013, n.d.; WHO, 2012), (2) psychological first aid, as identified in the three Ls (Look, Listen and Link) (WHO, 2014), and (3) layers in the intervention pyramid identified by the Inter-Agency Standing Committee (IASC) guidelines for mental health and psychosocial support in emergency settings (IASC Working Group, 2007; Kuriansky, 2011b), for example layer i., basic support and security and layer ii., community and family support, for a wide variety of community groups, (not to either stimulate or treat serious psychological problems). As such, the exercises are meant for empowerment and strengths-building.

The intervention protocol has been implemented widely as part of the GKCP, an international project whereby youth from different countries who have been impacted by trauma are connected to each other (Kuriansky, 2010a, 2010c, 2010d, 2012b, 2012c, 2012d; UNISDR, 2015b). Benefits include involving local people to help; following a step model, being culturally sensitive, working in the local language, and being sustainable (IASC Working Group, 2007; Kuriansky, 2010a, 2010c, 2010d; Jean-Charles, 2011a, 2011b; Kuriansky & Jean-Charles, 2012; Kuriansky, Lytle, & Chiu, 2011). As the aim is to provide support, rather than therapy, trainees do not need extensive experience and are given encouragement and reassurance of their ability to offer support.

IMMEDIATE AND LONG-TERM NEEDS

Much research and practice has shown that despite general resilience of survivors after environmental disasters, the mental health and well-being of those at all levels of exposure, including children as well as adults, are impacted not only immediately but also long term, making effective intervention programs that support survivors and helpers alike essential (Alexander, 2005; Başloğlu, Kiliç, Şalcioğlu, & Livanou, 2004; Liu et al., 2011; Kuriansky, 2012a, 2012b, 2012c, 2012d, 2012e, 2013a, 2013b, 2013c, 2013d, 2013e, 2014; Kuriansky & Nemeth, 2013; Nolen-Hoeksema & Morrow, 1991; Roussos et al., 2005; Satapathy & Subhasis, 2009; Save the Children, 2012; Thienkrua et al., 2006; Wang et al., 2009). The TTT workshops described in this chapter were designed to address these needs.

VALUE OF HELPING AND VOLUNTEERING

Enlisting helpers, particularly who are volunteers, is essential in many crises, especially in low-resource developing countries—as is the case in Haiti and Sierra Leone. While it is increasingly recognized that psychological first aid and psychosocial support are essential after a disaster, capacity to achieve this is often limited. The model of enlisting community volunteers described in this project offers a solution to this problem. Research has shown the positive psychological and physical effects on individuals from volunteering and altruistic behavior (Brown, Nesse, Vinokur, & Smith, 2003; Morrow-Howell, Hinterlong, Rozario, & Tang, 2003; Musick, Herzog, & House, 1999; Schwartz, Keyl, Marcum, & Bode, 2009; Schwartz, Meisenhelder, Ma, & Reed, 2003; Smith, 1981; Willigen, 2000; Young & Glasgow, 1998). Psychological benefits include that helping others can lower one's own depressive symptoms, enhance self-worth, and induce greater calmness (Krause, Herzog, & Baker, 1992; Luks, 1988).

THE MEANING OF HELPING

A "helper" is self-descriptive as anyone who offers assistance. A volunteer can be defined as "an individual engaging in behavior that is not biosocially determined (e.g., eating and sleeping), economically necessitated (e.g., paid work, housework, and home repair), or sociopolitically compelled (e.g., paying one's taxes and clothing oneself before appearing in public), but rather someone who is primarily motivated by the expectation of contributing to some purpose even if material incentive is offered (Smith, 1981). In the present projects, volunteer helpers (students and community members) in Haiti were referred to as "comforters" (i.e., supporters); in the trainings during the Ebola epidemic, one group of trainees were community volunteers, while another two groups of trainees were employees of organizations. In all cases, however, they were motivated to help, to learn new approaches, and to work with children.

TRAIN-THE-TRAINERS PROGRAMS AFTER DISASTERS

The following are reports about the TTT programs in select interventions, including several after natural disasters in Haiti and several during the Ebola epidemic in Sierra Leone.

Train-the-trainers Missions after the Natural Disasters in Haiti

The TTT projects in Haiti were carried out over a number of years following the January 12, 2010, earthquake, and another TTT was implemented immediately after the hurricane in September-October 2016. These are described below.

On January 12, 2010, a catastrophic earthquake with a magnitude of 7.0 on the Richter scale occurred on the island of Haiti. An estimated 320,000 people perished, hundreds were injured, and over a million people were displaced (BBC News, 2010). The destruction of buildings and livelihoods was extensive, causing severe problems for a country that was already one of the poorest in the world (U.S. Fund for UNICEF, n.d.). The world humanitarian community responded by pledging funds and sending food and medical supplies, though psychosocial needs were also dire and underserved.

The first and third authors of this chapter traveled to Haiti immediately after the earthquake, to mobilize psychosocial support, as a continuation of their collaboration prior to this event on the mental health needs of Haiti after floods in the country, given the general lack of psychological services (Jean-Charles, 2011b; Kuriansky, 2010a, 2010b, 2010c, 2010d; Luce, 2010). Such a mission was also consistent with their professional roles, in that the first author is a psychologist who has responded to many disasters, terror attacks, and emergencies worldwide (e.g., Kuriansky, 2005, 2007, 2010d, 2011a, 2012a, 2012c, 2017b); she is also the main representative of a psychology nongovernmental organization accredited at the UN, the International Association of Applied Psychology, for which the third author is an associate representative, as well as a native of Haiti and a Catholic priest from a local church ministry. Immediately after the quake, and over the course of several subsequent years, they mobilized groups of student volunteers to participate in workshops based on the TTT model, giving them skills to support others in crisis (Kuriansky, Zinsou, Arunagiri, et al., 2015). At this time, volunteers were recruited to participate to help survivors. The training was conducted over a course of two days after the trauma, primarily in French (locally spoken) (Kuriansky, 2010a, 2010b, 2010d). The trainees then provided simple emotional support to the innumerable suffering patients at the hospital, lying injured in the grass, tents, and halls. As described above, given these activities, the trainee/helpers have been referred to as "comforters." Data about the experience of these helpers was collected when members of the team returned to Haiti to conduct further workshops six months later, including another TTT with a group of students who then conducted the workshop with a group of over 100 children from a church community. (Kuriansky & Daisey, 2011)

In keeping with the intention to continue capacity building, team members reconvened three years later in Port-au-Prince, in June 2014, to conduct another TTT and assessment with a group of volunteers (some of whom were in the original group), who then conducted a workshop with children from the same church community. This training was concurrent with the fourth annual conference of the Center for Training in Mental Health and Spirituality, known as CESSA (according to its French name, Centre de Spiritualité, d'Evangélisation et de Santé Mentale), which was founded in response to the psychosocial needs revealed by the earthquake (Jean-Charles, 2011a, 2011b).

The trainees were students and practitioners in psychology and related fields recruited by team member Father Wismick, who was familiar with the volunteers and their motivation to participate. The purpose of the intervention was to further build capacity of human resources and the professional community in Haiti to offer psychosocial services, particularly for children, for the purposes of both long-term recovery from the trauma and resilience building for the community in general. The TTT was again led by the first author of this chapter, Kuriansky, in the local French language, using a training manual she developed, assisted by the fourth author of this chapter who also led the music cultural activities. The training was held over a weekend, before the workshop with the children, which was subsequently conducted by the trainees.

TTT Mission after Hurricane Matthew in Haiti

Hurricane Matthew, the worst natural disaster to affect Haiti since the 2010 earthquake, struck the southwestern coast of Haiti near Les Anglais on October 4, 2016, and continued wreaking havoc northward along Haiti's Tiburon Peninsula (Ahmed, 2016; Stewart, 2017). According to a report by the UN

Office for the Coordination of Humanitarian Affairs (OCHA, 2016), the category 4 hurricane left at least 1.4 million Haitians in need of assistance and approximately 750,000 Haitians in need of serious humanitarian aid. Of the 585 deaths directly caused by Hurricane Matthew throughout several countries—Haiti, as well as in neighboring Dominican Republic, St. Vincent and the Grenadines islands, and the southern shores of the United States—546 (93.3 percent) of those deaths occurred in Haiti (Stewart, 2017). Hurricane-force winds and heavy rainfall devastated the western coast, destroying infrastructure, buildings, agriculture, and food and safe water sources, with total damage to the region estimated at US$1.9 billion or approximately 10 percent of Haiti's GDP (Stewart, 2017). As in the case of the 2010 earthquake, thousands of families were left with damaged or destroyed homes, and children experienced disruption to their education. As is common in natural disasters impacting low-resource countries with limited infrastructure, the hurricane's effects additionally led to an outbreak of cholera among nearly 10,000 Haitians (Stewart, 2017). The massive desolation to the coast led to a global call for humanitarian aid to provide clean water, food, and medical services to the most affected regions. While not the primary focus of aid workers in such situations, critically, Haitians directly and indirectly (through family members and friends living in the south) impacted by the hurricane were also at heightened risk for psychological sequelae of mass trauma exposure. This is escalated by the repeated trauma, from the long-lasting effects and ongoing recovery from the earlier 2010 natural disaster, and even floods in Haiti before that.

To address the psychosocial needs of Haitians in the wake of Hurricane Matthew's destruction, the first three authors of this chapter led a team of 14 student volunteers from the third author's CESSA from Port-au-Prince, to implement a three-day TTT mission at two locations in the south of Haiti: Les Cayes and Torbeck. It is noted that several volunteers in this group had been in previous TTT programs, after the 2010 earthquake. Travel conditions were so extreme, with prevalent flooding and mudslides, that the van, like other vehicles, was temporarily stuck in pooled water and mud until several CESSA volunteers pushed the van to safety through knee-high water and mud, in torrential rain. Housing for the team was also hazardous, given mud and ongoing downpour and wind. Severe weather continued, making transportation to the workshop by community members perilous, signifying impressive commitment that at least 50 volunteers showed up for the training on two occasions.

Upon arrival in Les Cayes, the master trainers set up in the nursing school (associated with L'Université Notre-Dame d'Haïti, of which the third author was the vice provost).The stepped TTT pyramid model was implemented on two occasions in this location, using the following three steps:

1. The master trainers (i.e., authors of this chapter) trained the student trainee team on how to (a) teach the techniques selected for the workshop based on cultural appropriateness and (b) process the lessons and psychological principles underlying the techniques;
2. The trainee team then acted as master trainers with local community members who voluntarily attended the workshops (recruited by a local minister and member of the CESSA team, with strong community connections);
3. Finally, those community leaders led the workshop with local children.

Another TTT was implemented at another location, L'Université Notre-Dame d'Haïti school of agriculture in Torbeck, following the same stepped pyramid pattern, with community leaders and children.

As in the case of the above-described TTT after the earthquake, the goal of the stepped TTT pyramid model was to create an efficient resilience building and empowerment program that could be sustained by local community members.

Train-the-trainers Programs in an Epidemic

The following are reports of the TTT programs conducted during the Ebola epidemic in a West African country among the three countries hardest hit by the outbreak, specifically in Sierra Leone. During the deadly Ebola epidemic, the first author went to Sierra Leone to provide psychosocial assistance and developed and implemented training programs for other health care providers specially to work with children (Kuriansky, Polizer, & Zinsou, 2016).

Three TTT projects were implemented in January 2015, about nine months after the outbreak, when the viral epidemic was still serious (e.g., about 29 deaths a day vs. 90 deaths a day two weeks prior to the first workshop). These were co-developed and co-facilitated with a senior staff from IsraAID, an international relief nongovernmental organization with extensive experience in emergency psychosocial response, TTT1 was implemented with a group of community volunteers, the majority with minimal or no experience in psychosocial work but all of whom were highly motivated to work with children, held in a village a few miles outside the capital city of Freetown, organized by a partner, CARITAS, who implemented the workshop the next day with a group of children; TTT2 was implemented with the staff of the Children's Welfare Society whose work involved the support of children's protection and rights and whose director strongly requested the training. The techniques were similar to the ones described above in the Haiti trainings, with a few added techniques applicable to the Ebola situation (e.g., stamping out stigma that was prevalent in the situation) (Kuriansky, Polizer, & Zinsou, 2016). TTT3 was implemented with a group of participants from around the country of Sierra Leone who were in a two-day workshop about child protection and other methods to cope with Ebola, including about health practices and nutrition, organized by UNICEF, and who were meant to carry their training lessons to their district communities.

The children for the workshops in TTT1 included children who were survivors of Ebola and also others whose family had been affected (e.g., whose parents or relatives had died of Ebola and who therefore who had quarantined for the required period for observation).

RESULTS

Haiti Post-Earthquake

In 2011, data was collected retrospectively (due to logistics) from local Haitian helpers (see Kuriansky, Lytle, & Chiu, 2011 for more details) who had been trained to be supporters immediately after the earthquake in 2010. In 2014, helpers (some of whom were in the original group) fully completed a pre-post questionnaire after conducting a workshop with children from the same church community as in 2011. The comparison of this data is described later below.

The assessment protocol included a combination of quantitative and open-ended self-report questionnaires, including measures of symptoms during the earthquake (adapted from the Depression, Anxiety, and Stress Scale: Australian Centre for Post-traumatic Mental Health, n.d.; Henry & Crawford, 2005; Lovibond & Lovibond, 1995; Psychology Foundation of Australia, 2010), the Immediate Impact of Earthquake (adapted from the Impact of Event Scale–Revised: Christenson & Marren, 2013; Weiss & Marmar, 1997), Family and Friend Support (adapted from the Crisis Support Scale: Elklit, Schmidt, Pedersen, & Jind, 2001; Joseph, Williams, & Yule, 1992), the Impact of Helping (adapted from the Professional Quality of Life Scale–Version 5 (ProQOL): Stamm, 2010), PTG (adapted from the PTG Inventory (PTGI): Tedeschi & Calhoun, 2004a, 2004b), and a background questionnaire (see Kuriansky, Zinsou, Arunagiri, et al., 2015 for more detail). The post-training questionnaire repeated relevant questions from the pre-training questionnaire, including questions about helpfulness of the training, what trainees particularly liked, further training/experiences they would like, and any other suggestions.

The hypothesis was posed that helping others would be a positive experience for the helpers, reflected in both quantitative scores and qualitative responses. Across the repeated implementations of the post-earthquake workshops, results confirmed that the trainees were helped themselves by participating in the training; not only did they recognize the value of the training and working with children, but, equally important, they felt better about themselves and more empowered.

The results of the 2014 evaluation showed positive trends on all dimensions measured. With regard to perceived value of training and working with children, participants gave both quantitative and qualitative responses about the value of the training. When asked to rate the benefits of the training to their professional and personal lives on a scale of "1" to "10" with "10" being the highest, the average scores rated were "9.5" and "9.4," respectively, indicating a very high-perceived benefit of the experience on both aspects of their lives. When asked what they particularly liked in the workshop, a majority of the trainees answered "everything"; in addition, almost every exercise was mentioned as having a positive impact, including those targeted to self-esteem, personal strength, resiliency, energy, breathing and trust, as well as the games, songs, dances, and geography lesson. Examples of responses included "The trust exercise really helped me especially in my personal life" and "I like everything, especially the therapeutic exercises."

Open-ended unstructured interviews conducted with the 2014 trainees after the workshop confirmed and reinforced the quantitative and qualitative results from the questionnaires reported above about the perceived and experienced benefits and value of the training to the trainees on many levels. Increased self-efficacy was revealed in statements like, "I learned how we, the young professionals, can help the children to move forward" and "I now have the capacity to help others and children." Many trainees spontaneously mentioned wanting the program to continue and also being further motivated to pursue more study in helping professions, like the field of psychology. Regarding the style of the training, they specifically mentioned appreciating how "animated" and "energetic" the experience was. Personal growth was evident in statements like "I learned so much about how to be strong facing difficulties and surmounting sadness. Trainees further expressed greatly enjoying the experience and feeling "love" for each other and for the trainers.

Trainees rated high satisfaction, comfort, and motivation working with children even before the 2014 training (5.6 on a scale of 1 to 7). Ratings related to individual questions on these issues were high, both before and after the training (e.g., on rating the degree of interest in working with children). Responses included, "Children are a gift from God," "I enjoy working with children," and "I need to give my all to bring them a little bit of smiling." That working with children was specifically appealing to them was evident in responses like "I want to learn to surpass my difficulties and see the good moments of life and help the young get over difficulties and discover the good moments of life" and "I relive my childhood when I help children." After the training, the participants' satisfaction in working with children was especially evident. This satisfaction from working with and helping children was consistent with self-report ratings about motivation and enjoyment in working with children. Several trainees mentioned that children are the future, and in helping them, they feel they are helping their community and their country (e.g., "I think I have to be useful to the community and with the children it will be important" and "I'm interested in helping the youth because it is important to participate in the transformation of the country and it will be achieved with the youth").

The trainers/chapter authors hypothesized that the 2014 trainees would be motivated to continue this healing work, especially given its simplicity, effectiveness, helpfulness, and fun experienced by the children and the trainees themselves. This was overwhelmingly revealed in the qualitative answers and interviews, a crucial finding, given the necessity of having sustainability in the training. This was evident in both answers on the questionnaire that reflected interest in further training and in interviews about how they would apply what they had learned. For example, trainees expressed interest in conducting workshops using this model in their church, school, and community settings, as well as with children in a foster home and in a research study about abused children.

With regard to psychosocial outcomes, self-report ratings of the 2010 helpers on the Impact of Helping scale showed an average score on the Compassion Scale (37.04) consistent with the norm. Additionally, participants as a whole did not appear to be suffering from Compassion Fatigue, given that their average score on the Burnout subscale was low (i.e., 18.91) and that half the participants rated similarly low on the other component of Compassion Fatigue (i.e., the subscale of secondary trauma), indicating that individuals did not feel hopelessness or that their effort makes no difference. The other half of participants rated "average" scores on Compassion Fatigue, with none rating "high" on this scale. Any high scores on this scale, especially if also reflected in answers by individuals on other ratings, would identify those who could especially benefit from clinical help. They did, however, score above average on the Secondary Traumatic Stress subscale on the Impact of Helping scale, (i.e., a mean of 14.9 compared to the norm score of 13). This can be explained by the compounding of stress by being exposed to the same trauma as the children they were helping; however, this did not appear to distract from their motivation to help.

Similarly positive results were revealed among 2014 helpers, as scores on the Compassion subscale of the Impact of Helping scale revealed that 80 percent of the trainees' scores rated in the "high" category before the training (i.e., that they had a high degree of compassion compared to the norm on the scale). This increased to 90 percent rated as "high" after the training, with no trainees' scores in the "low" category on the scale. On the Burnout subscale, all trainees' ratings were in the "low" category before the training (i.e., indicating low experience of burnout), except for one subject who rated "average." After the training, all trainees' ratings of burnout were "low." On the Secondary Trauma subscale, trainees' ratings were higher than on the Burnout scale (i.e., half the trainees rated "low" and half rated as "average"); however, there was no increase (i.e., no change) in this score after the training. Two trainees did specifically describe upset about others' suffering, saying, "To see them [children] suffer, traumatized, is traumatizing" and "I could not watch suffering."

Ratings about self-esteem and feeling strong showed a trend toward improvement but were already at a high level among the 2014 trainees. Ratings on the WHO-5 Well-being Index (Bech, 2004; Snoek, 2006) showed higher ratings than the cutoff score (i.e., of "13") and a trend toward an increase in the average total score for the group, from 17.7 to 20.5, suggesting an improvement in well-being, specifically feeling more calm and having more interesting things in their daily life. Additionally, scores on other questions revealed trends toward a change in sense of connection in a positive direction, for example caring for others and being cared for by others, including how much they think others would help them. An important finding was that the ratings and perceived sense of empowerment in helping children were linked to an increased sense of community and connection with others, both with their peers and with fellow trainees and with the children they were serving. This was reflected in the trainees' answers on the questionnaire and also in their feedback and interviews.

Another important outcome of the 2014 training was an increase in perceived control. Initially, trainees reported feeling equally responsible for themselves (e.g., having free will), and believing that fate (or God) determines outcomes. After the training, however, there was a trend in reporting that fate and luck were less important determinants and that personal effort counted in determining outcomes.

Self-care is a crucial aspect of providing care to others, especially in emergency situations (Office of Emergency Preparedness and Response, 2013). The training stimulated attention to, and ideas about, self-care. Before the 2014 training, several trainees reported needing help in handling/regulating their feelings (e.g., frustration, anger, and impatience), and problems with money, family, and teachers. Responses about self-care activities included getting support from others (e.g., family), relaxation exercises, sports, study, and spiritual activities (e.g., prayer and meditation). After the training, many trainees added that they would use activities learned in the workshop, for example breathing exercises for relaxation, and that they would "talk to friends" and "feel my own strength."

The extent to which helping others helped themselves was evident in responses after the 2014 training. When asked about what they can do to help themselves, many trainees gave the following responses on the theme: "I feel good when I help others" (e.g., in Haiti, in French: "Je veux devenir plus fort pour aider plus les autres"), "Thank you for the chance to do something for others," and "I am inspired to help others as I know it will also help me." These responses further support the commonsense observation that volunteers who are from the community and who also experienced the traumatic event (even not to the same degree) can be especially helped by helping others, thus, increasing psychosocial community capacity in low-resource settings.

Trainees showed eagerness to participate and to learn in the training, to work with children, and to serve their community. Their responses revealed that they gained professional competence (e.g., learning more skills), personal benefits (e.g., well-being and self-confidence), and even spiritual awareness about the equality among people (consistent with the fact that traumas can equalize social strata when affecting richer and poorer indiscriminately) and about higher power. The 2011 self-report ratings revealed above-average scores (mean of 76.38) for participants on the PTGI. This finding is consistent with past research on PTG (Calhoun & Tedeschi, 1998, 2004; Linley & Joseph, 2004). The association between helping others and PTG on several levels is suggested by participants' spontaneous comments about helping, for example "I believe that I was born to help everyone in need any way that I can," "I have a new sense of solidarity," "The earthquake has affected my relationship with others because now I understand others better and I realize there is no such thing as superiority on this earth," and "Now my first priorities are God, my family, and friends, instead of unimportant materials that will remain on earth when I die."

Haiti Post-Hurricane, 2016

Fourteen Haitian volunteers (five females, nine males; M_{age} = 29.21 years, SD_{age} = 3.73 years, age range: 23–35 years) trained to deliver TTT workshops shortly in the wake of Hurricane Matthew fully completed a pre-post questionnaire similar to that administered in 2014 (see above). Overall, responses reflected that volunteers valued the training and showed improvement on a number of psychosocial aspects. A series of paired samples *t*-tests were conducted in the case of pre-post comparisons and one-sample *t*-tests comparing the group average to the scale midpoint for single time point data to elucidate meaningful patterns. Consistent with social science research reporting standards, results were considered statistically significant if $p < .05$, marginally significant if $p < .10$, or trending toward significance if $p < .20$.

Consistent with Haiti post-earthquake trainees, participants' quantitative and qualitative responses reflected their high valuation of the training and their ability to help children. Volunteers' qualitative responses on the pre-questionnaire to the question "Why did you want to come on this mission?"

reflected their motivation to participate in the mission to help their fellow Haitians as several trainees echoed the sentiment of wanting to "help my brothers and sisters recover." Another student additionally emphasized the potential for professional growth, expressing the desire "to reinforce my competencies and to help people in trauma."

Quantitative responses also reflected a marginally significant increased interest in working with people in trauma (mean change from 6.21 to 6.27 on a 1 to 7 scale, $p = .054$) and a nonsignificant trend toward increased knowledge about helping people in trauma (5.29 to 5.86, $p = .135$). Additionally, volunteers indicated significant increased knowledge (5.93 to 6.36, $p = .028$) and comfort (5.94 to 6.50, $p = .026$) working with children specifically. The training was also perceived as helpful for trainees' professional lives (6.29 on a 1 to 7 scale, $p < .001$) and their personal lives (6.21, $p < .001$), with mean scores significantly above the scale midpoint of 4. Participants' qualitative responses included: "It enriched my knowledge and made me develop a new talent," "This is the lesson that shows that it is in unity we can build," and "Personally, it helped me understand others in difficulty and to help them move forward, to live and to understand the events." Importantly, not only did trainees benefit from the training with respect to knowledge and comfort, but they also indicated a significantly high degree of liking and enjoyment for the training (mean 6.57 on a 1 to 7 scale, $p < .001$) and expressed that many of the exercises made them more "connected to other people." All participants indicated interest in all of the activities conducted throughout the workshops and a desire for more training in the future to strengthen their helping skills.

Regarding psychosocial outcomes, trainees also appeared to have gained a greater sense of personal agency through the training. That is, while still espousing strong beliefs in the power of God and fate, volunteers tended to feel more in control of their lives post-training (mean increase from 4.86 to 5.79 on a 1 to 7 scale, $p = .155$), though this effect was not statistically significant. The training appeared to have provided volunteers with better skills to combat hardship in their own lives, with one volunteer stating "I will know how to get control of my life better because I am more prepared to face any possible situation thanks to the training."

Well-being was also positively impacted by the training, as the mean score for all the respondents on the WHO five-question Quality of Life scale (Bech, 2004; Snoek, 2006) significantly increased from 3.83 to 4.20 on a 0 to 5 scale, $p = .015$. This finding suggests that the experience of learning new skills and helping their compatriots positively impacted volunteers' mental health and well-being. Again underscoring the therapeutic effect of the training on helpers themselves, trainees reported feeling significantly more calm (mean change of 7.43 to 8.36 on a 0 to 10 scale, $p = .031$), safe (6.64 to 7.86, $p = .015$), and hopeful (7.93 to 8.71, $p = .035$).

Self-care was similarly impacted by training, as post-questionnaire qualitative responses reflected the importance of spirituality (e.g., "Going to church: This is the place where I regain new energy to move forward") and helping others (e.g., "I love helping others, my life is for helping them"). Other common themes that emerged across volunteers were the importance of prayer, meditation, and music, which is not surprising, given their important role in Haitian culture.

Unfortunately, it was not possible to collect data from the community trainees; however, given the results of the initial trainee group and the anecdotal responses of the community trainees, it is hypothesized that the positive impact on the latter group would be at least as much, if not greater.

Sierra Leone, West Africa, 2014–2015 Ebola Epidemic

A pre-post questionnaire and unstructured interview modeled after the post-disaster Haiti assessment materials was implemented in the case of TTT projects in Sierra Leone during the Ebola epidemic, in order to assess aspects of the outcome of the training. This was carried out for two of the three training groups, given logistical restrictions. Only anecdotal reports from selected participants from the third trainee group were available.

Regarding the perceived value of the training and working with children, the TTT1 trainees' scores revealed that they gained from the training, both personally and professionally (reflected in the fact that all participants rated the helpfulness at nearly the highest level). Trainees further rated that the training prepared them to help children (reflected in a mean score of 6.4 out of a total of 7). The trainees ratings revealed that they really liked the training (on several questions related to this issue, all trainees rated the highest number) and all the activities, specifically mentioning activities like creating safe space and boosting trust. According to the pre-post ratings, the training dramatically increased the trainees' comfort level in leading workshops (i.e., the mean score increased dramatically from 3.6 to 6.8). Two-thirds of TTT2 trainees increased their rating about skills involved in providing psychosocial support for children, and three-quarters of respondents rated that they increased their knowledge. Almost 90 percent of TTT2 respondents rated that they increased in their comfort leading workshops with children.

In TTT1, the mean rating of interest in working with children was 6.6 in pre-evaluation and 7 in the post-evaluation, on a Likert scale of 1 to 7; but since the rating was so high in the pretest, there was little room for improvement. This was also the case for TTT2 participants' high ratings of their interest working with children (7 on scale 1 to 7).

Further supporting the perceived value of training among trainees, all TTT1 participants indicated that they would be interested in future training.

Specifications included the following: "It will help me widen my knowledge," "I want to learn new things as it will expand my experience," and "We'll help our community."

With regard to psychosocial outcomes, almost 90 percent of TTT2 trainees increased in their self-rating of feeling good about themselves and feeling powerful. All trainees rated an increase in their feeling of safety, and three-quarters of trainees increased in their reported level of trust in others. Participants' ratings of feeling connected to others started out high (8.4 on a scale of 1 to 10) but still increased to 9.1 post-training. The mean score for all the respondents on the WHO five-question Quality of Life scale increased from 3.7 to 4.575, even though the scale does not lend itself to change over several hours.

Reactions of the participants of the TTT3 trainees to the workshop were highly positive. Among the comments were: "[The workshop is] very special, and I am impressed with the methods used in this training. Most of the exercises have to do with empowering children, to be resilient, and to cope with each other in this everyday life, which to me, is also very useful." Another participant said, "These are activities we can always use in the case of Ebola in the care centers, and even outside of Ebola in the children's clubs that we work with. These children will like them, and they will give them more meaning, to help them recover and integrate them into their communities." Another trainee said, "The workshop was really, really, useful. It's going to add to whatever I have in stock. These are brilliant activities. They are going to build children's confidence, to build their resilience, to cope positively. That's what I'm going to take back to my community."

A further comment was, "This workshop really helped us to learn so many things that we'll go back and teach to our staff that the running of the OICC. We hope, with this training, we'll be able to empower our staff at the OICC, help them with all these kids, to take care of these children, help the children to feel at home, just don't be stigmatized, build up their confidence, give them the psycho-social force."

Other responses were: "The exercises and practices give us lots of confidence, as we'll be working with children in the OICC, through child-friendly ways, where we can use the various training materials that we have seen today" and "Most of these children have faced with the fact that they have lost one of their parents, or their parents have been taken to the treatment centers, and so, they want their parents to come back; but in the in between time, we can help them with these activities, I think will help them change their mindsets, giving them hope, and feeling their confidence again" and "We are so grateful for this training and hope that subsequent visits will help us to build more on these training. We know this is something new for Sierra Leone. When we should do these things, to help us in our work and to handle situations. So this was a great time."

The trainees reported liking various techniques, including those targeted to community cohesion, building trust, leadership, and feeling strong.

DISCUSSION OF EFFICACY OF TTT MODEL IN NATURAL DISASTERS AND EPIDEMICS

The present research presents promising preliminary evidence on the positive impact of applying a stepped TTT model in post-disaster and epidemic contexts on the well-being of diverse groups of community-based trainees in low-resource settings and emergency conditions. This is consistent with research showing that givers see their ability to give support as evidence of their own recovery (Henderson, 1995). This dynamic reflects psychological principles of relationships between helper and recipient, including identification, reciprocity, projection and vicarious learning, as well as the processes of (1) projecting outward and then reflecting inward and (2) externalizing personal pain, ultimately allowing for shared experience, personal processing, and renewed meaning, leading to healing.

The value placed on helping is consistent particularly in the Haitian culture with considerable faith in God, which no doubt increased the commitment to, and benefits from, the act of helping. This is consistent with research showing that volunteering in a religious context has a positive impact on mental health (Wilson & Musick, 1999).

The cultural context of any natural disaster or epidemic is important. Commitment to helping others and religious beliefs in Haiti may increase trainees desire to "Do God's work" and may be greater when compared to comforters and trainees in more individualistic or less-religious cultures. The influence of belief in traditional practices and indigenous healers in West Africa deserves consideration with regard to its impact on helping others. Despite any variations, the results and experience of the current projects suggest that the positive effects and PTG of helping may be a universal phenomenon.

The quantitative and qualitative results from the questionnaires showed the positive impact of the training, both in the structured self-reports and in the open-ended interviews as well as in clinical observations by the senior project team. Clearly, a more scientific assessment with a more rigid methodology and larger sample size, built into the available time of the training and practicality of the logistics, with follow-up, would be valuable to be able to establish this model as a "best practice"; however, the present preliminary research suggests the value of this model, especially in light of the "face" validity yielded by the qualitative answers and positive feedback, regarding both the ease of the trainees' learning the workshop material in such a short period of time, their enthusiasm in doing the workshop with the children, and the positive reports of all involved (i.e., the trainees, children, and teachers). The results also underscore what has been shown repeatedly in other research as well as in the first author's work, particularly regarding recovery from trauma, crisis, or environmental disaster and the value of the group approach and the importance of community in healing (Clayton, Manning, & Hodge, 2014; Kuriansky, 2012b, 2013b; Kuriansky & Nemeth, 2013).

It is worthwhile to note that the training was a holistic experience, creating a cycle of positivity for all involved. Similar to the beneficiaries of the training, the trainers and all the workshop team members also reported having an exceptionally positive and rewarding experience that was both professionally useful and personally satisfying. As described above, they spontaneously expressed feeling very bonded with everyone involved, being "touched" by everything that happened, and feeling "love," "caring," and great appreciation for the trainees, children, and each other. Similar to the trainees, they felt very satisfied and fulfilled from helping and committed to continuing to serve.

In summary, community volunteers have a considerable impact on building civil society, especially in the case of rebuilding after a disaster. The psychological benefits of such service accrue to those helped and to the helpers, including inoculating stress, strengthening personal efficacy, and increasing social and community ties. When a developing (or even, developed) nation is hit by a devastating environmental disaster, stepped pyramid training programs such as this one that mobilize the resources of local students studying psychology-related subjects, as well as teachers and community members interested in helping, can offer valuable support for rebuilding the community and needed sustainability. This approach can further strengthen the helpers' own resilience, especially when they have been similarly affected by the disaster. Training such helpers builds the human capacity of the community to serve survivors and pass along this learning to others. Such an approach holds great promise for the implementation of the new SDGs identified by the UN, which includes the promotion of people's mental health and well-being, and of the Sendai Framework that calls for psychosocial recovery programs.

The current comparison also reveals that many characteristics of interventions and assessments that are appropriate for disaster interventions for children and adults appear to be applicable in the case of disease epidemics, given that the circumstances of the two traumatic events have many overlapping features. For example, it is useful to apply a TTT model, utilizing community volunteers, in order to expand local capacity. Also, minimally trained but highly motivated individuals can be very effective in helping children become more resilient in the face of such large-scale traumatic events. Similar concepts are also applicable in both situations, namely creating safety for children, facilitating empowerment and self-efficacy in the face of grief and loss, and reestablishing connections with support systems. Despite these similarities, a major factor idiosyncratic to the Ebola epidemic is the widespread discrimination and stigma that survivors and others were subjected to, and that of course must be addressed in the workshops, and measured. Training modules to address this crucial issue were included in the programs described here.

Overall, the present findings, though preliminary and pilot in nature, with convenience samples as opposed to rigorous sample selection and scientific methodology, provide highly useful indications about the value of volunteering and helping behavior for the helper in both post-disaster and epidemic contexts. Comforters were able to aid community members and children through grief, trauma, and loss, which also helped the comforters address their own suffering. The results show that such trainings are valuable for helpers on both personal and professional levels. The present explorations support, and are supported by, research that volunteering can have significant positive effects on people's physical and psychological health (Grimm, Spring, & Dietz, 2007). The act of volunteering can help helpers cope and adapt, gain new perspectives on life, and increase social integration. In addition, volunteers can become "supporters" shortly after a disaster or in the height of an epidemic, offering emotional support with training in simple psychological first aid techniques. These outcomes are highly important in the aftermath of disasters and epidemics, when resources, including human capital, are limited. Emphasizing the direct as well as indirect and vicarious benefits of such helping can encourage larger numbers of volunteers in such direct situations.

FURTHER DISCUSSION

TTT Following the IASC Guidelines

The experiences described in this chapter follow the IASC guidelines (IASC Working Group, 2007), in that the trainees were trained in simple techniques that are on the first level of the guidelines, namely to provide general support. Thus, the techniques (described below), while grounded in sound psychological principles, are simple to administer, do not require advanced clinical skills, and are not meant to trigger deeper psychological issues.

Process of Mourning Disrupted in Epidemics and Natural Disasters

Since the present model addresses the base level of the IASC guidelines, it is not intended to arouse emotions that cannot be dealt with on the more preliminary level. Yet, in major natural disasters and epidemics, trainees must be sensitized to the deep mourning of survivors, even though this issue may not be addressed in an intensive way, in order not to trigger complex and deep feelings of loss and concomitant emotions that cannot be dealt with in this context.

The stages of mourning that crosses all situations have been established (Kübler-Ross, 2005). These include shock, depression/anger, and finally acceptance and resolution, despite the fact that every loss can have its individual meaning or aspects.

In the case of epidemics and natural disasters, an important similarity is that loved ones' bodies may not be available for natural or cultural traditions of burial or ceremonies. This disrupts the process of being able to mourn loved ones, a process that is crucial for healing. In the crisis of the Asian tsunami, bodies were swept into the water and unrecovered. Also, thousands of corpses were scooped up and dumped into piles. This prevented many families from identifying their dead loved ones and performing ceremonial rites, for example rites consistent with the Hindu tradition in Sri Lanka.

The same mass collection and disposal of corpses was done after the Haiti earthquake in 2010. Bodies were even placed in group graves on the grounds of hospitals after the injured died.

In the case of the Ebola epidemic, the cultural practice of preparing the dead was a cause of transmission of the virus. In other words, ritualistic cleansing, wrapping, and preparing the body involved coming into contact with body fluids (sweat, blood, saliva) that spreads the virus. This practice caused the ongoing perpetuation of the viral spread and was the reason many members of one family succumbed to the infection. Convincing the population to stop this practice was exceptionally difficult, especially by "outsiders" who were resented for their advice by the locals. Only when local healers and spiritual and community leaders advised the villagers to stop this practice did the epidemic start ceasing to spread.

An important communal way to honor the dead and bring some semblance of closure is collective mass memorials. One such memorial was held on the site where bodies were piled outside Port-au-Prince Haiti on 1 February after the 2010 earthquake. In New York, an author of this chapter attended another mass memorial for missing loved ones, at St. Francis of Assisi Church, led by the Revered Retired Archbishop of Port-au-Prince, Francois Wolf Ligonde (who had presided over the iconic Roman Catholic Notre Dame Cathedral in Port-au-Prince for 41 years until the new Archbishop Joseph Serge Miot took over). In the quake, Miot's body was tragically hurled from a balcony but retrieved from ruins at the cathedral grounds.

Complex Tragedies and Repeated Training

In certain incidences, including those reported above, communities have been assaulted by double trauma. For example, the people of Sierra Leone and Liberia endured the Ebola epidemic occurring after years of civil war and also the HIV/AIDS epidemic. Hurricane Matthew hit the island of Haiti in 2016 only six years after the devastating earthquake in 2010; similarly, the state of Louisiana in the United States was hit by Hurricane Katrina in 2004, then Hurricane Matthew in 2016, and then the floods of Hurricane Harvey in 2017 (though occurring mainly in Texas).

These double (or triple) traumas exacerbate the emotional trauma of the survivors. But it is also possible that trainees from earlier missions are again available in later incidences. This was the case, for example, with the mission to the south of Haiti immediately after Hurricane Matthew, when six of the student trainees were again in the trainee group, who had been in the trainee group for the missions after the 2010 Haiti earthquake, since they were still students or still involved in some leadership capacity with the Center for Spirituality and Mental Health.

Importance of Community Connection

Extensive research shows the value of social support and family and community ties in recovery from trauma (Dougall, Hyman, Hayward, et al., 2001; Walsh, 2002, 2007; Kuriansky, 2012; Landau & Saul, 2004). The emphasis on the individual in the context of his/her community and environment reflects an "ecological" approach, becoming increasingly popular in the field of environmental psychology and ecological psychology (Kahn & Hasbach, 2012; Kuriansky, 2012a; Nemeth, Hamilton, & Kuriansky, 2012). Activities in the trainings intentionally demonstrate the importance of people working together; and trainees anecdotally responded highly positively to these experiences in all the trainings related to the epidemic and the natural disasters.

COMMUNITY VOLUNTEERS AND STUDENTS ARE AVAILABLE AND VIABLE IN DISASTER RESPONSE

Contrary to the belief that people in the world are becoming inured to disasters—due in part to their prevalence—and more withdrawn in terms of reaching out to help others, a surge in altruism has emerged. Reports of the generous and positive response to the appeal for helpers from the community (to aid in rescue of survivors) from the recent hurricanes that hit the Caribbean Islands and parts of the U.S. hard in 2017 showed an influx of altruistic volunteers.

Experience as well as many reports have shown that volunteers from the community who are not expertly trained in a particular role can function in the midst of a disaster, when supervised or overseen by an expert. (Becker, 2006, 2007; Booth-Kewley et al. 2001; James & Noel, 2013; James et al., 2012; Jones, Weiss, & Chitalu, 2015; McCabe et al., 2012; Kuriansky, Zinsou, Arunagiri, et al., 2015; Tobias et al., 2012; Weiss et al., 2014; Williams et al., 2014; Yarber et al., 2015; Yu et al., 2014). This applies to mental health helpers, as for rescuers and health assistants. This was the case for the authors and their colleagues providing trainings in Haiti after the 2010 Haiti earthquake as well as the hurricane in 2016.

The initial cohort of 30 students after the Haiti earthquake of 2010 had very little training in psychological principles and counseling, but were committed to help others. As was mentioned above, they are referred to as "comforters" since they were trained to mainly provide comforting to patients (through acts like giving them water, holding their hand, and offering an "ear," "heart," and empathy, to talk if the person cared to), rather than any professional counseling. In the Haiti mission of 2016, the group of student trainees were more advanced in their psychological training, as they were in various stages of schooling in the mental health field in Haiti universities and at the Center of Spirituality and Mental Health established by the third author of this chapter.

It is significant that the trainees in all situations, regardless of level of background or experience in psychosocial work, required little assistance in implementing the activities with the children. This indicates their quick learning from the training within even one day and validates the intention of the TTT program that it can be easily learned and implemented by a group of volunteers.

Other Related TTT projects

Other TTT workshops have been conducted by the first author in diverse settings and with diverse populations worldwide post-disaster, following a similar methodology, with similar techniques. These will be mentioned, but not elaborated here, as the workshop content was more varied, or only anecdotal reactions of trainees are available, given logistical concerns.

Group TTT Working with Refugees

In a pilot project, a group of volunteers were trained in the similar model of the training programs above, to work with children Syrian refugees, living in Jordan. The model program was considered to be applicable as it addressed the specific reported issues of the population of refugees. These include a lack of a sense of safety, anxieties, and insecurities (Porter & Haslam, 2005; Kuriansky, 2017b). The trainees were an international group who were volunteers for the Atlantic Humanitarian Relief organization, comprised mainly of medical professionals who make annual missions to Jordan to administer emergency medical attention to Syrian refugees living outside of camps where medical care is more Readily provided. The main author trained a group of seven volunteers, in the model described above, who then led a group of children in the techniques. Logistics of the mission (including time available and necessity of translation of any assessment protocol) made the administration of questionnaire impractical. Therefore, only informal reports were available and documented. All of the trainees reported enthusiasm to learn, and to administer, the model, and noted the potential value to the children in building their sense of security, confidence, and self-esteem. The children in the group all responded positively, in participating actively in the techniques, and expressing some sense of joy, noted by the author as relief from the stresses of refugeeism.

A TTT Model for Teachers

The above model was also applied in a setting not immediately affected by disaster or epidemic, but that is worthwhile to report as it suggests the wide interest of the model to cohorts. Specifically, the main author conducted two trainings using the techniques with teachers and counselors who attended her sessions as part of the Caribbean Well-Being Conference (Kuriansky, 2017e). Comments from the participants were that the training was "enlightening," "fun," "affirming," and "interesting tools to use." Many anticipated applying the model, saying, for example, "I think I will introduce them [the techniques] during staff meetings… Also I can share them with the teachers so that they could pass it down to the children and the class." Many participants found particular appeal in the activities that encourage community cohesion.

Workshops after Hurricanes Katrina and Matthew in Louisiana

A series of workshops were also conducted in post-disaster situations after hurricanes Katrina and Matthew that hit the state of Louisiana, conducted by the first author in collaboration with a colleague who is a neuropsychologist, expert in trauma and resilience, and native of the state (thus, familiar with the local culture). Participants were community members who were in varied positions, for example students, church leaders, or aid workers. While these cohorts were also convenience samples, and not comparable to the groups reported above, and the techniques were only partly comparable (i.e., those taught by the first author, while other techniques were included by the co-trainer), it is worthwhile to note their outcome, as they lend support to the outcomes and discussion reported above. The results of pre-post assessments of participants in anniversary training workshops (held on the anniversary of the traumatic event when emotions are expected to be re-triggered) showed that participants made positive changes from feeling isolated to feeling connected, from hostility to cooperation, from a sense of victimization to feeling empowered (Kuriansky & Nemeth, 2013; Nemeth, Kuriansky, Reeder, et al., 2013).

One participant said, "I feel new hope…Everything has been taken from me, but now I have new confidence and self-esteem that I can do something and others are joining me. I am not alone." Another trainee, a social worker who participated in the workshop in her role as deputy executive director of Louisiana Spirit Hurricane Recovery Program (a FEMA-funded grant program for crisis counseling which co-sponsored the workshops) but also as an evacuee herself, said, "This workshop gives people a sense of power that they know they can go out and help someone else by teaching them these simple exercises."

Participants particularly responded to the activity of making soft stuffed pillows and drawing a bird and messages of hope on the material, which not only reflected the psychological construct of contact comfort, similar to the function of teddy bears for children, but served as the foundation for discussion about deeper feelings of comfort. This activity is part of the GKCP described above, and was included in the above trainings when time allowed. Exchanging of the object also facilitated discussion and group cohesion that is known to be healing. For example, one church leader reflected about how the activity can bond the parishioners further to deal with the trauma (Kuriansky & Nemeth, 2016).

LIMITATIONS

The comparisons drawn in this chapter must be considered in the context that they are drawn from diverse cultural settings, and from convenience samples, with participants self-selected or selected according to varying criteria, and with varying demographic characteristics (e.g., age, background, and degree of exposure). Also, sample sizes varied (e.g., being large or small in Sierra Leone according to the number of the staff or volunteers invited or available). Notably, the recruitment of 30 students after the 2010 Haiti disaster, and the large number of community members who showed up for the training in 2016 during the hurricane in Haiti, was deemed impressive, given the severity of the ongoing disaster, deaths of potentially eligible trainees, dangerous weather conditions, and difficulties in transportation. Also, some trainees were already predisposed to be interested and committed to work with children, given their job (e.g., as in the case of the staff in Sierra Leone working in the field of child welfare and protection).

Limitations in examinations as this one are commonly caused by constraints inherent in the logistics of an ongoing crisis or posttrauma situation, which makes empirical methodology and data collection difficult, as research must take a back seat to clinical needs for survivors' healing. Language also presented challenges, since parts of the Haiti questionnaires were not in the native Creole language, and only some trainees could be supervised while filling out the forms, given multiple responsibilities of the team (e.g., attending to the child participants and conducting clinical interviews). While the language of Sierra Leone is Krio (not exactly equivalent to Creole), more of the trainees and community people spoke English than in the community trainee group in Haiti. Validated assessment protocols, culturally relevant and reliable in cross-cultural contexts, need to be designed for such research, as these are not available to date. The present examination highlights the importance of such measures being developed.

Thus, only suggestions, rather than definitive conclusions, can be drawn. However, given the lack of study on this particular topic, namely comparing natural disasters and epidemics, it is valuable to consider the implications of the available data and these pilot efforts, to motivate empirical study.

POLICY IMPLICATIONS

The two international instruments described above (the UN Agenda 2030 and the Sendai Framework for Disaster Risk Reduction) are valuable in urging attention by government and nongovernment entities to psychosocial issues and psychosocial resilience-building after both epidemics and natural disasters. In the recent review of SDG 3 by governments in July 2017, some voluntary reviews of governments did mention the importance of psychosocial issues (Otto, Kuriansky, & Otto, 2017; UNDESA, n.d.). While this is somewhat encouraging, much more awareness and advocacy with governments need to be done to heighten their attention to this issue.

The results reported above show the impact of the training on skills building, and for diverse beneficiaries; therefore, the TTT approach and specific activities show promise for contributing to the achievement of Goal 4 of the SDGs, namely education for all. This is further supported by the fact that a version of the TTT, as noted above, was applied to an academic training setting (in St. Martin), with teachers and other education staff, who reported that they could see the usefulness of adapting the program to their context. Further, the community cohesion activities (e.g., creating a web with yarn) in the program elicit messages about acceptance and respect for differences among people, that relates to SDG 16 about peaceful societies. Further support for this point is that comments from participants about this activity include, as in the setting mentioned above, variations of the observations that "We are all different sizes, colors and shapes, but we are connected," "We are all together," "We must work together and accept each other as we are," and "We are one world."

Further, while the word "resilience" has become more commonplace in discussions and documents at the UN, this word usually refers to structural resilience, (e.g., distance of buildings to waterfronts and use of disaster-proof materials). Given the extent of human suffering and long-term sequelae compared to the availability and access to mental health support, more advocacy and action must be done to close this gap and highlight the importance of "psychosocial resilience." The first author has done a considerable amount of this advocacy, for example starting from UN Disaster Risk Reduction meetings in 2007 and including at the Third UN World Conference on Disaster Risk Reduction in Sendai Japan in 2014, and with the second author at the World Conference on Disaster Risk Reduction in Cancún, Mexico in 2016. A major lesson long-term and collaborative effort among many stakeholders is necessary.

Based on the above reports, psychosocial support can valuably be provided in the cases of natural disasters or epidemics through TTT programs that offer capacity building especially in low-resource communities and countries. A registry of potential volunteers and community leaders should be kept and adequate finding provided as part of disaster preparedness. Coordination should be maintained with community resources like schools, hospitals, community centers, and religious institutions, especially in cultures that are religiously oriented.

The present report underscores the importance of community connection in resilience and recovery when facing natural disasters or an epidemic. A resilient and empowered community is capable of collective PTG (Kuriansky, 2012b) in that large-scale destruction in a tragedy or health crisis reminds citizens of the universality of pain, suffering, and grief, and offers individuals, a community, and a country, a chance to create a new foundation, a stronger commitment to diversity, more connection among the citizens, better health practices, and more awareness of interdependence that redefines social structures, government policies, and how resources are to be used and shared.

The present chapter reinforces the authors' position that practical programs, enlightened policies, and a paradigm shift must include psychosocial resilience, which will facilitate the development of sustainable psychosocial resilience and well-being for children and adult survivors of disaster and epidemics who are served, and who can also provide valuable human capital in local communities to provide needed support (Kuriansky, Zinsou, Arunagiri, et al., 2015). Recommendations for disaster relief policy in the case of natural disasters can similarly be applied in response to epidemics. These include the following: psychosocial relief and psychological first aid should be an integral part of immediate disaster relief operations and integrated into primary health care; interventions specifically tailored to children—who are especially at risk—should be made widely available; plans, programs, and policies need to take a long-term view and to ensure such psychosocial help continues years after a disaster; and research to establish best practices should be conducted.

REFERENCES

Alexander, D. (2005). Early mental health intervention after disasters. *Advances in Psychiatric Treatment, 11*(1), 12–18.

Ahmed, A. (2016). Hurricane Matthew makes old problems worse for Haitians. *The New York Times.* Retrieved from https://nyti.ms/2dI37LU

American Psychological Association (APA) (n.d.). The Road to resilience. Retrieved January 21, 2015, from http://www.apa.org/helpcenter/road-resilience.aspx

Australian Centre for Posttraumatic Mental Health (n.d.). *Depression Anxiety and Stress Scale (DASS).* Retrieved September 14, 2014, from http://www.acpmh.unimelb.edu.au/site_resources/TrainingInitiativeDocuments/follow-up/DASS.pdf

Australian Centre for Posttraumatic Mental Health (n.d.). *Depression Anxiety and Stress Scale (DASS).* Retrieved September 14, 2014, from http://www.acpmh.unimelb.edu.au/site_resources/TrainingInitiativeDocuments/follow-up/DASS.pdf

Başloğlu, M., Kiliç, C., Şalcioğlu, E., & Livanou, M. (2004). Prevalence of posttraumatic stress disorder in earthquake survivors in Turkey: An epidemiological study. *Journal of Traumatic Stress, 17*, 133–141.

BBC News. (2010, February 12). Haiti will not die, President Rene Preval insists. *BBC News Home.* Retrieved July 30, 2011, from http://news.bbc.co.uk/2/hi/americas/8511997.stm

Bech, P. (2004). Measuring the dimensions of psychological general well-being by the WHO-5. *QoL Newsletter, 32*, 15–16.

Becker, S. M. (2006). Psychosocial care for adult and child survivors of the 2004 tsunami disaster in India. *American Journal of Public Health, 96*(8), 1397–1398.

Becker, S. M. (2007). Psychosocial care for adult and child survivors of the tsunami disaster in India. *Journal of Child and Adolescent Psychiatric Nursing, 20*(3), 148–155.

Booth-Kewley, S., Gilman, P. A., Shaffer, R. A., & Brodine, S. K. (2001). Evaluation of a sexually transmitted disease/human immunodeficiency virus prevention train-the-trainer program. *Military Medicine, 166*(4), 304–310.

Brown, S., Nesse, R., Vinokur, A., & Smith, D. (2003). Providing social support may be more beneficial than receiving it: Results from a prospective study of mortality. *Psychological Science, 14*(4), 320–327.

Calhoun, L. G., & Tedeschi, R. G. (1998). *Facilitating posttraumatic growth: A clinician's guide*. London, UK: Lawrence Erlbaum Associates.

Calhoun, L. G., & Tedeschi, R. G. (2004). The foundations of posttraumatic growth: Newconsiderations. *Psychological Inquiry, 15*, 93–102.

Christenson, S., & Marren, J. (2013). The Impact of Event Scale. *Try This: Best Practices to Nursing Care in Older Adults, 19*. Retrieved September 13, 2014, from http://consultgerirn.org/uploads/File/trythis/try_this_19.pdf

Clayton, S., Manning, C., & Hodge, C. (2014). *Beyond storms and droughts: The Psychological impacts of climate change*. Washington, DC: American Psychological Association and ecoAmerica. Retrieved April 10, 2015, from http://ecoamerica.org/wp-content/uploads/2014/06/eA_Beyond_Storms_and_Droughts_Psych_Impacts_of_Climate_Change.pdf

Dougall, A. L., Hyman, K. B., Hayward, M. C., McFeeley, S., & Baum, A. (2001). Optimism and traumatic stress: The importance of social support and coping. *Journal of Applied Social Psychology, 31*, 223–245. doi: 10.1111/j.1559-1816.2001.tb00195.x.

Elklit, A., Schmidt Pedersen, S., & Jind, L. (2001). The Crisis Support Scale: Psychometric qualities and further validation. *Personality and Individual Differences, 31*(8), 1291–1302.

Furr, J. M., Comer, J. S., Edmunds, J. M., & Kendall, P. C. (2010). Disasters and youth: A meta-analytic examination of posttraumatic stress. *Journal of Consulting and Clinical Psychology, 78*(6), 765–780.

Goldstein, S., & Brooks, R. B. (Eds.). (2005). *Handbook of resilience in children*. New York: Kluwer Academic/Plenum Publishers.

Grimm, R., Jr., Spring, K., & Dietz, N. (2007). The health benefits of volunteering: A review of recent research. Retrieved on August 30, 2017 from https://www.nationalservice.gov/pdf/07_0506_hbr.pdf

Henderson, A. (1995). Abused women and peer-provided social support: The nature and dynamics of reciprocity in a crisis setting. *Issues in Mental Health Nursing, 16*, 117.

Henry, J. D., & Crawford, J. R. (2005). The short-form version of the Depression Anxiety Stress Scales (DASS-21): Construct validity and normative data in a large non-clinical sample. *British Journal of Clinical Psychology, 44*(2), 227–239.

Inter-Agency Standing Committee (IASC) Working Group. (2007). *IASC guidelines on mental health and psychosocial support in emergency settings*. Geneva: IASC.

IsraAID (2014–2015). IsraAID; Sierra Leone. Retrieved January 25, 2015 at: http://israaid.co.il/projects/sierra-leone

James, L. E., & Noel, J. R. (2013). Lay mental health in the aftermath of disaster: Preliminary evaluation of an intervention for Haiti earthquake survivors. *International Perspectives in Psychology: Research, Practice, Consultation, 1*(2), 110–126.

James, L. E., Noel, J. R., Favorite, T. K., & Jean, J. S. (2012). Challenges of postdisaster intervention in cultural context: The implementation of a lay mental health worker project in postearthquake Haiti. *International Perspectives in Psychology: Research, Practice, Consultation, 1*(2), 110–126.

Jean-Charles, W. (2011a, Fall). First international conference on restoring life and maintaining hope in Port-au-Prince: Establishing a new "Center for Spirituality and Mental Health" in Haiti. *International Psychology Bulletin,* 15(4), 39–41. Retrieved September 12, 2014, from http://internationalpsychology.files.wordpress.com/2013/01/ipb_fall_2011-10-28-1_final.pdf

Jean-Charles, W. (2011b, January-March). Rebati: After the earthquake, the IAAP UN team continues to remember Haiti. *IAAP Bulletin of the International Association of Applied Psychology, 23*(1–2), 33–35.

Jean-Charles, W. (2015, March 16). *The Global Kids Connect Project in Haiti: Overview and outcome*. Panel presentation at the session on Volunteering to Build Back Better, Children and Youth Forum, World Conference on Disaster Risk Reduction, Tohoku University, Sendai, Japan.

Jean-Charles, W., Kuriansky, J., & Margevich, A. K. (2016, November). *Resilience, spirituality and community: Foundations and applications in Haiti.* Paper presented at the Caribbean Regional Conference of Psychology, Port-au-Prince, Haiti.

Jones, D., Weiss, S., & Chitalu, N. (2015). HIV prevention in resource limited settings: A case study of challenges and opportunities for implementation. *International Journal of Behavioral Medicine, 22*(3), 384–392.

Joseph, S., Williams, R., & Yule, W. (1992). Crisis support, attributional style, coping style and post-traumatic symptoms. *Personality and Individual Differences, 13*(11), 1249–1251.

Kahn, P. H., Jr., & Hasbach, P. H. (2012). *Ecopsychology: Science, totems, and the technological species*. Cambridge, MA: MIT Press.

Koller, D. F., Nicholas, D. B., Goldie, R. S., & Gearing, R. (2006). Bowlby and Robertson revisited: The impact of isolation on hospitalized children during SARS. *Journal of Developmental and Behavioral Pediatrics, 27*(2), 134–140.

Kouadio, I. K., Aljunid, S., Kamigaki, T., Hammad, K., & Oshitani, H. (2012). Infectious diseases following natural disasters: Prevention and control measures. *Expert Review of Anti-infective Therapy, 10*(1), 95–104.

Krause, N., Herzog, A. R., & Baker, E., (1992). Providing support to others and wellbeing in later life. *Journal of Gerontology: Psychological Sciences, 47*, 300–311.

Kübler-Ross, E. (2005). *On grief and grieving: Finding the meaning of grief through the five stages of loss*. New York: Simon & Schuster Ltd.

Kuriansky, J. (Producer). (2005). *Tsunami 2004 in Sri Lanka Dr. Judy with Children.* [Video]. Retrieved April 6, 2015, fromhttps://www.youtube.com/watch?v=VQxwYLu1lwM&feature=youtu.be

Kuriansky, J. (2007). Healing after a terror event on campus in Israel: Unique workshops and allied techniques for international Jewish and Arab students, staff and extended community. In J. Kuriansky (Ed.), *Beyond bullets and bombs: Grassroots peacebuilding between Israelis and Palestinians* (pp. 315–325). Westport, CT: Praeger.

Kuriansky, J. (2008). A clinical toolbox for cross-cultural counseling and training. In U. P. Gielen, J. G. Draguns, & J. M. Fish (Eds.), *Principles of multicultural counseling and therapy* (pp. 295–330). New York: Taylor and Francis/Routledge.

Kuriansky, J. (2010a). Bringing emotional First Aid and Hope to Haiti. http://www.beliefnet.com/Inspiration/2010/02/Bringing-Emotional-First-Aid-and-Hope-to-Haiti.aspx?p=5

Kuriansky, J. (2010b, Spring). Haiti pre-and post-Earthquake: Tracing professional and personal commitment past, present and future. *International Psychology Bulletin. 14*(2), 29–37. Retrieved from http://internationalpsychology.files.wordpress.com/2013/01/ipb_spring_2010_4_27_10.pdf

Kuriansky, J. (2010c). Stories of Haiti. Retrieved March 21, 2015, from http://www.humnews.com/humnews/2010/4/13/stories-of-haitiapril-13-2010.html

Kuriansky, J. (Producer) (2010d). *Haiti after 2010 Earthquake Dr. Judy mission.* [Video]. Retrieved April 7, 2015, from https://youtu.be/e7jLW4K0QWE

Kuriansky, J. (2011a). Advancing the UN MDGs by a model program for Girls Empowerment, HIV/AIDS prevention and entrepreneurship: IAAP project in Lesotho Africa. *The IAAP Bulletin of the International Association of Applied Psychology, 23* (1–2, January/March), 21–23.

Kuriansky, J. (2011b). Guidelines for mental health and psychosocial support in response to emergencies: Experience and encouragement for advocacy. *The IAAP Bulletin of the International Association of Applied Psychology, 23*(1–2), 31–33.

Kuriansky, J. (2012a). *Helping children recover from natural disasters: Principles and practice from professional and personal experiences in the field in China, Sri Lanka, Haiti and Japan, skills building and psycho-educational techniques.* Presentation at the International Conference for Chinese Psychology and Health in Global & Fourth Congress of the IACMSP.

Kuriansky, J. (2012b). Our communities: Healing after environmental disasters. pp. 141–167. In Nemeth, D. G., Hamilton, R. B. & Kuriansky, J. (Eds.) *Living in an Environmentally Traumatized World: Healing Ourselves and Our Planet.* Santa Barbara, California: Praeger Press.

Kuriansky, J. (2012c). Recovery efforts for Japan after the 3/11 devastating tsunami/earthquake. *Bulletin of the International Association of Applied Psychology, 24*(2–3), Part 22. Retrieved March 30, 2015, from http://www.iaapsy.org/Portals/1/Archive/Publications/newsletters/July2012.pdf

Kuriansky, J. (2012d). Report: Soothing Sendai. Retrieved March 30, 2015, from http://www.humnews.com/the-view-from-here/2012/3/22/soothing-sendai-report.html

Kuriansky, J. (2012e). Train, retain, gain: Youth volunteer leadership for intercultural cooperation to build stronger societies. Workshop presented at the DPI/NGO conference, Bonn, Germany. *Bulletin of the International Association of Applied Psychology, 24*(2–3): 23–26.

Kuriansky, J. (2013a). Helping kids cope with the Oklahoma tornado and other traumas: 7 techniques. *Huffington Post.* Retrieved February 13, 2013, from http://www.huffingtonpost.com/judy-kuriansky-phd/helping-kids-cope-with-the-oklahoma-tornado_b_3322238.html

Kuriansky, J. (2013b). Superstorm Sandy 2012: A psychologist first responder's personal account and lessons learned about the impact on emotions and ecology. *Ecopsychology, 5*(S1): S-30–S-37. doi:10.1089/eco.2013.0010. Accessible at: ftp://authors:w3stra1n@journals-ftp.wbrt.com/Distribution/ECO-2013-0010-Kuriansky_1P.pdf

Kuriansky, J. (2013c). Superstorm Sandy: Coping with the one-year anniversary. *CitizensMagazine*. Retrieved March 30, 2015, from https://statenislandpolitics.wordpress.com/2013/10/26/drjudy/

Kuriansky, J. (2013d). Talking to kids about the anniversary of Superstorm Sandy. *Huffington Post*. Retrieved March 30, 2015, from http://www.huffingtonpost.com/judy-kuriansky-phd/talking-to-kids-about-the-anniversary-of-superstorm-sandy_b_4167294.htm

Kuriansky, J. (2013e). Thoughts on Katrina vs. Sandy (Essays on nature-induced, humaninduced, and nature + human-induced environmental trauma). *Ecopsychology, 5*(S1): S-20–S-26. doi:10.1089/eco.2013.0039. Accessed March 30, 2015 at: http://online.liebertpub.com/doi/abs/10.1089/eco.2013.0039?src=recsys

Kuriansky, J. (2014). *Building resilience in children coping after disaster and living in crisis: Applied models in Haiti, Japan and Africa*. Presentation at the Louisiana Psychological Association, on "Resiliency, mindfulness and resolve: Coping with the hand you're dealt." New Orleans, Louisiana.

Kuriansky, J. (2015, March 16). [Video]. Dr. Judy Kuriansky: Statement at World Conference on Disaster Risk Reduction, Sendai Japan 2015. Presented at the High level Multi-Stakeholder Partnership Dialogue, World Conference on Disaster Risk Reduction, Sendai, Japan, March 14–18. Retrieved on April 10, 2015, from https://youtu.be/R72sDJ1xVZg

Kuriansky, J. (2016). Report of the IAAP United Nations team: Success in the New Global Agenda Advocacy. *Bulletin of the International Association of Applied Psychology, 28*(1–2).

Kuriansky, J. (2017a, July). *Mental health and wellbeing: Advances at the United Nations and in civil society initiatives, importance and impact for psychologists in Europe and Worldwide*. Paper presented at the European Federation of Psychologists' Association's 15th European Congress of Psychology, Amsterdam, The Netherlands.

Kuriansky, J. (2017b, July). *Psychosocial Intervention during a medical mission for Syrian refugee children in Jordan: Experiences and lessons learned and importance for the people, psychology professionals and the international community*. Symposium conducted at the European Federation of Psychologists' Association's 15th European Congress of Psychology, Amsterdam, The Netherlands.

Kuriansky, J. (2017c, July). *Call to action for psychologists in achieving mental health and well-being in the global agenda*. Symposium conducted at the European Federation of Psychologists' Association's 15th European Congress of Psychology, Amsterdam, The Netherlands.

Kuriansky, J. (2017d, July). *Mental health and well-being, Advances at the United Nations and events impacting psychotherapy*. Paper presented at the 8th congress of the World Council for Psychotherapy, Paris, France.

Kuriansky, J. (2017e, August). *A unique train-the-trainers model for community intervention for wellbeing and resilience post-disaster*. Workshops presented at the Caribbean Well-being Conference, University of St. Martin, Philipsburg, St. Martin.

Kuriansky, J., & Berry, M. O. (2011a). Advancing the UN MDGS by a model program for girls empowerment, HIV/AIDS prevention and entrepreneurship: IAAP Project in Lesotho Africa. *IAAP Bulletin, 23*(1–2) January/April. Retrieved April 7, 2015, from www.iaapsy.org/Portals/1/Bulletin/apnl_v23_i1-2.pdf

Kuriansky, J., & Berry, M. O. (2011b). The Girls Empowerment Programme: A multistakeholder camp model in Africa addressing the United Nations Millennium Development Goals. *Centerpoint Now.* New York: The World Council for Peoples of the United Nations.

Kuriansky, J., & Daisey, R. (n.d.). *Tanzania workshop Dr. Judy Kuriansky & Russell Daisey and children* [Video]. Retrieved April 7, 2015, from https://www.youtube.com/watch?v=3poxmUe6Nz8&feature=youtu.be

Kuriansky, J., & Daisey, R. (Producers) (2011). Global Kids Connect Project. [Video]. Retrieved April 7, 2015, from http://youtu.be/VUOOVjkK5-Q

Kuriansky, J., & Jean-Charles, W. (2012). Haiti Rebati: Update on activities rebuilding Haiti through the Global Kids Connect Project. *Bulletin of the International Association of Applied Psychology, 24*, 2–3 July/October. Retrieved January 31, 2015, from http://www.iaapsy.org/Portals/1/Archive/Publications/newsletters/July2012.pdf, pp.116–124. Part 21.

Kuriansky, J., Jean-Charles, W., & Margevich, A. K. (2017, May). *Community psychosocial resilience and recovery from natural disasters: The case of Haiti.* IGNITE Stage presented at the 5th biennial Global Platform for Disaster Risk Reduction, Cancún, Mexico.

Kuriansky, J., Jean-Charles, W., Nemeth, D., & Margevich, A. K. (2017, August). *Providing spiritually oriented psychosocial support after the doubly devastating hurricane in Haiti.* Poster session presented at the 125th annual convention of the American Psychological Association (Division 36), Washington, DC.

Kuriansky, J., Lytle, M., & Chiu, A. (2011, March 11). *Models addressing the UN MDGs(Millennium Development Goals): Outcome of projects in Africa and Haiti.* Paper presented at symposium at the Eastern Psychological Association, Cambridge, MA.

Kuriansky, J., & Margevich, A. (Producers) (2016). Haiti Post-2016 Hurricane: Community training workshop for children. [Video]. Retrieved January 12, 2017, from https://www.youtube.com/watch?v=W14x9_nwVfQ

Kuriansky, J., & Margevich, A. K. (2017a, May). Community psychosocial resilience and recovery from natural disasters. In United Nations Major Group for Children and Youth, *Inter-generational dialogues*. Interactive session conducted at the 5th biennial Global Platform for Disaster Risk Reduction, Cancún, Mexico.

Kuriansky, J., & Margevich, A. K. (2017b, July). *Mental health and well-being: Advances at the United Nations and events impacting psychotherapy.* Symposium conducted at the 8th congress of the World Council for Psychotherapy, Paris, France.

Kuriansky, J., Margevich, A. K., Jean-Charles, W., & Nemeth, D., (2017, July). *Psychosocial support & resilience in cultures in repeated trauma: Lessons from earthquakes to floods.* Symposium conducted at the 8th congress of the World Council for Psychotherapy, Paris, France.

Kuriansky, J., & Nemeth, D. G. (2013, September). A model for post-environmental disaster wellness workshops: Preparing individuals and communities for hurricane anniversary reactions. *Ecopsychology, 5*(Suppl. 1): S38–S45. doi:10.1089/eco.2013.0006.

Kuriansky, J., & Nemeth, D. G. (2016, December). A training workshop to build personal and community resilience while helping children after a natural disaster. Workshop conducted in Baton Rouge, Louisiana.

Kuriansky, J., Polizer, Y., & Jean-Charles, W. (2015, March 16). *Youth and mental health: Workshop of techniques*. Presentation at the Children and Youth Conference, World Conference on Disaster Risk Reduction, Tohoku University, Sendai, Japan.

Kuriansky, J., Polizer, Y., & Milissen, L. (2015). *Children coping with the Ebola epidemic: The Resilience and Empowerment Training and Workshop*. Unpublished manuscript.

Kuriansky, J., Polizer, Y., & Zinsou, J. (2016). Children and Ebola: A model resilience and empowerment training and workshop. In J. Kuriansky (Ed.), *The Psychosocial aspects of a deadly epidemic: What Ebola has taught us about holistic healing*. Santa Barbara, California: ABC-CLIO/Praeger.

Kuriansky, J., Wu, L-Y., Bao, C., Chand, D., Kong, S., Spooner, N., & Mao, S. (2015). Interventions by international and national organizations for psychosocial support after the Sichuan Earthquake in China: A review and implications for sustainable development. In D. G. Nemeth, J. Kuriansky, & R. Hamilton (Eds., Volume 11: Interventions and Policy). *Ecopsychology: Advances in the intersection of psychology and environmental protection*. Santa Barbara, California: ABC-CLIO/Praeger.

Kuriansky, J., Zinsou, J., Arunagiri, V., Douyon, C., Chiu, A., Jean-Charles, W. Daisey, R., & Midy, T. (2015) Effects of helping in a train-the-trainers program for youth in the Global Kids Connect Project after the 2010 Haiti earthquake: A paradigm shift to sustainable development. In D. G. Nemeth, J. Kuriansky, & R. Hamilton (Eds., Volume 11: Interventions and Policy). *Ecopsychology: Advances in the intersection of psychology and environmental protection*. Santa Barbara, California: ABC-CLIO/Praeger.

Landau, J., & Saul, J. (2004). Family and community resilience in response to disaster. In F. Walsh & M. McGoldrick (Eds.), *Living beyond loss: Death in the family* (pp. 285–302). New York: W. W. Norton & Company.

Linley, P. A., & Joseph, S. (2004). Positive change following trauma and adversity. *Journal of Traumatic Stress, 17,* 11–21.

Liu, M., Wang, L., Shi, Z., Zhang, Z., Zhang, K., & Shen, J. (2011). Mental health problems among children one-year after Sichuan earthquake in China: A follow-up study. *PLOS One, 6*(2), e14706.

Lovibond, S. H., & Lovibond, P. F. (1995). *Manual for the Depression Anxiety Stress Scales*. (2nd ed.). Sydney, Australia: Psychology Foundation of Australia.

Luce, J. (2010). Dr. Judy on the trauma of disasters—like Haitian earthquake. Huffington Post. Retrieved April 6, 2015, from http://www.huffingtonpost.com/jim-luce/dr-judy-on-the-trauma-of_b_461779.html

Luks, A. (1988, October). Helper's high. *Psychology Today*, 39–40.

Margevich, A. K., Kuriansky, J., & Jean-Charles, W. (2017a, July). *Providing psychosocial support in a culture doubly devastated by natural disaster: The case of Haiti*. Poster session presented at the European Federation of Psychologists' Association's 15th European Congress of Psychology, Amsterdam, The Netherlands.

Margevich, A. K., Kuriansky, J., & Jean-Charles, W. (2017b, July). *Post-disaster psychosocial support in Haiti following Hurricane Matthew*. Poster session presented at the World Council for Psychotherapy's 8th World Congress for Psychotherapy, Paris, France.

Masten, A. S. (2011). Resilience in children threatened by extreme adversity: Frameworks for research, practice, and translational synergy. *Development and Psychopathology, 23*(2), 493–506.

McCabe, O. L., Marum, F., Mosley, A., Gwon, H. S., Langlieb, A., Everly, G. S. Jr., ... Links, J. M. (2012). Community capacity-building in disaster mental health resilience: A pilot study of an academic/faith partnership model. *International Journal of Emergency Mental Health and Human Resilience, 14*(2), 112–122.

Ministry of Social Welfare, Gender and Children's Affairs. (2014). *Training Manual: Psychosocial Support for Ebola-Affected Communities in Sierra Leone*. Government of Sierra Leone. http://mswgca.gov.sl/Ebola/index.html?undefined.

Mohdin, A. (2014). Ebola crisis: View on disability, soothing Ebola's mental scars. SciDevNet. Retrieved from http://www.scidev.net/global/disease/analysis-blog/focus-on-disability-soothing-ebola-s-mental-scars.html

Morrow-Howell, N., Hinterlong, J., Rozario, P., & Tang, F. (2003). Effects of volunteering on the well-being of older adults. *The Journal of Gerontology, 58B*, S137–S145.

Musick, M. A., Herzog, A. R., & House, J. S. (1999). Volunteering and mortality among older adults: Findings from a national sample. *Journal of Gerontology: Social Sciences, 54B*, S173–S180.

Nemeth, D. G., Hamilton, R. B., & Kuriansky, J. (Eds.). (2012). *Living in an environmentally traumatized world: Healing ourselves and our planet*. Santa Barbara, CA: ABC-CLIO/Praeger.

Nemeth, D. G., Kuriansky, J., Reeder, K. P., Lewis, A., Marceaux, K., Whittington, T., Olivier, T.W., May, N.E., & Safier, J.A. (2012). Addressing anniversary reactions of trauma through group process: The Hurricane Katrina Anniversary Wellness Workshops. *International Journal of Group Psychotherapy, 62*(1), 129–141.

Nemeth, D. G., & Olivier, T. W. (2017). *Innovative approaches to individual and community resilience: From theory to practice*. Chennai, India: Elsevier.

Nemeth, R. B. Hamilton, & J. Kuriansky (Eds.), *Living in an environmentally traumatized world: Healing ourselves and our planet* (pp. 141–167). Santa Barbara, CA: ABC-CLIO/Praeger.

Neria, Y., Nandi, A., & Galea, S. (2008). Post-traumatic stress disorder following disasters: A systematic review. *Psychological Medicine, 38*(4), 467–480.

Nolen-Hoeksema, S., & Morrow, J. (1991). A prospective study of depression and posttraumatic stress symptoms after a natural disaster: The 1989 Loma Prieta earthquake. *Journal of Personality and Social Psychology, 61*(1), 115.

Office of Emergency Preparedness and Response. (2013). Maintaining responder resilience through extreme disaster: Self care beyond lip service. New York DMH

Responder, *3*(4), 1–2. Retrieved from https://www.omh.ny.gov/omhweb/disaster_resources/health_responder/DMH_responder_fall2013.pdf

Otto, C., Kuriansky, J., & Otto, J. (2017). *Mental health and well-being at the heart of the 2030 Agenda: Realizing the promise*. Unpublished manuscript.

Pajares, F., & Urdan, T. (2006). *Self-efficacy beliefs of adolescents: A volume in adolescence and education*. Charlotte, NC: Information Age Publishing, Inc.

Porter, M., & Haslam, N. (2005). Predisplacement and postdisplacement factors associated with mental health of refugees and internally displaced persons: A meta-analysis. *JAMA: The Journal of the American Medical Association, 294*(5), 602–612.

Psychology Foundation of Australia (2010, March 30). Depression Anxiety Stress Scales DASS. *The School of Psychology—UNSW*. Retrieved July 15, 2011, from http://www2.psy.unsw.edu.au/groups/dass/

Qian, Y., Gao, J., Wu, H., Zhong, J., Wang, Y., Li, W., et al. (2011). Exploration of post earthquake long-term psychological aid model: A one-year review of one foundation-Peking University children's psychological wellbeing recovery program. *Chinese Mental Health Journal, 25*(8). [in Chinese with English abstract].

Reifels, L., Bassilios, B., Forbes, D., Creamer, M., Wade, D., Coates, S., … Pirkis, J. (2014). A systematic approach to building the mental health response capacity of practitioners in a postdisaster context. *Advances in Mental Health, 11*(3), 246–256.

Roussos, A., Goenjian, A., Steinberg, A., Sotiropoulou, C., Kakaki, M., & Kabakos, C. (2005). Posttraumatic stress and depressive reactions among children and adolescents after the 1999 earthquake in Ano Liosia, Greece. *American Journal of Psychiatry, 162*, 530–537. doi:10.1176/appi.ajp.162.3.530.

Satapathy, S., & Subhasis, B. (2009). Disaster psychosocial and mental health support in South and South-East Asian countries: A synthesis. *Journal of South Asian Disaster Studies, 2*(1), 21–45.

Save the Children (2012, May). *Facilitator handbook 2: Workshop tracks*. Retrieved from http://pscentre.org/wp-content/uploads/Facilitator-handbook-2.pdf

Schwartz, C. E., Keyl, P. M., Marcum, J. P., & Bode, R. (2009). Helping others shows differential benefits on health and well-being for male and female teens. *Journal of Happiness Studies, 10*, 431–448.

Schwartz, C., Meisenhelder, J., Ma, Y., & Reed, G. (2003). Altruistic social interest behaviors are associated with better mental health. *Psychosomatic Medicine, 65*, 778–785.

Shih, M. (2004). Positive stigma: Examining resilience and empowerment in overcoming stigma. *The ANNALS of the American Academy of Political and Social Science, 591*(1), 175–185. doi: 10.1177/0002716203260099.

Silverman, W. K., & La Greca, A. M. (2002). Children experiencing disasters: Definitions, reactions, and predictors of outcomes. In A. M. La Greca, W. K. Silverman, E. M. Vernberg, & M. C. Roberts (Eds.), *Helping children cope with disasters and terrorism* (pp. 11–33). Washington, DC: American Psychological Association. doi: http://dx.doi.org/10.1037/10454-001.

Smith, D. (1981). Altruism, volunteers, and volunteerism. *Nonprofit and Voluntary Sector Quarterly, 10*, 21–36.

Snoek, F. (2006). WHO-Five Well-Being Index. Retrieved April 6, 2015, fromhttp://www.dawnstudy.com/News_and_activities/Documents/WHO-5.pdf

Spiegel, P. B., Le, P., Ververs, M.-T., & Salama, P. (2007). Occurrence and overlap of natural disasters, complex emergencies and epidemics during the past decade (1995–2004). *Conflict and Health, 1*(2), 1–9.

Stamm, B. H. (2010). The Concise ProQOL manual (2nd ed.). Pocatello, ID: Proqol.org.Retrieved July 16, 2011, from http://www.proqol.org/uploads/ProQOL_Concise_2ndEd_12-2010.pdf

Stewart, S. (2017). National Hurricane Center Tropical Cyclone Report: Hurricane Matthew. *National Weather Service*. Retrieved from http://www.nhc.noaa.gov/data/tcr/AL142016_Matthew.pdf

Sundram, S., Karim, M. E., Ladrido-Ignacio, L., Maramis, A., Mufti, K. A., Nagaraja, D., … Wahab, M. A. (2008). Psychosocial responses to disaster: An Asian perspective. *Asian Journal of Psychiatry, 1*(1), 7–14.

Tedeschi, R. G., & Calhoun, L. G. (2004a). Posttraumatic growth: Conceptual foundations and empirical evidence. *Psychological Inquiry, 15*(1), 1–18.

Tedeschi, R. G., & Calhoun, L. G. (2004b). *Posttraumatic growth: Conceptual foundation and empirical evidence*. Philadelphia, PA: Lawrence Erlbaum Associates.

Thienkrua, W., Cardozo B. L., Chakkraband, M. L., Guadamuz, T. E., Pengjuntr, W., et al. (2006). Symptoms of posttraumatic stress disorder and depression among children in tsunami-affected areas in southern Thailand. *Journal of the American Medical Association, 296*(5), 549–559.

Tobias, C. R., Downes, A., Eddens, S., & Ruiz, J. (2012). Building blocks for peer success: Lessons learned from a train-the-trainer program. *AIDS Patient Care and STDs, 26*(1), 53–59.

U.S. Department of Veterans Affairs National Center for Posttraumatic Stress Disorder (PTSD). (2010, February). *Mental health reactions after disaster*. Retrieved from https://www.ptsd.va.gov/professional/pages/handouts-pdf/Reactions.pdf

U.S. Fund for United Nations Children's Fund (UNICEF). (n.d.). *UNICEF urgently appeals for aid for Haiti following devastating earthquake.* Retrieved March 30, 2015, from: http://www.abc3340.com/story/11812079/unicef-urgently-appeals-for-aid-to-haiti-following-devastating-earthquake

United Nations Children's Fund (UNICEF). (n.d.). *A practical guide for establishing child friendly spaces*. Retrieved March 21, 2015, from http://www.unicefinemergencies.com/downloads/eresource/docs/MHPSS/A%20Practical%20Guide%20to%20Developing%20Child%20Friendly%20Spaces%20-%20UNICEF.pdf

United Nations Children's Fund (UNICEF). (2013). *Mental health and psychosocial support in humanitarian action.* Retrieved March 21, 2015, from http://www.unicefinemergencies.com/downloads/eresource/mhpss.html

United Nations Children's Fund (UNICEF) & United Nations International Strategy for Disaster Risk Reduction (UNISDR). (2011, December). *Children and disaster: Building resilience through education.*

United Nations International Strategy for Disaster Risk Reduction (UNISDR). (2015a, 18March). *Sendai Framework for Disaster Risk Reduction 2015-2030.* Retrieved from http://www.wcdrr.org/uploads/Sendai_Framework_for_Disaster_Risk_Reduction_2015-2030.pdf

United Nations International Strategy for Disaster Risk Reduction (UNISDR) (Producer). (2015b). *WCDRR: The Global Kids Connect Project: A model programme to promote resilience, Judy Kuriansky.* Retrieved April 3, 2015, from https://www.youtube.com/watch?v=NM2DYaB4OYM&index=73&list=PLBDwPnveHho_fXUfFQaVkUGb1v4EcAcyO

United Nations, Department of Economic and Social Affairs (UNDESA). (n.d.). *Sustainable development knowledge platform.* Retrieved April 3, 2015, from https://sustainabledevelopment.un.org/sdgsproposal

United Nations, Department of Economic and Social Affairs (UNDESA). (n.d.). *Sustainable development knowledge platform: Outcome document—Open Working Group on sustainable development goals.* Retrieved September 30, 2014, from http://sustainabledevelopment.un.org/focussdgs.html

United Nations, Department of Economic and Social Affairs (UNDESA). (n.d.). *Sustainable development knowledge platform: Outcome document—High level political forum.* Retrieved August 30, 2017, from https://sustainabledevelopment.un.org/hlpf

United Nations, Department of Economic and Social Affairs (UNDESA). (2015). *Sustainable development knowledge platform: Outcome document—Transforming our world: The 2030 agenda for sustainable development.* Retrieved August 30, 2017 from https://sustainabledevelopment.un.org/post2015/transformingourworld

United Nations, Office for the Coordination of Humanitarian Affairs (UNOCHA). (2016, October). *Haiti: Struggling to survive.* Retrieved on August 30, 2017 from http://www.unocha.org/country/top-stories/all-stories/haiti-struggling-survive

Walsh, F. (2002). A family resilience framework: Innovative practice applications. *Family Relations, 51*, 130–137. doi: 10.1111/j.1741-3729.2002.00130.x.

Walsh, F. (2007). Traumatic loss and major disasters: Strengthening family and community resilience. *Family Process, 46*, 207–227. doi: 10.1111/j.1545-5300.2007.00205.x.

Wang, L., Zhang, Y., Wang, W., Shi, Z., Shen, J., Li, M., & Xin, Y. (2009). Symptoms of posttraumatic stress disorder among adult survivors three months after the Sichuan earthquake in China. *Journal of Traumatic Stress, 22*(5), 444–450.

Weiss, D. S., & Marmar, C. R. (1997). The Impact of Event Scale—Revised. In J. P. Wilson, & T. M. Keane (Eds.), *Assessing psychological trauma and PTSD: A practitioner's handbook* (pp. 399–411). New York: Guilford Press.

Weiss, S. M., Tobin, J. N., Lopez, M., Simons, H., Cook, R., & Jones, D. L. (2014). Translating an evidence-based behavioral intervention for women living with HIV into practice: The SMART/EST Women's Program. *International Journal of Behavioral Medicine, 22*(3), 415–424.

Williams, A. B., Le, S. T., Colby, D., Le, T. T. T., Pollack, T., & Cosimi, L. (2014). Effectiveness of train-the-trainer HIV education: A model from Vietnam. *JANAC: Journal of the Association of Nurses in AIDS Care, 25*(4), 341–350.

Willigen, M. (2000). Differential benefit of volunteering across the life course. *The Journals of Gerontology, 55B*, S308–S318.
Wilson, J., & Musick, M. (1999). The effects of volunteering on the volunteer. *Law and Contemporary Problems, 62*, 141–168.
Wir, K. (2017). Maximizing children's resilience. *Monitor on Psychology, 48*(8), 40–46.*Contemporary Problems, 62*, 141–168.
World Health Organization (WHO). (2012). *Mental health and psychosocial support for conflict related sexual violence: Principles and interventions.* http://www.unicef.org/protection/files/Summary_EN_.pdf
World Health Organization (WHO). (2014). *Psychological first aid during Ebola viral disease outbreaks.* Retrieved March 21, 2015 from http://apps.who.int/iris/bitstream/10665/131682/1/9789241548847_eng.pd
World Health Organization (WHO). (2016a). *Ebola data and statistics.* Retrieved August 30, 2017 from http://apps.who.int/gho/data/view.ebola-sitrep.ebola-summary-latest?lang=en
World Health Organization (WHO). (2016b). *Zika situation report.* Retrieved August 30, 2017 from http://www.who.int/emergencies/zika-virus/situation-report/23-june-2016/en/
World Vision. (2016, June). *What's a child friendly space?* Retrieved August 30, 2017 from http://www.worldvision.ca/stories/disaster-relief/whats-a-child-friendly-space
Yarber, L., Brownson, C. A., Jacob, R. R., Baker, E. A., Jones, E., Baumann, C., ... Brownson, R. C. (2015). Evaluating a train-the trainer approach for improving capacity for evidence-based decision making in public health. *BM Health Services Research, 15*, 547–557.
Young, F., & Glasgow, N. (1998). Voluntary social participation and health. *Research on Aging, 20*, 339–362.
Yu, X., Lau, J. T. F., Mak, W. W. S., Cheng, Y., Lv, Y., & Zhang, J. (2014). A pilot theory based intervention to improve resilience, psychosocial well-being, and quality of life among people living with HIV in rural China. *Journal of Sex and Marital Therapy, 40*(1), 1–16.

Index

7-Step Integrative Healing Model, xxiii, 131–35

Abi-Hashem, Naji, 105–6
absorption, 63, 125
Abu-Baker, Khawla, 146
acceptance:
Cambodians, 45–46;
Haitians, 34;
hurricane survivors, 139;
Indian undergraduates, 13–14
acculturation stress:
Syrian refugees, 116
adaptation, 63–64;
sociocultural, 113–14;
Syrian refugees, 115–16;
adolescent resilience:
and authoritative parenting, 79–80;
and Chinese cultural beliefs, 78;
and parental role models, 79;
in sexual abuse survivors, 91
adjustment. *See* adaptation
adult resilience measure-28 (ARM-28), 7, 26;
Haitian PTG study, 28, *29*, 30;
Indian undergraduates' PTG study, 10–11
adversity. *See* trauma
Alliant International University, 43
altruism:
Cambodians, 48;
community volunteers, 166–67, 175–76;
disaster survivors, 147;
Haitians, 35;
Syrian refugees, 120–21
American University of Phnom Penh, 43
appreciation of life:
Haitians, 31–32;
Indian undergraduates, 12
ARM-28. *See* adult resilience measure-28
Armenia:
1988 earthquake, 136–37;
genocide, 142–45
Artz, Lillian, 88
Association for Trauma Outreach and Prevention, 131

Bio-Psychosocial and Spiritual Model. *See* 7-Step Integrative Healing Model
Braun, Virginia, 93
breathing exercises, 135, 166
Buddhism, 13, 52, 53, 78, 134
burnout:
community volunteers (TTT-trained), 165–66

Cambodia:
posttraumatic era, 39–41
Cardona, S., 65–66
CARITAS, 162
Castañeda, Tannia de, xxii, 64–67
caste-based violence:
India, xxii, 4–5
CBAS. *See* Chinese Beliefs about Adversity Scale
Centro de Estudios para la Cooperación Internacional (CECI), 64
children:
community volunteers (TTT-trained) work with, 164–65, 167–68, 169, 170
child resilience:
Caucasian, 79–80;
Chinese, 80;
and psychosocial assistance, 155–57;
Syrian, 120–21, 122
child sexual abuse (CSA):
South Africa, 87–88, 94–95;
South African studies, xxiii, 89, 90, 91–93;
South African survivors' resilience, 90–91, 94–99
China:
cultural beliefs about adversity, 78–82;
parenting styles, 80
students' resilience, 81–82;
Chinese Beliefs about Adversity Scale (CBAS), 78
Church:
role in healing/recovery process, 33, 169
citizen security:
Guatemala, 61–62
Clarke, Victoria, 93
climate change:
Guatemala, 62–63
collective mass memorials, 174
community healing:
tsunami survivors, 142
community volunteering/volunteers, 158–59;
burnout, 165–66;
compassion fatigue, 165;
Train-the-Trainers program, xxiii, 156–57, 159–63, 169–70, 176;
and value of helping, 171;
viability in disaster response, 175–76;
working with children, 164–65, 167–68, 169, 170
compassion fatigue, 165
Conecta-Tec, 70
Confucianism, 78
contentment:
Indian undergraduates, 12
coping styles/mechanisms, 125;
negative/unhealthy, 119–20;
positive/healthy, 120–21
courage, 50;
Cambodians, 48–49
CSA. *See* child sexual abuse
cultural beliefs/contexts:
and coping behaviour/resources, 75–76, 89;
relevance to helping professionals, 81–82;
and South African coping behaviour/resources, 90–91, 94–99;
and Taiwanese coping behaviour/resources, 77–81;
and trauma, 110–11

Daisey, Russell, 160
Dalits, 5
destiny, 78;
Community volunteers' (TTT-trained) view of, 166, 168;
hurricane survivors' view of, 139
didactic information, 135
dissonance, 68
Domhardt, Matthias, 91
Dunkle, Kristin, 88

earthquake:
Armenia (1988), 136–37;

Haiti (2010), xxii, 22–23, 159–60, 163–67, 176;
Taiwan (921 Earthquake), 79
Ebola epidemic, 162–63, 169–71, 174
education:
Guatemala, 62
education outreach:
and Guatemalan street-connected children, 67–69;
Syrian refugees, 122;
and violence prevention in Guatemala, 64–67
Eisenberg, Nancy, 80
Elon University, 65
emotional disclosure, 134;
hurricane survivors, 138;
tsunami survivors, 141–42
emotional support/warmth, 80
emotional trauma:
Syrian refugees, 114–15
empathy:
Cambodians, 48;
defined, 14;
in group setting, 134, 141;
Haitians, 35;
Indian undergraduates, 14–15;
tsunami survivors, 141
endurance:
Chinese beliefs about, 78, 82
epidemics:
cholera in Haiti (2010), 161;
incidence, 151–52;
and mourning, 174;
vis-à-vis natural disasters, 154–55
Eschenauer, Robert, 81–82

family and friends:
desire to be closer, 14, 47;
desire to spend more time with, 141–42;
extended family networks, 97, 99;
trauma transmission through family interactions, 41;
"treat them right", 35–36
family support:
Caucasian children, 80;
Chinese immigrants, 82;
disaster survivors, 147;
Guatemalans, 67, 68;
Indians, 15
fate. *See* destiny
fear:
Cambodians, 40, 48–49;
tsunami survivors, 141
Fegert, Jörg M., 91
forgiveness, 134, 135;
measures, 133;
meditation exercises, 135
Frankl, Victor, 134, 147

gender-based violence:
India, 3–4;
South Africa, 88, 97
general health questionnaire-28 (GHQ-28), 7;
Indian undergraduates' PTG study, 9–11
genocide:
of Armenians, 142–45
GHQ-28. *See* general health questionnaire-28
GKCP. *See* Global Kids Connect Project
Global Kids Connect Project (GKCP), 157, 178
gratitude for life:
Guatemalan at-risk youth, 64, 65;
Indian undergraduates, 12–13
Grazioso, María del Pilar, xxii, 64–66
grounded theory for posttraumatic growth model, 8, 11, 27–28, 44
Guatemala, xxii, 59–60;
climate change, 62–63;
economics, 60–61;
education, 62;
health, 61;
innovation, 70;
MPP Project, 61–62;
political conditions, 63;

Violence Prevention Program (VPP), 64–67
guilt:
tsunami survivors, 141

Haffejee, Sadiyya, 91
Haiti:
2010 earthquake, xxii, 22–23, 159–60, 163–67;
2016 Hurricane Matthew, xxii, 23, 160–62, 167–69, 175;
history, 21–22;
post-disaster psychosocial support, xxiii, 159–62, 176;
post-disaster psychosocial support outcomes, 163–69;
value of helping/volunteering, 171
Hakka people:
cultural beliefs about adversity, 79
happiness:
Guatemalan at-risk youth, 64, 65;
Haitians' perception, 33–34
healing and recovery process:
Cambodians, 40;
Haitians, 32–33;
Indian undergraduates, 15–16
health:
Guatemala, 61
hegemonic masculinity:
and violence, 88, 97
Hinduism, 13
humanitarian outreach relief missions. *See* Meaningfulworld
human strengths, xiv, xvii–xviii, xx–xxi
hurricane:
Andrew in Florida (1992), 137–39;
Katrina and Matthew in Louisiana, 177–78;
Matthew in Haiti (2016), xxii, 23, 160–62, 167–69, 175;
Harvey in Texas (2017), 175–76

IASC. *See* Inter-Agency Standing Committee
India:
demographics, 1–2;
gender-based violence, 3–4;
Jat agitation (2016), xxii, 4–5;
natural disasters, 3;
political violence, 2–3;
road traffic accidents, 3
Inter-Agency Standing Committee (IASC) guidelines, 157;
and Train-the-Trainer program, 173–74
intergenerational trauma:
American Armenians, 145;
Cambodians, 40–41;
Turkish Americans, 145
international psychology, xvii
interpersonal growth:
Cambodians, 46–48;
Haitians, 35–36;
importance, 134–35;
Indian undergraduates, 14–15
IsraAID, 157
Israel-Palestine conflict, 145–47

Jean-Charles, Wismick, 159, 161
Jefferis, Tamlynn, 90
Jewkes, Rachel, 88

Kalayjian, Ani, 131, 143–44. See *also* 7-Step Integrative Healing Model
karma:
Cambodians' belief, 51–52;
Hurricane Andrew survivors' belief, 139
Khmer Rouge, 39, 40, 41, 52
kindness, 35–36, 48, 90
Kuriansky, Judy, 153, 157, 159, 161, 162, 177, 180.

Lebanon:
outreach to Syrian refugees, 117, 121–22;
resiliency, 118, 125;
social dilemmas and refugee problem, 117–19, 125;
Syrian elite in, 117;
Syrian refugee population, 116–17

LEC. *See* life events checklist
Lee, Tak Yan, 78
life:
"live in the moment to the fullest", 32;
"not take for granted", 31–32;
"peace and freedom to enjoy life", 33
life events checklist (LEC), 6, 25
life priorities, shift in:
Cambodians, 49–50;
Indian undergraduates, 12–13
Li, Ming-hui, 81–82
Lutz, Goldbeck, 91

Malindi, Macalane Junel, 90
Margevich, Alexandra, 151
Masten, Ann S., 91
Meaningfulworld outreach missions, 131–33;
9/11 attacks, New York, 139–40;
Armenian earthquake (1988), 136–37;
Hurricane Andrew in Florida (1992), 138;
tsunami in Sri Lanka (2004/2005), 140–42
meaning in life questionnaire (MLQ), 26, 133;
Haitian PTG study, 28–30
meaning making, 116, 134–35;
9/11 survivors, 140;
Armenian earthquake (1988) survivors, 136–37;
disaster survivors, 147–48;
Hurricane Andrew (1992) survivors, 138–39;
Sri Lankan tsunami (2004/2005) survivors, 141–42
medical interventions/treatment:
Indian undergraduates, 15–16
mental health:
Chinese immigrants, 82;
Guatemalan at-risk youth, 69;
and UN 2030 Agenda for Sustainable Development, 153
mental health care and services:
Hurricane Andrew survivors, 138;
Syrian refugees, 116, 125–26;
therapeutic encounter guidelines, 122–24.
See also 7-Step Integrative Healing Model
mental trauma:
Syrian refugees, 114–15
MLQ. *See* meaning in life questionnaire
money:
as source of happiness, 33–34
Mónico, Carmen, 65–66
Morrell, Robert, 88
mourning, 173–74
moving on/forward in life:
Haitians, 34;
Indian undergraduates, 15
Münzer, Annika, 91

natural disasters:
epidemics vis-à-vis, 154–55;
incidence, 151–52;
India, 3;
and mourning, 174;
and psychosocial support (TTT model), xxiii, 152, 171–73;
survivors' accounts, 132;
Taiwan, 77, 79.
See also earthquake; hurricane
new experiences/possibilities:
9/11 survivors, 140;
Cambodians, 50
nightmares, 133;
and 7-Step Integrative Healing Model, 134, 135;
Cambodians, 40;
hurricane survivors, 138;
Syrians, 115
tsunami survivors, 141;

Oldfield, Jeremy, 67–69
Oritz, Emily, 67–69
Oshio, Atsushi, 6–7

Palestinians:
Israeli discriminatory practices against, 146–47
parental attachment:
and mental health of Guatemalan at-risk youth, 69
parenting style:
and child/adolescent resilience, 79–80
patriarchy:
and gender-based violence, 88, 97
peer attachment/support:
and mental health of Guatemalan at-risk youth, 69;
and sexually abused children, 96, 98–99
personal growth/strength:
Cambodians, 44–46;
community volunteers (TTT-trained), 164;
defined, 13;
Haitians, 34–35;
Indian undergraduates, 13–14;
refugee women, 64;
youth, 67
Phasha, Nareadi, 90
political trauma:
India, 2–3
positive psychology, xvii-xviii
posttraumatic growth (PTG):
Cambodians, 52–54;
cross-cultural and international perspectives, xviii, 39;
cross-cultural scholarship/studies, xx–xxi, 6–7, 16–17;
facilitating factors, 48–50;
four-category model, 16–17;
Haitians, 36–37;
and helping others, 167;
Indian undergraduates, 1, 16–17;
Tedeschi and Calhoun model, 11, 39, 43–44, 45, 46, 49, 53
posttraumatic growth inventory (PTGI) scale, 6–7, 25–26;
Haitian study, 28–30;
Indian undergraduates' study, 9, 10–11
posttraumatic stress disorder (PTSD), 40, 111;
Armenian genocide survivors, 143;
Cambodians, 41;
and fear, 48–49;
Hurricane Andrew survivors, 138;
mental health professionals, after 9/11 attacks, 139–40
prayers:
Haitians' belief in, 32–33, 169
problem-solving:
cross-cultural context, 81–82
psychosocial caregiving/support:
children, 155–56;
Syrian refugees, 116.
See also Train-the-Trainers program
Psychotraumatology and Human Rights conference (1999), 143–44
PTGI scale. *See* posttraumatic growth inventory scale
PTSD. *See* posttraumatic stress disorder

reconciliation:
Armenian-Turkish dialogue, 145
recovery. *See* healing and recovery process
refugees:
El Salvadorian women, 64;
Guatemalan women, 64.
See also Syrian refugees
religion. *See* spiritual/religious change
research methodologies, xxii;
Cambodian PTG study, 41–44;
Haitian PTG study, 23–31;
Indian undergraduates' PTG study, 5–11;
South African sexually abused children's resilience study, 91–93
resilience, 152–53, 180;
atypical, 99, 100;
contextualized studies, 59; 63–71

cross-cultural and international perspectives, xviii;
cross-cultural scholarship/studies, xix–xxi;
defined, 60, 75, 121, 153;
Resilience Research Centre-Adult Resilience Measure-28 (RRC-ARM-28), 67
respect for elders, 96, 97, 99
road accidents:
India, 3
RRC-ARM-28. *See* Resilience Research Centre-Adult Resilience Measure-28
RTI International, 61, 64

safe space:
Guatemalan youth at-risk, 68
satisfaction with life:
Guatemalan at-risk youth, 64, 65;
Indian undergraduates, 12
satisfaction with life scale (SWLS), 26;
Haitian study, 28–30
Saz, Marco, 64–66
school connectedness:
and mental health of Guatemalan at-risk youth, 69
SCYP. *See* street connected young people
Sekweyiya, Yandisa, 88
self-actualization:
Cambodians, 46;
defined, 46
self-care:
community volunteers (TTT-trained), 166, 169
self-efficacy:
Cambodians, 44–45;
community volunteers (TTT-trained), 172;
cross-cultural context, 81–82;
Guatemalan at-risk youth, 64, 65
self-esteem:
community volunteers (TTT-trained), 166, 171;
Indian undergraduates, 13
Sendai Framework for Disaster Risk Reduction, 153–54, 179
sense of coherence, 80
sexual violence:
and patriarchy, 88, 97.
See also child sexual abuse
shame:
and child sexual abuse survivors, 98;
Chinese cultural beliefs about, 82
Shek, Daniel T. L., 78
shock:
tsunami survivors, 141
Sierra Leone:
post-Ebola outbreak psychosocial support, xxiii, 162–63, 169–71
Sirikantraporn, Jill, xix, xxii
skill development:
Guatemalan street-connected young people, 68
sleep disturbances:
Cambodians, 40;
tsunami survivors, 141
social ecological resilience, 75, 89;
relevance for helping professions, 81–82, 99–100;
sexually abused South African girls, 90, 91, 94–99;
Taiwanese, 77–81
socialization:
Syrian refugees, 120
social support, 100;
Cambodia, 47–48;
and Caucasian children, 80;
Haiti, 33;
importance, 175;
India, 15;
in Lebanon for Syrian refugees, 121–22;
and sexually abused South African children, 96, 98–99
South Africa, 90, 97;
social workers:
as resilience enablers, 96, 98

sociocultural adaptation:
Syrian refugees, 113–14, 116
socioemotional intervention:
Guatemala, 64–65, 67
South Africa:
child sexual abuse, 87–88, 94–95;
Ubuntu philosophy, 90, 96–97, 99;
virginity tests, 98
spiritual/religious change:
Cambodians, 50–52, 53;
Haitians, 32–33;
hurricane survivors, 139;
Indian undergraduates, 16;
and self-acceptance, 13;
Syrian refugees, 120
Sri Lanka:
2004/2005 tsunami, 140–42
Stevenson, Andrew, 67–69
street-connected young people (SCYP):
Guatemala, education outreach for, 67–69;
South Africa, 90
students:
PTG of Indian undergraduates, 5–17;
resilience in cross-cultural context, 81–82;
viability in disaster response, 175–76
substance abuse, 134;
hurricane survivors, 138;
South Africa, 88
suicide:
Indian undergraduates, 5
SWLS. *See* satisfaction with life scale
Syria:
civil war, 106–7, 111–13;
contemporary society, 113–14;
history and national profile, 107–10
Syrian refugees, 105;
adjustment, 115–16;
mental-emotional trauma, 114–15;
sociocultural adaptation, 113–14, 116;
trauma, 111, 125
Syrian refugees in Jordan:
psychosocial assistance, 176–77
Syrian refugees in Lebanon, xxiii, 116–19;
coping mechanisms, 119–21, 125;
and Lebanese outreach, 121–22

Taiwan:
history, 76–77;
natural disasters, 77, 79;
sociocultural context and influences, xxii–xxiii, 77–82
Taku, Kanaka, 6–7
Taoism, 78
teachers:
as resilience enablers, 94–95, 96, 98–99;
Train-the-Trainers model, 177, 179–80
terrorism:
9/11 attacks, 139–40
Theron, Linda, 90, 91
traditional healers:
and cultural subversion, 95, 97–98
Train-the-Trainers (TTT) program, 152;
and children's needs, 156–57;
efficacy, 171–73;
and IASC guidelines, 173–74;
limitations, 178–79;
outcomes, 154, 163–71;
policy implications, 179–81;
post-2010 Haiti earthquake, 159–60, 163–67;
post-2014 Ebola outbreak in Sierra Leone, 162–63, 169–71;
post-2016 Haiti Hurricane Matthew, 160–62, 167–69;
sustainability, 165, 169–70, 175;
and Syrian refugees, 176–77;
for teachers, 177, 179–80
trait resilience:
cross-cultural context, 81–82
transformative capacity, 64
trauma:
assessment, 134;
Cambodians, 39–41;
and Chinese cultural beliefs, 77–81;

and cultural beliefs/contexts, 75–76, 110–11;
defined/notion, 2, 110;
double/triple, 175;
Harvard Trauma Questionnaire. Part Four, 133;
Syrians, 111, 114–15, 124–25
trauma-based cultural syndrome:
baksbat (broken courage), 40, 49;
defined, 40;
kyol goeu (wind overload), 40
tsunami:
2004/2005 Sri Lanka, 140–42;
"giant monster", 142
TTT program. *See* Train-the-Trainers program
Turkey:
denial of Armenian genocide, 143–45

Ungar, Michael, 60, 89
UNICEF, 157, 163
United Nations:
2030 Agenda for Sustainable Development, 153, 179
United States:
9/11 attacks, 139–40;
Hurricane Andrew in Florida (1992), 137–39;
Hurricane Harvey in Texas (2017), 175–76;
Hurricane Katrina and Matthew in Louisiana, 177–78;
students' resilience, 81–82;
Universidad del Valle de Guatemala (UVG), 64, 65
USAID, 64

Vemula, Rohith, 5
violence:
9/11 attacks, 139–40;
caste-based, xxii, 4–5;
gender-based, 3–4, 88, 97;
and hegemonic masculinities, 88, 97;
political, 2–3, 63;
prevention, 64–67;
sexual, 87–88
virginity:
South African context, 98

wars/armed conflicts:
Guatemala, 63;
India, 2–3;
Syria, 106–7, 111–13
well-being:
community volunteers (TTT-trained), 168
work ethic, 147
Wright, Margaret, 91

Yang, Yan, 81–82
youth at-risk, Guatemalan:
mental health and resilience, 69;
risks and challenges, 66, 67;
street-connected youth, 67–69;
Violence Prevention Program (VPP), 64–67
youth, Cambodian:
intergenerational trauma, 40–41
youth, Syrian:
resilience, 120

About the Editors and Contributors

EDITORS

Grant J. Rich received his PhD in Psychology: Human Development from the University of Chicago. His work focuses on optimal cross-cultural human development, international positive psychology, mixed methods, history of psychology, and integrating traditional and contemporary healing modalities. He is senior editor of *Pathfinders in International Psychology* (2015) and *Internationalizing the Teaching of Psychology* (2017). He was editor of APA Division 52's *International Psychology Bulletin* (2010–2014), and received the President's Award for Extraordinary Service: APA Division of International Psychology (2014). A fellow of the American Psychological Association, the Society for the Teaching of Psychology, and the Society for Media Psychology and Technology, he has taught at several institutions around the globe, including in Alaska, Cambodia, and India. He has authored dozens of articles and chapters, written nearly 100 reviews, and presented at numerous international conferences ranging from Africa and Europe, to Mexico and the Caribbean, to the Middle East. A board-certified massage therapist (NCBTMB), he is editor of the academic research book, *Massage Therapy: The Evidence for Practice* (2002). He has served on medical missions internationally and traveled to over 22 nations. Recently, he has published articles in the *Journal of Positive Psychology* (2016), the *Journal of Humanistic Psychology* (2017), and the *American Psychologist* (2016).

Dr. Skultip (Jill) Sirikantraporn is a licensed psychologist in California and New York with research interests in trauma, resilience, and posttraumatic growth in the context of cross-cultural and international psychology. She is cochair of the webinar committee of APA Division 52 (International

Psychology). She has published on the topic of resilience among marginalized populations, including injection drug users, patients with co-occurring disorders, new immigrants, and Southeast Asian immigrants. Originally from Southeast Asia (Thailand), she has several ongoing projects collaborating with professionals in Thailand, Cambodia, Malaysia, and India to expand and deepen psychological knowledge in the context of these cultures.

CONTRIBUTORS

Dr. Naji Abi-Hashem is a clinical and cultural psychologist, author, public speaker, consultant, visiting professor, and a caregiver at large. Formerly, a staff psychologist with the Minirth-Meier New Life Clinics and affiliated hospitals in Seattle, Washington, USA, conducting inpatient and outpatient therapies. He is an active member or a diplomate in a number of professional associations and has served on the Board of Directors for about ten national and international organizations. He was also a scholar in residence at two graduate schools in Pasadena and Berkeley, California, USA. Dr. Abi-Hashem writes and speaks on matters related to psychology, social issues, counseling, cross-cultural work, immigration, geopolitics, Middle Eastern studies, religious faith and worldview, globalization, loss, grief, trauma, spirituality, psychotherapy, pastoral care, fundamentalism, and radicalism. So far, he has made about 90 academic presentations at professional conventions and has authored about 90 publications in the form of journal articles, book chapters, encyclopedia entries, training videos, and general essays. Currently, he is an associate with Member Care International and divides his time between Beirut, Lebanon, and the United States.

Julie C. Badaracco received her MA in psychology and is currently working to complete her doctoral degree in psychology from the California School of Professional Psychology at Alliant International University. Her research focuses on ethnic minorities, acculturation, posttraumatic growth, and resiliency. Ms. Badaracco has worked in various community mental health clinics and programs including the Kids & Teens in Court Program, Vista Balboa Crisis Center, and Catholic Charities. She strives to continue serving underserved communities as well as doing research that will benefit the most vulnerable of populations.

Tannia de Castañeda is a PhD candidate in applied psychology and holds a master's degree in psychological counseling and mental health at Universidad del Valle de Guatemala (UVG). She is a distinguished professor in the Department of Psychology, Social Sciences Faculty at UVG. Her research explores resilience processes in Guatemalan youth in contexts of adversity and the influence of educational opportunities and socioemotional interventions that support positive adjustment and well-being in young people. She is also a specialist in consulting programs in areas related to human development, psychological counseling, business management (organizational counseling), and entrepreneurship. She also has a professional background in the field of business administration, and has training in personality development and human relations. She has experience in the design of educational innovation programs that integrate psychology and technologies.

Russell Daisey is a music therapist and internationally known pianist and singer-songwriter. An NGO professional affiliate at the United Nations of the International Association of Applied Psychology, he is cofounder with Dr. Judy Kuriansky of the Stand Up for Peace and Global Kids Connect Projects. He produced concerts globally, including after 9/11; earthquakes in Haiti and Japan; International Congresses of Applied Psychology in Cape Town and Paris; the European Congress of Psychology in Stockholm; UN DPI/NGO conference in Mexico City; and the First Hiroshima International Peace Summit in Japan with HH the Dalai Lama and Archbishop Desmond Tutu.

Dr. Daria Diakonova-Curtis is a postdoctoral fellow at the Department of Psychology at St. Petersburg State University in St. Petersburg, Russia, and Research Coordinator as well as 2017 Humanitarian Relief Mission to Armenia Participant with the Association for Trauma Outreach & Prevention, Meaningfulworld. She is the recipient of the Paul Werner Dissertation Award and APA's Division of International Psychology's Graduate Student Research Award, of which she is now chair. She has presented at the United Nations, as well as international and regional conferences, on issues of cross-cultural health, resilience, and human rights.

Sadiyya Haffejee is a community-counseling psychologist, registered with Health Professional Council of South Africa. She is the supervising psychologist at a child and youth care center, where she is involved in supervision of intern psychologists, providing therapeutic services to youth in care, monitoring and evaluating interventions, and conducting research on resilience processes of youth transitioning out of care. Sadiyya is also a doctoral candidate at the University of North West and her research is focused on exploring resilience processes in sexually abused African girls through the use of participatory research methods. Other research interests include gender violence, social justice, community psychology, and innovative, participatory methods of data collection.

Ching-Yu Huang received her PhD in social and developmental psychology from University of Cambridge in 2013. After finishing her PhD, she went to Taiwan for a postdoctoral research fellowship at the Children and Family Research Center, National Taiwan University, where she conducted research on domestic violence in Taiwan, as well as provided consultancy and trainings to social workers, police officers, and prosecutors about forensic interview practice for child witnesses and victims. Thereafter, she went to Alliant International University, San Diego, USA, to further conduct research in child custody evaluation, and on effects of adverse experiences on child development. She joined Bournemouth University in January 2017 as a lecturer in psychology, and is currently involved in various research projects in developmental psychology, cross-cultural psychology, applied forensic psychology, domestic violence, and children's social and emotional development.

Nashaw Jafari received her master's degree in clinical psychology from Alliant International University, where she studied integrative and multicultural psychology. She researched trauma, resiliency, and posttraumatic growth. She completed her undergraduate studies at Soka University of America, where she researched factors in psychological well-being in emerging adulthood and identification with all of humanity. She has presented her research findings at the Western Psychological Association and Society of Cross-Cultural Research conferences. She is passionate about giving back to her community and served as a board member on Community Action Partnership, an organization that empowers people in economically disadvantaged areas.

Dr. Wismick Jean-Charles, Haitian priest, is the current vice president of the University of Notre-Dame, in Haiti. He received his doctorate in psychology from Fordham University, New York. He also holds a master's degree in counseling psychology, and education. Dr. Jean-Charles is the founder of Center of Spirituality and Mental Health (CESSA for the French name) in Haiti, which blends spirituality with contemporary psychology. He has published many articles and delivered numerous invited presentations at national and international conferences in the areas of post-disaster and spirituality. Prior to working in his new role of vice president of the Catholic University of Notre-Dame, Dr. Jean-Charles taught at Fordham University and Montclair State University, USA.

Dr. Ani Kalayjian, EdD, DDL, RN-BC, BCETS, DSc (Hon), founder and president of the Association for Trauma Outreach and Prevention, Meaningfulworld, is a graduate from Teachers College, Columbia University, with master's and doctoral degrees and honorary doctor of science degree from LIU. She has been consulting at UN since 1988. She has received Alumni of the Year Award from TC Columbia University, ANA Human Rights Award, APA Div. 52 Mentoring Award, and Humanitarian Award from University of Missouri, and Pakistan Social Council. She is the author of an internationally acclaimed book on *Disaster & Mass Trauma*, Chief Editor of an international book on *Forgiveness & Reconciliation: Psychological pathways to conflict transformation and peace building* (Springer Publishing), and Chief Editor of II Volumes on *Emotional Healing around the World: Rituals and practices for resilience and meaning-making* (Greenwood, ABC-CLIO, 2010). She has produced a meditation CD, on Ancestral Healing and Transforming Generational Trauma, and eight films on Humanitarian Outreach Projects.

Dr. Judy Kuriansky is an international clinical psychologist and humanitarian who has held workshops and trainings worldwide, including after disasters in Sri Lanka, Haiti, China, Japan, Australia, and the United States. She is on the adjunct faculty at Columbia University Teachers College and honorary professor at Peking Health Sciences Center in China, and is also an award-winning journalist, pioneer radio talk show host, and television commentator. Her many books address ecopsychology, Middle East peace, and psychosocial issues in Ebola. She partnered with the UN Ambassador of Palau to advocate successfully for mental health and well-being to be included in the UN Global Agenda 2030.

Dr. Alexandra Margevich is an experimental social psychologist who holds a BA from McGill University in 2010, with a major in psychology and a minor in behavioral science and cultural anthropology. She holds an MA in clinical psychology from Columbia University (2012) and a PhD in social psychology from Rutgers University (2017). She has served as a research associate for the Rutgers Implicit Social Cognition Lab and the Rutgers Center for Law, Inequality and Metropolitan Equity. She has additionally worked as an intern and youth representative for the International Association of Applied Psychology at the United Nations.

María del Pilar Grazioso is Director of the doctoral program in Applied Psychology and the master's program in Community Psychology at Universidad del Valle de Guatemala and co-coordinates Proyecto Aiglé, Guatemala. She has coordinated and supervised community and clinical internships, research projects and administrated programs at the undergraduate and graduate level. She received the Division 52 Outstanding International Psychologist Award in 2010 and was recognized by the Colegio de Psicólogos de Guatemala. She has served in several leadership positions in the Interamerican Society of Psychology, worked as editor for several journals and as associate editor of the *Wiley-Blackwell Encyclopedia of Gender and Sexuality Studies*. Currently, she is Faculty Advisor for the Psi Chi, Guatemalan Chapter, and serves as Guatemala Liaison for Div 52 of the American Psychological Association.

Dr. Chris Stout is a licensed clinical psychologist, Founding Director of the Center for Global Initiatives, VP of Research and Data Analytics, at ATI Holdings, LLC, and on faculty at the College of Medicine at the University of Illinois at Chicago. He served as NGO Special Representative to the United Nations and was one of the World Economic Forum's Global Leaders of Tomorrow and Invited Faculty in Davos. He was invited by the Club de Madrid and Safe-Democracy to serve on the Madrid-11 Countering Terrorism Task Force. He has published over 35 books, including two Amazon best sellers; his works have been translated into eight languages. He has received five humanitarian awards and four additional doctorates (honoris causa) for his work in global health and humanitarian intervention. He also blogs in these areas as a LinkedIn Influencer. He is listed in TED Conferences Founder Richard Saul Wurman's "Who's Really Who, 1000: The Most Creative Individuals in America."

Linda Theron, D.Ed., is a full professor in the Department of Educational Psychology, Faculty of Education, University of Pretoria, and an extraordinary professor in Optentia Research Focus Area, North-West University, South Africa. She is registered with the Health Professions Council of South Africa as an educational psychologist. Her research explores the resilience processes of South African young people challenged by chronic adversity and accounts for how sociocultural contexts shape these processes of resilience (see www.Lindatheron.org). Together with Dr. Michael Ungar (Resilience Research Centre, Canada), Linda was the principal co-investigator of the 5-country Pathways to Resilience Study (2009–2015). In 2013, she received the Education Association of South Africa's research medal for her rich contributions to understanding, and promoting, resilience processes that support the positive adjustment of South African youth. She is lead editor of *Youth Resilience and Culture: Complexities and Commonalities* (Springer, 2015) and an associate journal editor of *Child Abuse & Neglect* (Elsevier).

Lightning Source UK Ltd.
Milton Keynes UK
UKOW04n1614020118
315443UK00003B/85/P

9 781498 554831